An Inquiry Into The Genealogy And Present State Of Ancient Scottish Surnames: With The Origin And Descent Of The Highland Clans

William Buchanan

Nabu Public Domain Reprints:

You are holding a reproduction of an original work published before 1923 that is in the public domain in the United States of America, and possibly other countries. You may freely copy and distribute this work as no entity (individual or corporate) has a copyright on the body of the work. This book may contain prior copyright references, and library stamps (as most of these works were scanned from library copies). These have been scanned and retained as part of the historical artifact.

This book may have occasional imperfections such as missing or blurred pages, poor pictures, errant marks, etc. that were either part of the original artifact, or were introduced by the scanning process. We believe this work is culturally important, and despite the imperfections, have elected to bring it back into print as part of our continuing commitment to the preservation of printed works worldwide. We appreciate your understanding of the imperfections in the preservation process, and hope you enjoy this valuable book.

B.G. ex dono G.P. Aug.

AN INQUIRY

INTO THE

GENEALOGY and PRESENT STATE

OF

Ancient Scottish Surnames:

WITH THE

ORIGIN AND DESCENT

OF THE

HIGHLAND CLANS;

AND

FAMILY OF BUCHANAN.

By WILLIAM BUCHANAN OF AUCHMAR.

EDINBURGH:

PRINTED AND SOLD BY WILLIAM AULD,
TURK'S CLOSE, LAWN-MARKET.

M,DCC,LXXV.

CONTENTS.

AN INQUIRY into the Genealogy and present State of Ancient SCOTTISH SURNAMES. 1

Origin of the Family of Murray   19
Origin of the Family of Stewart   28
Origin of the Family of Douglas   33
Origin of the Family of Wymefs   34
Origin of the Family of Campbell   ib
Origin of the Family of Ogilvie   48
Origin of the Family of Kennedy   49
Origin of the Family of Graham   ib
Origin of the Family of Seaton   54
Origin of the Family of Levingston   55
Origin of the Family of Hamilton   57
Origin of the Family of Hepburn.   ib
Origin of the Family of Gray   ib
Origin of the Family of Frafer   59
Origin of the Family of Sinclair   60
Origin of the Family of Ramfay   60
Origin of the Family of Carnegie   ib
Origin of the Family of Munroe   ib
Origin of the Family of Grant   61
Origin of the Family of Menzies   ib

CONTENTS.

An Account of the MacDonalds	62
An Account of the Surname of MacDougal; particularly of Lorn.	79
An Account of the Surname of MacNeil	85
An Account of the Surname of MacLean or MacGillean	89
An Account of the Surname of MacLeods	98
An Account of the MacIntoshes and MacPhersons	102
An Account of the Robertsons or Clan Donnochie	109
An Account of the Surname of MacFarlane	111
An Account of the Surname of Cameron	125
An Account of the Surname of MacLauchlan	131
An Account of the Surname of MacNaughtan	133
An Account of the Surname of MacGregor	137
An Account of the Surname of Colquhoun: And the ancient Lairds of Luss, before the assumption of that Surname	142
An acconnt of the Surname of Lamond	151
An Account of the Surname of MacAulay	156

CONTENTS.

An Historical and Genealogical Essay upon the Family and Surname of BUCHANAN   1
An Account of the Family of Auchmar   55
An Account of the Family of Spittel   65
An Account of the Old Family of Arnpryor   71
An Account of the Family of Drumikill   80
An Account of Mr George Buchanan   101
An Account of the Family of Carbeth   108
An Account of the Family of Lenny   120
An Account of the Family of Auchneiven   138
An Account of Buchanan of Miltoun; also of Buchanan of Cashill, Arduill and Sallochie   144
An Account of the MacAuselans   152
An Account of the MacMillans   157
An Account of the MacColmans   164
An Account of the Origin of the Spittels   168
An Account of the Origin of the MacMaurices, MacAndeoirs, MacChruiters, and MacGreusichs   173
The Martial Atchievements of the Family of Buchanan   178
The Learned Men of the Name of Buchanan   191

THE PREFACE.

THE Subject of the following Book may possibly appear a little too confined to the most part of Readers, in regard the affairs of Private Families can be of so very little concern to the Publick; and besides Genealogies themselves are commonly reckoned so dry and tasteless a thing, that very few people think it worth while to be at much pains about them. It is not my design to answer all the arguments may be urged on this head. I persuade myself, no man thinks it lost labour to enquire into the descent of Princes, and other eminent Personages; and why should it be looked on as altogether unnecessary to know that of Private Families, especially when they have produced Persons of extraordinary characters and reputation in the world? The Publick Historians cannot be supposed to know any thing of such minute passages, without the help of such private memorials; and therefore it is necessary, that some or other should take upon them that lower employment, of gathering together the materials, that may be serviceable to the higher order of Writers. Instead therefore of incurring censure for the choice of my subject, I ought rather to have the thanks of my Readers, for not going out of my depth, by undertaking what I had not sufficient abilities for.

None of my Readers need be afraid of being imposed upon in my management of this Work. For tho' indeed in some cases, where authentick records could not be had, I have been obliged to take up with the best attested, and most generally received traditional accounts; yet for the most part I am supported in what I say, by ancient charters of uncontested authority. And besides, whenever I am obliged to make use of tradition, I always advertise my Reader of it; and giving him the most probable account to confirm my own opinion, leave him to make what judgement he pleaseth himself upon the matter.

In the Account of the HIGHLAND CLANS, the curious will find something that has not yet been touched upon by any of our Writers, and which may be agreeable to such as are fond of our Scottish Antiquities; there being not only an abstract of all that our Historians have delivered unto us on that subject, but also all the old uncontroverted traditions we have among us relating thereto, which, tho' they cannot be vouched by written authorities, yet it would be over great incredulity to pay no manner of regard to them; especially since we have for the most part no better documents for the origine of most nations in Europe.

The PREFACE.

The Family of BUCHANAN has had the honour to produce a great many persons, that make a very considerable figure in our History; and as it is natural for us to be curious about the smallest circumstances relating to great men, those of that temper will here find what in a great measure may serve to gratify such their curiosity. Besides, this Family is now grown so very numerous, that it cannot but be of very great use to those of the name, or that are any way allied to it, to have a full and distinct account of its affairs. So that tho' perhaps this Treatise may not be of such general use, yet it will at least serve them for whom I principally intended it; to wit, those of the Name and Family of BUCHANAN.

In giving an account of the Family of BUCHANAN, I have been very exact in looking over the writings belonging to it, now in the hands of his Grace the Duke of Montrose, which the Laird of Gorthy was pleased to supply me with. This account, though a great many documents are lost, has been of considerable use to me: as has also the Tree of the Family of Buchanan in Lenny's hands, which tho' a great part of it is cut off, and some of it contradictory to more certain evidents, yet is in the main a very valuable piece of antiquity. I have had also the perusal of all the writings in the hands of the Buchanans of Drumikill, Lenny, Carbeth, Spittel, Auchneiven, and Gartinstarry, which though very distinct, yet would not have been full enough, had I not obtained an ancient Chartulary among the Records of Dunbarton-shire, containing the whole progress of the Earls of Lennox and their vassals, from the beginning of the reign of King Alexander the second anno 1214, till the latter end of King Robert the third's reign, which has been of singular service to me. The Chartulary of Paisley has also furnished me with several things very useful for my purpose.

Some people indeed of the name of BUCHANAN, from what inducement I will not pretend to determine, have been pleased to refuse me the necessary helps for giving an account of their families: If I have therefore been any ways defective in what relates to them, they have none but themselves to blame for it, who have deprived me of the means whereby I can do them justice, which was my sole intention in undertaking this Work.

I do not think myself obliged to make any apology for the stile of the ensuing sheets. The subject of them exclude every thing of labour and elegance. All that can be looked for in them is plainness and perspicuity, both which it has been my greatest pains to endeavour after. If I have succeeded, so as to satisfy those for whom I chiefly intended these sheets, I am content, and shall desire no other reward for my labours, than that they will charitably excuse whatever errors I may have fallen into, on account of the sincerity, and honesty of my intentions. I submit the whole to the candid Reader, and shall no longer detain him from the perusal of the Work.

AN INQUIRY

INTO THE

GENEALOGY and PRESENT STATE

OF

Ancient SCOTTISH Surnames:

WITH THE

ORIGIN AND DESCENT

OF THE

HIGHLAND CLANS.

By WILLIAM BUCHANAN of AUCHMAR.

[FIRST PUBLISHED IN THE YEAR 1723.]

EDINBURGH:

PRINTED AND SOLD BY WILLIAM AULD,
TURK'S CLOSE, LAWN-MARKET.

M,DCC,LXXV.

AN INQUIRY

INTO THE

Genealogy and present State

OF

Ancient Scottish Surnames.

INTENDING to give an account of the origin of some of the most considerable CLANS in Scotland, I think it necessary to advertise the readers in the entry, that they are not to expect such distinct and well vouched relations of things transacted at so great a distance of time, as in matters of more recent memory. The history of all nations and people in their origin depends upon the authority of immemorial tradition, which if it be not a good one, is at least the only one can be obtained in all such cases. I have therefore made use of it in the enfuing Treatife, wherever more authentick Documents were wanting, and when other circumftances give the ftrength of probability to the traditional accounts.

The exiftence of any Surnames as now ufed before the reign of King Malcolm Canmore, which commenced in the year 1057, is vigoroufly controverted by a great many of this age; and that the firft furnames which commenced in, or fhortly after that reign, were local furnames, or thefe denominated from the lands firft acquired by the affumers of thefe furnames. This fuppofition upon due examination will be found of no great weight, if the leaft regard be had to our public hiftories, and fome other records; there being no defignation more frequently mentioned in our hiftories than that of *Phylarchæ*, or Cheiftians of tribes, which in all rational probability can admit of no other conftruction than Chiefs of furnames or clans, agreeable to thofe of that ftation in thefe modern ages. It is very abfurd to affert, that there were cheiftians of tribes in thefe times, and yet allow them no tribes to be cheiftians of; which is the fame thing in effect as to call one by the name of a King, and yet allow him to have no kingdom; or to speak of a General, and at the same time deny him any soldiers. Tho' it may be urged against this assertion, that these *Phylarchæ* were the King's governours of provinces, inhabited by tribes of different denominations: Yet this is no way probable, it being evident from our history, that in the reign of King Eugenius VIII, about the year 740, Murdoc was Governor of the province of Galloway, and in the reign of King Solvatheus anno 770, Cullan Governor of Argyle, and Duchal Governor of Athole. All these being designed by the particular provinces governed by them, and existing in the same ages, that the *Phylarchæ* were not only existing, but in their full splendor, as they continued for many ages thereafter, and of a quite different office and designation, sufficiently demonstrates the *Phylarchæ* to have been different from the governors of provinces. Nor could these have been governors or captains of the two or three tribes of the Brigantes and Silures, to which by some the Iceni are added, into which the Scottish people were in ancient times divided, in regard the *Phylarchæ* are said to be very numerous, being Councellors in civil, and Captains in martial affairs under our Scottish Kings. Whereas if there had only been Captains of these tribes, their number had been no more than three, which is highly improbable, and the more so, in regard only the first of these three tribes is mentioned, or applied ordinarily to the Scots, by any unexceptionable authors. Much less are we to rely on these newly invented fictitious names of Gadeni, Novantes, Ladeni, and such like names of tribes assigned to the ancient inhabitants of each province, or shire in this kingdom, to be met with in divers, especially of our modern writers, none of which hath the least signification in, or affinity with the undeniable native language used by those to whom these terms are given; whereas the term of *Gathelians* denoting their origin, and *Albinich* importing their country, tho' far more ancient terms than any of the other, are as yet in the native language retained by the progeny of the ancient Scots. So that it may be presumed the above names of the several tribes had not been so wholly disused, had the same ever been really in use, or of any import in their language; these terms seeming to have been invented by such as had little knowledge of the language, and other circumstances of those to whom they assigned them, and therefore no great reason to assign the *Phylarchæ* who had a real existence to these tribes, which in all appearance had no other than a fictitious one.

Nor can it be well imagined with what shew of reason it can be denied, that the ancient Scots were composed of divers surnames in common with other nations, such as the Grecians, who, tho' called by the general denomination of Grecians, and more particularly by their several provinces, as Beotians, Spartans, &c. yet at the same time surnames were in use among them; as the Heraclidæ, from their progenitor Hercules; Pelopidæ from Pelops; Mirmidons, so denominated from their frugality or laboriousness. Also among the Romans distinct surnames were no less frequent than among the former; as the Fabii from their ancestor Fabius; the Manlii Torquati so denominated from their ancestor Manlius Torquatus. Among the English the ancestor of the surname of Piercy, ancient Earls of Northumberland, obtained that surname upon account of their ancestor's piercing King Malcolm III. his eye with a spear at Alnwick. Also the Turnbulls in Scotland are said to have first got that surname from one of their ancestor's turning of a mad Bull, which made an attempt upon King Robert I. Nor were surnames in these more ancient times only used among the more polite nations, but also among the more barbarous; as the Acmenidæ among the Persians; Arsacidæ among the Parthians, and so in general among most of the known world. And it is very remarkable, that notwithstanding of the various revolutions, and grand mutations which have fallen upon the country and people of Italy, since the declination, at least extinction of the Roman Empire, yet some remainder of the ancient surnames with litttle variation continue as yet in that country; as some of the Vitellii, of which family was Aulus Vitellius, a Roman Emperor. And we find

Chiapinius Vitellius, a principal officer under the Prince of Parma in the wars of Flanders, not much above an age ago, being of that antient surname. The Irish also contend in their histories, that they can carry down the descent of the O'Neils, O'Donnells, O'Lauchlins, O'Brians, MacRories, and others termed by them the Mileian progeny, from certain sons of Mileius King of Spain, being Captain of the first colony of Gathelians, or Scots which from Spain first arrived, and settled in Ireland.

The Welch, and some English writers assert, that the ancestor of the surname of Tudor, of which was King Henry VII. was originally descended from Cadwallader last King of the Britons, who flourished about the 668 of the Christian Epocha. To instance the fondness of people's having the origin of their most famous men screued up to as great a pitch of antiquity as possible, yea, sometimes above measure, I observed in Harrison, an English Writer, the genealogy of Hengist first King of Kent, and planter of the Saxons in Britain, carried up to Noah, and names assigned to each of his progenitors through all that long pedigree. Tho' indeed I in no manner approve of such vain glory; I as little do so of the opinionativeness of some of our writers, who endeavour all they can to deprive their country of that which other nations esteem their honour, and which a great many upon much worse grounds, and much less satisfying authorities, use their utmost efforts in asserting, by extolling the antiquity of their nation, and surnames.

The principal reason of some people's decrying the antiquity of the last is, that those writers will not allow private evidences, judged by them the only infallible records, to have had any existence before the reign of King David I. and therefore what is recorded of any surnames is not to be relied on before that time. But as the first part of that supposition is not so infallible as these would make private evidents, so no more is the last part of it, it being well known, that there is lately found among our publick records a charter by King Duncan I. grand-father to King David, as also a charter by Ethelred, one of King Malcolm the third's sons, of lands called Admor, to the Culdees of St Andrews, granted in his father's time, and to which he is witness. And as these, so divers others of equal if not greater antiquity might be found upon due disquisition in our publick records, and some private hands. Yea *Speed*, and other English historians, mention that there is a charter in the publick records of that nation granted by King Athelstan to one Paulan a Saxon gentleman, of the lands of Rodham in York-shire, with divers others by King Edgar, Ethelred, and other Saxon Kings long before the reign of King David. So that if these Saxon Kings be allowed to have granted charters in those more ancient times, who received both their religion and letters from the Scots, I see no reason of denying those of this kingdom the same matter; tho' probably a great many of the most ancient have been cancelled, and others carried into foreign parts in the time of the wars after the death of King Alexander, and at the reformation.

And though there were no other record than our publick histories concerning divers of our surnames, and other affairs, if no credit muſt be allowed to any thing recorded therein before the reigns of King Malcolm III. and King David I. the loſs would be found much greater than could readily be compenſated by any ſuppoſition newly advanced, however ſpecious, tending to the ſubverſion of an hiſtory as well founded in all circumſtances as is requiſite for any of that kind.

To this therefore I ſhall appeal in relation to what I am to offer in further proſecution of the above mentioned ſubject, and by the ſame will endeavour to illuſtrate a good many of our moſt conſiderable ſurnames, whoſe progeny of the ſame denomination is found in this age to have exiſted in ſeveral junctures, and different reigns, divers ages before the time prefixed by thoſe modern writers.

My firſt inſtance is of the ſurname of Murray. Our hiſtorians relate a people of that denomination to have arrived in this kingdom in the reign of King Corbred I. and for poſſeſſions to have got Murray-land, retaining that name yet; of which tribe in regard of their armorial bearing, being Mollets, accounted by Heralds the moſt ancient, and that the ancient and once numerous surname of Sutherland is reputed a Branch of the same, the present surname of Murray may without the least inconsistency be not only presumed, but even admitted to be originally descended; especially seeing in the reign of King Donald V. anno 900, there is mention of a controversy maintained with much slaughter betwixt the Murrays and Rosses, both being considerable surnames at that time, which is more than two Centuries before the time assigned for the commencement of Surnames. And that which in a great measure confirms my allegation in relation to the Murrays, is, that among the first of our surnames that of Murray is found upon record by private evidents, and is thereby known to have been a potent and numerous name.

For further instances we have the Grahams in King Fergus the II's time, anno 404. Of which, with the Dunbars, there is again mention made in the reign of King Indulfus. Now as was before observed of the surname of Murray, the surname of Graham within so small a tract of time after this reign being found upon record by private evidents, leaves no room to doubt of its being the genuine offspring of those already mentioned. In the same manner also the Dunbars, of which the potent name of Hume is a branch, may be asserted to be the progeny of that considerable person of that name mentioned in the foresaid reign, notwithstanding of some late writer's asserting one Gospatrick, a Saxon, who left Northumberland, and settled in the Mers about the reign of King Malcolm IV. to be ancestor of the Dunbars. But the contrary plainly appears by the concurrent testimony of divers of our historians, who maintain that surname's descent from one properly called Barr, one of King Kenneth the Great's Captains, who in the wars against the Picts, and upon the subversion of that people, obtained an estate in the Mers, being a part of the Picts dominion, and upon the acquision of those lands named the same Dunbar, which in the ancient language imports the Fort or Habitation of Barr, whence his progeny assumed the surname of Dunbar. Nor does it infer any inconsistency, that the principal person of that name had besides his estate in the Mers the estate of Bengelly in Northumberland, of which he retained possession till the Scots were dispossest of that whole Province, by the unjust avarice of King Henry II. of England.

The third and most clearly documented instance of any hitherto advanced is, that of the illustrious surname of Douglas in King Solvathius' time in the year 770. Of which surname Sir William Douglas went Lieutenant to Prince William, King Achaius's brother, in the army sent by that King to the service of Charles the Great, First Emperor of the West, and King of France, upon the conclusion of the League betwixt France and Scotland; after which the said Sir William, having settled in Tuscany, was ancestor of the family of the Douglassii there, and in the Low countries, who have always retained the ancient surname and bearing of the family of Douglas in Scotland, and also a close correspondence therewith, as may be seen by the exquisite history of that surname here, as also by the history written by Umberto de Lorato of those others abroad, which could not have been very practicable to be so exactly done, had not the surname of Douglas been so denominated in the reign in which that brave gentleman, a branch thereof, left this kingdom. The progenitor of the surname of Douglas is reported by some antiquaries to have been a son of MacDuff Thane of Fife, who upon his so much signalizing himself in the battle against Donald Bain, obtained his surname, not from his black-grey armour alone, as is commonly asserted, but from his surname of MacDuff, or Duff, termed in Irish Du, or Duy, from whence and his grey armour he was upon that occasion termed Macduiglas, and thereafter more briefly and properly Douglas.

However this be, there are not other instances wanting to confirm what has been advanced on the present subject; such as the ancestor of the surname of Hay, who with his two sons by their valour gained that signal victory for the Scots against the Danes at the battle of Luncarty, in the reign of King Kenneth III. He by our historians is expresly asserted to be surnamed Hay at that occasion.

The ancestor of the surname of Keith is

also memorable in our history for killing of Camus the Danish General in the reign of King Malcolm II. We have also an account of Duncan MacDuff, who was Thane of Fife in the reign of MacBeath, and is recorded to have been a person of great power and authority, and chief of a numerous and potent surname, as the many considerable branches descended of that family near those times clearly evince, such as the Weymesses, MacIntoshes, and Shaws, with divers others. The first of these derive their surname from Caves, with which the sea-coasts of those lands first acquired by the progenitor of that name abounds; caves being termed in Irish *Uaimh*, which can be no other way rendered in English than Weymess. The surname of Hume has also the same etymology, all the difference being that the *H*, or note of aspiration, is more plainly pronounced in the last of these surnames.

These above adduced being not only of a date much more ancient than the period by some writers assigned for the commencement of surnames in general, but also in these times in which the said are found upon record both potent and numerous, which cannot be in reason thought to have been effected in an instant, or even a small tract of time; it seems therefore much more reasonable to presume, that they, with some others long ago extinct, or not expresly recorded, and others hereafter to be mentioned, were the genuine progeny of the *Phylarchæ*, and others anciently planted at several junctures in this kingdom, than to conclude them and all our other surnames in a manner upstarts, in regard each of them cannot (as I suppose few others can) produce such distinct evidents concerning their several origins, as may satisfy such as reject all that suits not their particular humours, however inconsistent with reason or the nature of the matter canvassed the same may sometimes fall out to be.

Next falls to be considered that assertion of local surnames derived from the lands of the assumers to have commenced in the reign of King Malcolm III. and to be the most ancient surnames, and that there was no other surname, or method of distinguishing persons in use before that time, but what was assumed either from bodily properties, applicable to particular persons, as

Roy, or *Baan*, from the Red or flaxen colour of a perſon's hair; *Balloch*, from ſpots on the face; *Bacah*, from a halt in one's leg: Or from ſome quality of mind, as *Coich*, mad or paſſionate, and ſuch like. It is alſo aſſerted, that theſe names then uſed were ſometimes derived from a perſon's father's Chriſtian name, as James ſon of John, with others of that kind, none of which were of longer duration than the perſon's own time ſo denominated. And ſo there was room left for new ſurnames each generation. All which, if true, would argue us to have been a more confuſed and rude ſet of people, than our very enemies could have wiſhed, or ever gave us out to be.

As to local ſurnames it is to be obſerved, that the greater part of them are derived from proper ſignificant terms in the Engliſh language, terminating moſtly in *town*, or ſome other term in that language; which language cannot be documented to have commenced in the reign of King Malcolm III. even in England, much leſs to have been either ſpoken, or underſtood in Scotland, over all which Iriſh was the native language used by the inhabitants then and for some ages thereafter, it being severely enacted, that none should either use or learn the Saxon, or Teutonick, which was that used in England, lest by that means there should be any correspondence with the Saxons when enemies. Yea so far was the mixture of Teutonick, and old Cimbrick, or Danish, from being either perfect or pleasant, that William the Norman Conqueror, upon his conquest of England, endeavoured all he could, as did also some of his successors, to suppress or abolish that language entirely, and bring the French in place thereof, which in a great measure was effected. So that it was at a long distance after his time ere that compound of the said three languages, and the Latin, termed now English, was introduced, and longer time ere the same was brought to any measure of perfection; so that it is somewhat ridiculous to assert, that Surnames which in the least can lay any just claim to antiquity, could be derived from any significant terms in a language scarcely known, and far less used in this kingdom before the reigns of King Alexander II. and III. who by their successive marriages with the daughters of the Kings of England, their frequent commerce and correspondence with that kingdom, and the resort of divers English to and settlement in this, made that language, tho' even in those times very unpolite, to be in some measure used here.

Nor will it be found upon record, that these local surnames are generally of a more ancient standing than the reign of the first of these two Kings; and even then the assumers of these local surnames had other surnames not only at the time, but also a good many for divers ages before the assumption of the local ones; as Houston's ancestor had that of Padvinan before that of Houston; Buchanan that of MacAuselan before that of Buchanan, and so a great many others. However in the reigns of King Alexander III. and King Robert I. the English language having become pretty much in use, it is probable those Kings, as did some of their successors, encouraged the assumers of new surnames from their lands, in order to carry off some dependants and cadets from the too numerous and potent Clans, by that means diminishing their numbers, and weakning their union, so formidable often to the Kings themselves, who rationally concluded, that few were so free of ambition, and careless of their own interest, as not to chuse to be a kind of Chief of his Sept, or at least expected some one of his progeny in a little time would be so, and to be in the King's favour and protection, rather than be subject to the imperious commands of their Chieftains, which often tended to the ruin of themselves and their dependants. Moreover many of English extract, who upon divers accounts settled in this kingdom, in the time of the wars betwixt the death of King Alexander III. and the beginning of the reign of King David II. judged it their interest to change their former, and assume new surnames from their lands, or some other occasion; by that means in some small process of time to bring in oblivion their extract and nation, both so justly odious at that time to the people they resided among. So that as the most probable time of the commencement of these surnames is hereby pointed out, so also the extract of them upon a due disquisition will be found to be English.

For further illustration of this subject, it is unanimously agreed to by our Historians, that upon the subversion of the Picts, being more than 200 years before the reign of King Malcolm III. a great part of the land possessed by the said people, obtained new denominations, from the proper names of those brave Captains to whom King Kenneth assigned the lands in recompence of their service in conquering the ancient possessors thereof; as for instance, that Peninsula formerly called *Ross*, was then called *Fife*, from the proper name of a Nobleman called Fife, whose surname was MacDuff, and whose progeny continued Thanes of that country for divers ages thereafter. As was at the same time the country called anciently *Horestia*, termed afterwards *Merns* and *Angus*, from the proper names of two brethren betwixt whom that country was divided.

Nor seems the other supposition concerning epithetical surnames to be much better founded, as derived from some properties of person's bodies, or qualities of their mind. These epithetical designations must be owned to have been in use in some preceeding ages, and even in the prefent in all places where the Irifh language is ufed, or prevails; though at the fame time there is not the leaft reafon of allowing thefe epithets to have been ever ufed in place of furnames, or that perfons fo defigned had no other furnames fave them, which indeed are moftly to be met with in private evidents, the clerks of which being moftly church-men, were fo ftupid, and fupinely negligent, and fo very carelefs of the inftruction or advantage of future ages, as for the moft part to neglect all other defignations of perfons, except thofe epithetical ones fo much ufed then, and by which perfons were well enough known, tho' of no longer duration than their own time; which feems neither to have been regarded nor confidered by thofe unthinking clerks, more than their frequent omiffion of inferting dates in charters, and other evidents written by them. So that if it be argued, that furnames did not commence, or that perfons had none becaufe not defigned by them in moft of thofe reputed unerring private evidents, it may as well be argued from the omiffion of inferting dates in thofe evidents, that no certain or stated epocha of time commenced, or was known at the time of writing those evidents in which the same is omitted. As these private records or evidents so much at present relied on, are most frequently defective in respect of the particulars above-mentioned and some others, so neither are our publick histories wholly free of such imperfections in relation to full designations of persons; as for instance that Donald Baan in King Solvathius' time by most of our Historians is no otherwise designed, and therefore by our modern writers judged to have had no other surname than the epithet of *Baan* assigned upon account of his flaxen hair; yet Archdean Ballenden, translator of Boetius's history, fully and truly designs him *Donald Baan MacDonald Governor of Jura.* He seems to have been tutor to the great Mac-Donald, while minor, or his deputy in some parts of his vast terriorities. Also another Donald is no other way designed by our Historians, than *Donald Balloch*, or *Spotted Donald*, who lived in the reign of King James I. and was brother to Alexander Lord of the Isles, who with his Clan are very well known to be MacDonalds for a great many ages before that time. Malcolm Beg, who succeeded to Gilbert laird of Buchanan in the office of Senescall or Chamberlain to the Earl of Lennox, in the latter part of the reign of King Alexander III. and beginning of King Robert I. is always designed, in all charters in which he is inserted granted by that Earl, *Malcolm Beg or Little*; yet he is found by very authentick documents in the hands of the Earl of Perth, and in the publick records, to have been surnamed *Drummond*, and one of the Earl's ancestors. The same Malcolm's father in a charter by the Earl of Lennox, in the reign of King Alexander II. is designed *Gilchrist Drummond*.

I have observed charters of no earlier dates than the reigns of King James V. and Queen Mary, with others in the two preceeding reigns, to be the most carlessly and rudely written, most confused and unexact in designations of persons inserted therein, and in divers other circumstances of any of the kind to be met with in any preceeding age, some being therein designed from epithets applicable to their fathers, as

John son of Black William, Thomas son of Long or Tall Donald, and such like. Yea in this present age there are two gentlemen of Sir Donald MacDonald's family, and Kepach's, termed Donald Gorm, or Blew Donald, whose progeny, if existing an age or two after this present, would with a deal of reason judge it most ridiculous in any to assert, that their ancestors were not of the surname of MacDonald, because more frequently designed, at least termed, by the epithet *Gorm*. So that it seems consistent with reason, that the asserters of epithets in place of surnames refuse the existence of any other surnames in these three last ages, in which those epithets are most frequent in evidents, or otherways allow persons to have had other surnames together with them in more ancient times.

THAT people known by the denomination of Scots, of which our Scottish nation is at present composed, may, in respect of the origin of the same, be divided into four different distinct classes, or divisions. The first of these classes consists of these surnames whose origin is purely Scottish, being the genuine progeny of the ancient Scots, which from Ireland at different junctures and occasions arrived and settled in Scotland. The second class is composed of such as came from South-Britain, or England, at the time of the four grand conquests of that kingdom, and upon some other accounts, and settled here. The third class or division consists of such French, as upon account of the mutual amity and correspondence commenced by the league betwixt Scotland and France, in Charles the Great and King Achaius' reigns, and continued for a great many ages thereafter, upon which, and divers other accounts, a great number of French settled in this nation, of whom are descended a great number of very confiderable families. The fourth and laft divifion, being the leaft of the four, confifts moftly of fuch Danes and Norveyians as were naturalized by our Scottifh Kings, and obtained poffeffions in this kingdom upon divers occafions, being upon the above accounts permitted to continue in this kingdom, after their country-men were obliged by King Alexander III. to yield or quitt their poffeffion of the Northern Ifles of Scotland, of which they had got a grant from Donald Baan the Ufurper, for their affiftance in fupporting him in his ufurpation, and by virtue of that grant, retained poffeffion for 200 years, till obliged to abandon thofe Ifles by King Alexander, about the year 1280. However divers of Danifh extract, having, by alliance, and other means, before the faid time, obtained confiderable eftates, were allowed to continue by the benevolence of King Alexander, and the fucceffive Kings of Scotland. So that thefe, with fome few others in conjunction with them, of different extracts from the three claffes above-mentioned, make up the fourth clafs or divifion of Scottifh furnames.

The first example by which I shall illustreat the class first mentioned, shall be the Surname of STEWART, being not only of an extract or descent purely Scottish, but also the only Scottish surname whose ancestor was an immediate son, or lineal descendant of the race of our ancient Scottish Kings. The time and manner of whose descent, tho' treated of by divers of much greater abilities than I can pretend to, nevertheless agreeable to the account given by our Seneciones or Shanachies, but especially according to that delivered by a certain genealogical account of that illustrious family, composed in the reign and dedicated to King Charles II. by an unknown author, (which little pamphlet is as well vouched, if not better, than any thing ever I could discover upon that subject), I shall deliver the origin of that Family in the manner following.

Kenneth the Great, King of the Scots, subverter of the Picts, had three sons, Constantine his successor, Ethus, and Gareth. This last had one son, Dorus, whom Mr Abercromby makes son to Ethus the Swift, being by that account grand-child to King

Kenneth, as well as by the other, the difference being concerning his father. Gareth, father to Dorus, was first Thane of Lochaber. Doire or Dorus had two sons; Kenneth, by some erroneously termed Murdac; and Ferquhard, father to Donald, who murdered King Duff, for which he and his progeny were exterminated. Kenneth had two sons; Murdac his successor, and Gareth Thane of Athol. Murdac was married to Dunclina, daughter to King Kenneth III. by whom he had two sons; Bancho his successor, and Alexander; also four daughters, the first married to one of the ancestors of the Douglasses, another to Donald Thane of Sutherland, the third to Angus ancestor of the Camerons, and the fourth to Malcolm MacRory, Lord of Bute.

Bancho, with three of his sons, and his brother-in-law Hugh Douglas, was murdered by order of the tyrant MacBeath, his fourth son Fleance having escaped, and fled to Wales. Bancho's two daughters were married to MacDuff Thane of Fife, and Frederick, ancestor of the Urquharts. Fleance, by Maria Mnesta, daughter to Griffith ap Lewellin, Prince of Wales, had

Walter, first of the surname of Stewart, being married to Christian, daughter to Allan Lord of Bretaign in France, by whom he had Allan his successor, who had two sons; Walter his successor founder of the Abbey of Paisley anno 1160, and Simon ancestor of the Boyds. Walter's successor was Allan the second, whose successor was Walter the third, High Justiciary of Scotland. He had two sons; Alexander his successor, and Robert Lord Torbolton, who by marriage of the heiress of Sir Robert Croc, obtained with her the estates of Croukstoun and Darnly, and was ancestor of the family of Darnly afterward of Lennox, notwithstanding that Mr Abercromby makes Allan, son of John commonly termed of Bute, ancestor of that family. Alexander had two sons, James his successor, and Walter, who by marriage of the heiress of Cummine Earl of Montieth, got that Earldom, and thereupon changed his surname to Montieth. He had two sons, Murdo his successor, and Sir John Montieth of Rusky, ancestor of the surname of Montieth, and who betrayed Sir William Wallace. Murdo Earl of Montieth had one son Allan, who, by marriage of the heiress of MacDuff Earl of Fife, obtained that Earldom, who having one daughter conveyed those estates by marriage to Robert Stewart, second son to King Robert II. and first of the Stewarts. Both estates, through forfaulter of Duke Murdo his son, fell to the crown. Alexander's third son, by Jean MacRory heiress of Bute, was John, killed at the battle of Falkirk anno 1298.

James High Stewart had one son, Walter, married to Marjory Bruce daughter to King Robert I. by whom he had one son, Robert, named Blear-eye: His mother when big with child of him, being killed by a fall from her horse, at that place of Renfrew-moor called Queen Blear-eye's Cross, the child by a Doctor there present was cut out of her belly, and the instrument with which the operation was performed having touched his eye, the same continued to be always tender thereafter, which give him the epithet of Blear-eye. Upon the death of his uncle King David II. without male-issue, he obtained the Crown of Scotland, by designation of King Robert II. of whose successors I refer to our publick histories.

The second principal branch of that great Family, was the Family of Lennox, lineally descended from Robert Lord Torbolton, already mentioned, his son being Allan first Lord Darnly, who had two sons, John his successor, and Allan, who acquired the lands of Faslane, and others in the Lennox. Allan of Faslane's son Walter, by marriage of Margaret heiress of Donald Lennox Earl of Lennox, obtained that Earldom, whose son Duncan Earl of Lennox had only two daughters, Isabel the eldest married to Murdo Duke of Albany, who with his father-in-law the Earl of Lennox, and his own two sons, Walter, and Alexander, was by order of King James I. executed anno 1424, and their estates forfaulted.

John second Lord Darnly had two sons, Allan his successor, and Robert, first Lord of Aubigny in France. Allan Lord Darnly married Lillias second daughter to the last mentioned Duncan Earl of Lennox, and by her by gift of her father's forfaulture got the Earldom of Lennox, whose issue enjoyed the same till the reign of King James VI. that the Earldom was conferred upon Esme Lord Aubigny, whose grand-child died without iffue in the reign of King Charles II. The Earldom having devolved upon an illegitimate fon of that King, he fold the fame lately, referving only the tittle. Of this family are defcended the Earls of Traquair and Galloway, with a great many others; the Earl of Moray being defcended of a fon of Murdo Duke of Albany, and the Earl of Bute of a fon of King Robert III.

Of all other ancient furnames of Scottifh defcent or origin, the heroick Surname of DOUGLAS juftly merits to be mentioned next to that of Stewart; but having briefly touched on that furname already, and there being a particular hiftory of the fame, I fhall infift no further thereon, than to declare that I agree with the fentiments of thofe Antiquaries who affert the progenitor of, and who firft affumed the Surname of Douglas to have been a fon of MacDuff Thane of Fife, for which there are divers arguments ufed not neceffary to be in this place enumerated.

From the same ancient Surname of Mac-Duff, as already hinted, is descended the Surname of WYMESS, the ancestor thereof being Eugenius son to Constantine third Earl of Fife, in the reign of King Alexander I. It is asserted the Lesley's and Abernethies are of the same stem with Wymess; but I could not obtain any exact account of the time and manner of the descent of either of these two last off that of MacDuff.

The next instance is of the surname of CAMPBELL, which is of an ancient Scottish origin, however otherwise asserted by some of our Historians. I shall briefly glance at the genealogy and some other matters relating to this surname, conform to two accounts of the same in Manuscript; the one of these composed by Mr Alexander Colvil, from evidents and other records of the family of Argyle; the other account by Neil MacEwan, who and his ancestors for divers ages have been Seneciones or Genealogists of the said family. This last derives the ancient surname of *Oduibhne*, now Campbell, from Mervie Moir, or Mervin the Great, son to the famous Arthur King of the Brittons, and of Elizabeth daughter to the King of France, which behoved to have been Childobert the fifth in defcent from Pharamond, who was contemporary with King Arthur.

Mervin is reported to have been a wild untractable man, and upon that account rejected by the Brittons, tho' neither this nor any other circumftance relating even to the exiftence of fuch a perfon is any way confiftent with probability; for tho' there be no great reafon of fo doing, yet there are a great many who doubt of the exiftence of King Arthur himfelf, in regard fome of his country-men in their writings have fo much blended the account of his life and actions with fo many ridiculous and monftrous fables, as have very much prejudged the credit due to his exiftence and heroick atchievements. This brave King is recorded to have begun his reign in the year 518, and in a reign of twenty-four years to have gained twelve victories, with the affiftance of Goranus King of the Scots, and Lothus King of the Picts, over the Saxons, till in the end he expelled moft part of them, and obliged fuch as stayed in his kingdom to be in subjection to him. But much prosperity having rendered him and his subjects too insolent, they endeavoured to defraud Mordred King of the Picts of the British Crown, which through defect of Arthur's issue justly belonged to him, which was the occasion of a bloody battle betwixt them, in which both these Kings lost their lives, and so shattered the state of the Brittons, that it could never be retrived thereafter, till in the end ruined by the Saxons. King Arthur was not only very much esteemed by the Brittons, but also by most others, being accounted one of the World's Nine Worthies, of which three were Jews, Joshua, David, and Judas Maccabeus; three Christians, Arthur of the Brittons, Charlemaign of France, and Godfrey of Bulloign; three Pagans, Alexander the Great, Julius Cæsar, and Hector of Troy. But as for Mervin this pretended son of King Arthur, there is no probable ground for the existence of any such person, it being plainly recorded by all such histories as make mention of this King, that he never had any issue, nor was ever married to any but his Queen Gwyvanor, who survived himself: Nor would the Brittish and French Histories have wholly ommitted a matter of that importance, were there the least ground for the same; neither would the Brittons, however wild or foolish he might be, have past by that King's son whom they so much valued, and confer their Crown upon one Constantine, a Nobleman who had no manner of pretence thereto; much less would Modred the Pictish King, being only King Arthur's cousin-german, contend for a Crown which by so plain a right pertained to another. So that although by this account the furname of Oduibhne is said to have got that denomination from the marriage of Ferithar Olla, the fourth in descent from Mervin, with a daughter of Diarmuid Oduibhne a principal Nobleman of Ireland, and to have not only obtained from this Diarmuid the denomination of Oduibhne, but also that of Siol Diarmuid, by which that surname is in Irish frequently designed; yet this supposition is wholly groundless, there being no instance of any ancient Scottish or Irish Surname's obtaining their ancient or principal denomination by any such means. Some of the progenitors of this surname are by the said account reported to have been married to grand-children of Con Centimachus, and Neil the Great, two of the most famous Kings that ever reigned in Ireland; so that if they were used to take denominations from such families as they married into, the same would much rather be assumed from names of one of those Kings, than from that of any Nobleman their subject.

But passing this topick, I come to the account most consistent with probability, in relation to the origin of that surname. The ancestor of the same was Diarmuid Oduibhne, who, as one of the principal *Phylarchæ* or Captains, came from Ireland with some of the Scots, who either in King Fergus's time, or in that of one of the two colonies which at different junctures came from that Kingdom, and settled in Argyle and the Isles adjacent. For tho' the generality of our Historians, more especially Genealogists, rather to please the taste of those of the modern times, than in any great measure to promote the truth, or at least probability, use their utmost efforts to afsign some plausible manner and stated period concerning the origin of ancient surnames; yet all amounts to no more than probable conjecture, supported only by probable and solid tradition, of which that most consistent with sound reason and probability ought most to obtain: So that in the accounts of the origin of this, or any other of our ancient Scottish Surnames, there is as little absurdity in presuming the same to be the offspring of those who first settled here, as by a specious kind of story to assert them descended at such a time, and from such a person, some eight or nine hundred, or a thousand years ago, there being as few written documents to confirm the last, as the first of these accounts. Nor is it in reason to be supposed, as I have hinted already, that the whole progeny of those Scots, who are recorded to have settled before, at, and in some process of time after the coming of King Fergus I. here, to be so totally mouldred away, and extinct, as that few or none of these surnames now in being, and of an ancient Scottish extract, can be pretended to be their genuine progeny; but that each surname must be put to the shift of framing a later origin for themselves, which when affected is not a whit better founded, nor more satisfactory to people of understanding than the former method; to which left I appear too closely to adhere, I shall relate the account most agreed to, conform to the more modern method of genealogizing, in relation to the origin of the above-mentioned surname.

Thus in place of Mervie, or as others call him Smervie Moir, supposed son of King Arthur, these other genealogists, with a greater shew of probability, mention Diarmuid Oduibhne, a very famous Irish Nobleman, and much celebrated for valour and other heroick atchievements by the Irish Historians, who having come to Scotland in the beginning of the reign of King Goranus, or Coranus, about the year 512, married a daughter of the said King, of whom he begot Ferithar Uor, or Ferithar the Dun. From this Diarmuid, according to the above Antiquaries, the Surname obtained the two designations of Oduibhne, and Siol Diarmuid, who flourished in, or some little time after that of King Arthur, which gave rise to the story of his being son to that King, as also of divers of his posterity's being called Arthurs, whence no inference can be deduced of their descent from King Arthur, that Christian name being used among the Irish long before King Arthur's time: As for instance Cormac MacArtur, son of Arthur, to-named Ulfada or Long Beard, King of Ireland, a great many years before the time of Arthur King of the Brittons: As also a great many others of account in Ireland in very ancient times. This Diarmuid seems either to have been of the same origin with the Sept of Scottish O-duibhns, and therefore to have been by them at the juncture assumed for *Phylarcha* or Cheiftain, or which is more probable to be lineally descended from the first Diarmuid, and upon account of the grandeur by marriage of the Scottish King's daughter, and other atchievements, to have been accounted the progenitor of that Surname, and from whom the same was first so denominated.

Ferithar Uor was married to a great grand-child of Neil the Great, to-named *Naoighealla* or Nine Hostages, whom he is recorded to have had in his custody at one

F

time from several Spanish and Brittish Princes, with whom he had been at variance, being thence termed Keeper of Nine Hostages, and one of the most famous of the Irish Kings. Ferithar Uor's successor was Duibhne, or Duina, an ordinary Christian name in those times. Duina's successor was called Arthur, whose mother was Murdac Thane of Murray's daughter. There is no account of the family this Arthur married into; however his successor called Ferithar Olla, or the Physician, is reported to have been married to one Diarmuid Oduibhn's daughter, which is a grand mistake, as already observed. Ferithar Olla's successor was Duibhne Faltdearge, or Duina Red Hair; he is said to have been married to a grand-child of Neil the Great, which is no less an error than that above-mentioned, as appears from the vast distance of time betwixt these two. His successor was Ferithar Fionruadh, or Whitish-Red. His successor was Duina Dearg, or Red, his son being Duibhne Doun, or Duina the Brown, from the colour of his hair. His successor was Diarmuid MacDuine or son of Duina.

This Diarmuid MacDuina had two sons: Arthur, with the Red Armour, either from artificial colour, or frequent colouring thereof with blood. The second son was Duina White-Tooth. The eldest of these called Art Armdhearg, or Arthur Red Armour, had three sons, Sir Paul Odnine or MacDuine Knight of Lochow, of which estate all his progenitors already mentioned were proprietors. This Sir Paul was termed Paul Ansporrain, or Paul with the Purse, being Treasurer to King Malcolm III. as is commonly alledged. His two brethren were Arthur Dreinuch, of whom descended MacArture of Inchdreiny, and others of that name upon Lochow-side. The other brother was called also Arthur, of whom descended the Family of Darnly in Lennox, lately extinct. Of the first of these two Arthurs descended also the Family of Strachur; which tho' recorded to be descended of one of the Knights of Lochow, some generations after the assumption of the Surname of Campbell; yet it is not so probable as the above descent, in regard of the long continued pretension of the Family of Strachur to more antiquity than that

F 2

of Argyle, which could be founded upon no other ground than that above related.

Diarmuid MacDuibhne's second son, Duina White-Tooth, had one son called Gillecollum, or Malcolm Oduibhne, who first married the Lord of Carrick's daughter, by whom he had three sons. The eldest of these Gilmorrie was ancestor of the MacNeachts of Lochaber, and other parts of Argyle-shire. The second son was Corcarua, ancestor of the MacUilins, or rather MacAilins in Ireland. The third son Duncan Drumanach, in regard he resided beyond Drumalbin, was, conform to this genealogy, ancestor of the Drummonds. But that Surname refuse this, and assert their ancestor to have come to Scotland with Queen Margaret Queen to King Malcolm III. and while the ship, in which the Queen was, happened to be in very much danger by a storm, that the dexterity of that gentleman in piloting the same was a great means of the preservation of the ship and passengers, whence he obtained the Surname of Drummond, importing the top of the waves, as is very much illustrated by the armorial bearing of that Surname, being Three Bars waved or undee.

Malcolm Oduin, after his first Lady's death, went to France, and married the Heiress of the Beauchamps, or as in Latin, *Campus Bellus*, being Niece to the Duke of Normandy. By her he had two sons, Dionysius and Archibald, who from the inheritance got with their mother, changed their Surname from Oduin to Campbell. Dionysius the eldest continued in France, and was ancestor of a Family designed Campbell in that Kingdom, of which Family was Count Tallard, a Mareschal of France, carried prisoner to England in the reign of Queen Anne, and divers others of quality. The second brother came to Scotland, as some say an Officer in William Duke of Normandy's army, at his Conquest of England, anno 1066. And coming to Argyle-shire, married his cousin Eva Oduin, only daughter to Sir Paul Oduibhne, or Paul Ansporrian. She being Heiress of Lochow, and he having retained this Surname of Campbell, as did his successors, the whole Clan of Oduibhne in a small tract of time, in compliance with their Chief, assumed that Surname, as did many others in this Kingdom upon the like occasion.

This Archibald, who first assumed the Surname of Campbell, his successor was called Duncan, who, by marriage of one called Dorothy MacFiachir Heiress of the upper part of the Barony of Lochow, united these two estates. He was succeeded by Colin the Bald, who married a Niece of King Alexander I. Or as others with no less probability assert, of King Alexander II. This Colin was instituted Master of the Household to the King, and the King's Lieutenant in the Shire of Argyle and West Isles. Colin's eldest son was Archibald. He had a second son Hugh, ancestor of the Old House of Loudon in the Shire of Air, they having got that estate by Crawford, Heiress thereof, as did her ancestor acquire the same by marriage of the only daughter of Sir James Loudon, Heiress of that estate. The race of the Old Campbells of Loudon terminating also in an Heiress in the reign of King Charles I. Campbell of Lawers, descended of a son of Glenorchy, by marriage of the said Heiress, obtained that estate, being afterwards Chancellor of Scotland, and grand-father to Hugh the present Earl. Colin the Bald had also two illegitimate sons, the eldest Taus Corr, or Thomas the Singular; he was ancestor of the MacTauses, or Thomsons of Argyle-shire; and some other parts. The name of the other illegitimate son was Iver of whom the MacIvers of Glasrie, and other parts.

Colin the Bald was succeeded by his son Archibald, who had two sons, Duncan his successor, and Dugal ancestor of the Old Family of Craignish. Archibald was succeeded by his son Duncan, whose successor was Dugal. His successor was Archibald, who married the Lord of Carrick's daughter, by whom he had Colin Moir, or the Great; being so both in body and spirit. He married a daughter of one Sir John Sinclair, by whom he had his successor Sir Neil. This Colin Moir was killed by his neighbour John MacDougal Lord of Lorn, at a place called the Strein, being a ridge of mountains betwixt Lorn and Lochow. It is thought the Family of Argyle derived the designation of MacCuillain Moir from this Collin; but I am more apt to believe that designation was derived from Colin first Earl of Argyle, and Chancellor of Scotland in the reign of King James II. Sir Neil was married to Lady Marjory Bruce, sister to King Robert, which was the occasion of the close adherence of Sir Neil, and his son Sir Colin, to the interest of that Prince, and performing many signal services to him and King David II. his son. Sir Neil had a son called Dugald, or rather Duncan, ancestor of MacDonachy now Campbell of Inverraw, and other gentlemen of that name, the said Duncan's mother being a daughter of Sir John Cameron, Lochiel's ancestor, and second Lady to Sir Neil. He had another son Sir John of Moulin, afterward Earl of Athole. The further account of this Surname is set forth at large in Mr Crawford's Peerage, to which I refer the reader.

There is also of ancient Scottish descent the Surname of OGILVIE, descended of Bredus a brother, or rather son to the Famous Gilchrist Earl of Angus, who flourished in the reign of King William of Scotland, and was married to that King's sister.

The Surname of KENNEDY is in like manner of great antiquity in this kingdom, being originally descended of that once potent Surname of the MacKennedy's of Ireland, of which Surname was that brave King Brian Kennedy, to-named Boraimh, or Taxer, being Contemporary with our King Malcolm II.

Thus having adduced a sufficient number of instances for the illustration of Surnames of an ancient Scottish descent, being the first class of Scottish Surnames, I shall next proceed to give instances of these whose descent is from England, being the second class of those Surnames, now reputed Scottish ones.

The first instance I shall adduce of the same is, the Surname of GRAHAM, which, according to Buchanan, and some others of our Historians and Antiquaries, is descended from one Fulgentius, a Nobleman lineally descended from the ancient Kings of the Brittons, who in the beginning of the third Century of the Christian Epocha, with an army of his country-men, attempting to free themselves and country from the Roman servitude, their just endeavours were nevertheless frustrated by the superior power of their adversaries, in which exigency Fulgentius, and divers of his associates, were obliged to flee for refuge to Donald, first of that name King of the Scots, then at war with the Romans, who not only gave a very kind reception to these strangers, but bestowed estates upon Fulgentius and some other principal men of them, whose posterity remained always thereafter in Scotland. The principal person of Fulgentius's progeny, having, after the fatal battle of Dun, in which Eugenius King of the Scots, with the greatest part of his nobility, and others of any account of the Scottish nation, were killed by Maximus the Roman Legat, in conjunction with the perfiduous Picts, gone with divers other Scots into Denmark, he continued there till the restoration of King Fergus II. anno 404, or as Boece 423.

That person of Fulgentius' race who went to Denmark, whose proper name was Græme, married in Denmark, and his daughter was married to King Fergus II. tho' others relate that Græme's daughter was mother to King Fergus, being married to Erthus his father, which carries little prabability, in regard Græme was not only a principal affiftant to King Fergus in his own life-time, but was after his death elected Governor, or Regent of the Kingdom, during the minority of his fon Eugenius, and having in that time broke over the wall of Abercorn, greatly harraffed the dominions of the Brittons; fo that from that adventure that wall is faid to have obtained the denomination retained as yet of *Graham's Dyke*, which denomination others affert to be taken from the Emperor Severus, who repaired that wall, which was firft begun by Julius Agricola in the reign of the Emperor Domitian. The reafon given for the laft is, that Severus being born in Africa, was of a very black and fwarthy complexion, and that thence the Dyke was termed *Grim's Dyke*, *Grim* in Irifh fignifying Black or Swarthy, whence the Scottifh word *Grim* is derived. However this be, the firft feems moft probable; nor can thefe great atchievements in Eugenius's minority be imputed to Græme, by reafon of his too great age, whereas the Tranflator of Boetius calls Fergus's mother Rocha, daughter to a Nobleman of Denmark, called Roricius, or rather Rodericus. And that which very much evinces Græme's origin as above afferted is, that his grandchild Eugenius, upon affumption of the government, (as our Hiftorians relate) gave, for pretence of the war commenced by him againft the Brittons, the reftitution of his grand-father Graham's lands.

Our hiftory gives no acount of the pofterity of this Græme for fome ages. The firft to be met with of them is that Graham who, with Dunbar and the forces of Lothian, appeared in the Rear of the Danes, when in battle with King Indulph and his Army, which was the occafion of the defeat of the firft. The next was Conftantine, married to Avila daughter to Kenneth one of the anceftors of the Stewarts, in the year 1030. And in the year 1125, William de Graham is witnefs to the Foundation Charter of Holy-rood-houfe in the reign of King David I. The faid William's fon, Sir David, got Charters of Charletoun, and other lands in Forfar-fhire, in the reign of King William of Scotland; as did his fon, another Sir David, from Malduin

Earl of Lennox, of the lands of Strablane, and from Patrick Dunbar Earl of Dunbar, or March, of the lands of Dundaff and Straithcarron, in the reign of King Alexander II. as did his succeffor, alfo David, the lands of Kincardine from Malife Foreteth Earl of Strathern, in the reign of King Alexander III. Before all which lands mentioned in the above Charters that Surname feems to have been in poffeffion of Abercorn, Eliestoun, and other lands in Lothian. And tho' one Muir is reported to to have had Abercorn in the reign of King Alexander III. yet in all probability he has had but fome part thereof, acquired from the Grahams, which after having continued fome little time with Muir returned to the Grahams again, and went from them with Margaret, heirefs thereof, to James brother to the Earl of Douglas, in the reign of King James I.

There were two principal Families of this name in the reign of King Alexander III. the one being of Abercorn. Both thefe are mentioned among the *Magnates Scotiæ* in cognition of the debate betwixt Bruce and Baliol anent the Scottifh Kingdom, as alfo inserted in that Famous Letter written by King Robert I. to the Pope in the year 1320. These two thereafter were united, when Patrick Graham of Eliestoun and Kilbride, second son to Sir Patrick Graham of Kincardine, in the reign of King Robert III. married the only daughter and heiress of David Earl of Strathern, and by her obtained that Earldom, whose son Malise was deprived of the same by King James I. in regard that estate was entailed to heirs-male; but he gave Malise in lieu of Strathern the Earldom of Monteith anno 1428, whose posterity continued for nine generations Earls thereof. William the ninth Earl, having no issue, disponed his estate to the Marquis of Montrose, and died anno 1694.

The first cadet of this Family was Sir John Graham of Kilbride, Gartmore's ancestor. And the last cadet of any repute was Walter, ancestor to Graham of Gartur.

The next in antiquity of Surnames thus descended, and who were obliged to leave their native Country by the Romans, are by some Antiquaries reported to be the SEATONS, tho' there be little to be found in any of our private records concerning that Surname till the reign of King David I. when Alexander de Seaton is mentioned, as also his son Philip, in a charter of those lands, which for the most part that family enjoyed till of late in the reign of King William. The famous and loyal Sir Christopher Seaton, who was married to Christian Bruce, Sister to King Robert I. is very much celebrated in the account of the wars managed after the death of King Alexander III. and no less so is that heroick action of his son Sir Alexander, in keeping of the town of Berwick, though at the expence of the lives of his two sons, both executed by the orders of that rigorous prince King Edward III.

Those Surnames which were obliged to abandon England through the tyranny and oppression of the Normans, upon the conquest of England, are so very numerous, that I can only mention some few instances of the same.

As first, the Levingstons, derived from Levingus, a proper name frequent among the Saxons: As was also Alphingus, or as it is ordinarily exprest Elphingus, ancestor of the Elphingstons. These with a great many others, ancestors of divers of our principal Surnames, came to Scotland with Edgar Atheling, and his sister Margaret, Queen to our King Malcolm III. some little time after the Norman Conquest, and were all courteously received, and many of them endowed with estates by that Magnificent Prince. The ancestor of the Levingstons having settled in West Lothian, denominated these lands first acquired by him Levingston from his own proper name, which continued to be so for some descents. The first of that Surname found mentioned in any private Record is called Levingus in the reign of King David I. This name was aggrandized by two several means; First, by Sir William Levingston's marriage with the Heiress of Callander, and with her obtaining that estate, in the reign of King David II. Secondly, by Sir Alexander this Sir William's grand child's being Governor of Scotland in the minority of King James II.

As the Levingstons gave denomination to their lands in West Lothian, so the ancestor of the Ephingstons after the same manner denominated the lands firſt acquired by him in Mid-Lothian, which by an heireſs in the reign of King James I. came to the Johnſtouns, that part of the eſtate in Stirlingſhire called formerly Airthbeg (as Mr Crawford aſſerts) being retained by the heir-male, and changed into that of Elphingſton.

The Hamiltons, Hepburns, Grays, and a great many others, are of a more late deſcent from England than theſe already mentioned. All I ſhall obſerve concerning them is, only in relation to that of HAMILTON, the deſcent of which from England ſeems to be of greater antiquity by far than what is generally aſſerted by our Hiſtorians; and I am more apt to join ſentiments with the author of the Engliſh Peerage, who affirms the anceſtor of the Hamiltons to have come to this kingdom in the reign of King William. And that which in a great meaſure confirms me in this opinion is, a Charter in the Regiſter of Dunbarton, pertaining to Hamilton of Bardowie, granted by Duncan Earl of Lennox to John Hamilton of Bathernock, now Bardowie, upon reſignation of John Hamilton his father, of thofe lands in the year 1394, and in the reign of King Robert III. So that the Lord Hamilton's fon, who married Galbraith heirefs of Bathernock, being named by all who write of that Surname David, and owned to be a later cadet than the anceftors of the Hamiltons of Prefton, Innerwick, Bathgate, and a great many others, evinces thefe writers either to be in an error in relation to the defcent of thofe of Bardowie, or which is more probable, in that of the furname in general, as to their anceftor's coming to Scotland in the reign of King Robert I. For tho' it be evident, that by fome feveral defcents Bardowie's anceftor is later than divers cadets of that Family, yet by the above charter in 1394, being only 88 years pofterior to the coronation of King Robert I. the grand-father of that John, in whofe favour that charter was granted, muft be allowed to have exifted at, if not before the coronation of the faid King, and confequently before the time allotted for the firft coming of the anceftor of the Surname of Hamilton to this Kingdom.

The next clafs of Scottifh Surnames is, thofe whofe defcent is from the French, being alfo a very confiderable part of our Scottifh Surnames. The firft inftance of thefe is the Surname of FRASER, fo denominated from the three Straw-berry leaves termed in French Frazes, which that Surname ufe for Armorial Bearing. Some other Surnames of a French extract have alfo obtained denominations from the fame caufe, as the Sharps, Purveffes, and others. The Frafers are faid to be defcended of Peter Count of Troile, who came to Scotland fome little time after the League betwixt Scotland and France. That Surname is not only found upon record, but to have been divided in divers great branches, or families, in the reigns of King Malcolm IV. and King William; one of which in the reign of the latter was Chancellor of Scotland. That great man and Loyal Patriot Sir Simon, fo famous in the reign of King Robert I. was Lord of Tweedale, and refided in Oliver-Caftle in that country.

The Tweedies, now poffeffors of that caftle and adjacent eftate, are fuppofed to be defcended of the ancient Frafers. Lovat's ancestor was also called Simon, his mother being a sister of King Robert I. From this last Simon the Lords Lovat are always termed MacShimes, or contractedly MacImmey, the same with Simpson, whose family is by far the most numerous of any other of that Surname.

The Sinclairs are also of a French descent, being Earls of Orkney, afterwards of Caithness; William, or rather Henry Earl of Orkney and Caithness being Chancellor in the reign of King James II. and of the greatest grandeur of any Nobleman of his age. Also the Montgomeries, as their arms and motto evince, are of a French, or as others assert of a Norman origin; as are also the Bruces; and the Baillies thought to be descended of the ancient Balliols; and the Browns; with a great many others too numerous to be here mentioned.

The fourth and last, and indeed the least class of Scottish Surnames is, those whose descent is from Denmark, and some other Northern Regions. Some Antiquaries, more especially our Heralds, presume the Ramseys, Carnegies, and Munroes, to have come originally from Germany, by reason of their armorial bearings. The Grants affert themfelves to be of a Danifh defcent from *Aquin de Grand* or *Grant*. Sir John de Grant is one of thefe mentioned in the debates which fell out after the death of King Alexander III. The Menzies alfo contend to be of a Danifh extract, as alfo fome others, more efpecially of the Clans, as fhall be hereafter fpecified.

Having thus briefly illuftrated, by inftances, the feveral claffes of Scottifh Surnames, I fhall proceed next to an account of the Clans, or thofe whofe Surnames commence with MAC, of which fuch as are nobilitated being fo fully treated of in the Scottifh peerage, fhall not therefore be touched in this place; nor the MacDowals of Galloway, MacIlvains, MacGuffogs, MacCullos, and fome others, who tho' of an ancient Scottifh extract, yet having no manner of correfpondence or agreement in language, habit, or any other circumftances, with thofe moft properly termed Clans, fhall not here be infifted upon. I fhall therefore confine myfelf wholly to the Highland Clans, which are ordinarily conjoined in our old records and Acts of Parliament.

AN
Account of the
MACDONALDS.

HAVING already offered some few arguments for evincing of some of the Clans, and other Surnames of a Scottish extract, to be the genuine progeny of the ancient Scots, who at different junctures planted the Western parts of Scotland, I shall not in this place further insist upon that subject, but proceed to an account of the MacDonalds, who, for many ages, were of the greatest esteem, and deservedly had the precedency of other Clans. For had not their fate been to be planted in the most remote corners of this kingdom, and by that means no object or occasion offered of exerting that valour and vigour so very natural to them, their actions had been recorded in as bright characters as those of the Douglasses, or any others of our heroick surnames.

The Chieftain or *Philarcha* of this Tribe or Clan, and from whom the principal men thereof are descended, according to Mr Welsh, and some other Irish, also some of our Scottish Seneciones or Genealogists, about a century before our Saviour's nativity, was Coll, to-named Vuais, who had two cousin-germans of the same name, they being by three several sons grand-children to Con Cenchathach, or Constantine Centimachus, King of Ireland, so-named from his fighting a hundred conflicts in his time against foreign invaders of his kingdom, and home-bred rebels, as the Irish History asserts. From these three Colls some of the most ancient of the Clans deduce their descent; and as these are termed Descendants of the Mileian Stem, so they are also designed *Sliochd nan Colluibh*, or the posterity of the Colls; in the like manner as the Campbells are designed both *Clanoduibhne*, and *Siol Diarmuid*, the children of Duina, and progeny of Dermud, two of the most famed of their ancestors.

Coll Vuais's son was called Gillebreid, or, as our Histories name him, Bredius. This Bredius, in the reign of King Ederus, about 54 years before our Saviour's nativity, with an army of his Islanders entered Morvern, and the other Western Continent, which having with great barbarity depopulated, he was in his return met by King Ederus with an army, and entirely defeated. Bredius hardly escaping by absconding himself in a cave, was thence termed *Bredius* or *Gillebreid of the Cave*. However after the King's departure he obtained new forces, by which he obliged the inhabitants of these parts to become his tributaries, in which he was not disturbed by King Ederus, then under some apprehensions of an invasion by Julius Cæsar, who at that juncture had invaded the South parts of Britain.

Bredius's son was called *Sumerledus*, from whom the Chieftains of that Clan were for some ages designed MacSoirles, or Sumerledsons, as Richard Southwell an English writer, in his account of the petty Kings, or Reguli of some of the Brittish Isles while under the dominion of the Norvegian Kings, asserts, who says, that those Reguli possest all the Isles round Britain, at least Scotland, except those possest by the son of

Sumerledus, being most of our Æbudæ, or Western Isles then possest by the MacDonalds.

Sumerled's son was called *Rannald;* Rannald's son was called *Donald,* which name continued for several successive generations, and from which that Clan obtained their denomination. The first of these Donalds of the Isles found upon record, was that Donald, who about the year 248 of the Christian Epocha, in the reign of King Findoch, made a descent upon the Continent of Argyle, but being defeated by the King, was killed with a great many more of his men: For revenge of whose death his son of the same name in the year 262, and first year of the reign of King Donald II. with an army entered the Continent, and being encountered with an army hastily levied by the King, that Prince was defeated by the Islanders. The King dying of his wounds in a few days, Donald of the Isles usurped the government, and retained the same for twelve years, at the end of which he was killed by Cratlinth, King Findoch's son, who kept down his successors, as did some of the succeeding

Kings. They made no great disturbance for a considerable time, till in the year 762, one of these Chiefs of the Isles, called Donald, made an insurrection, but was defeated by King Eugenius. That insurrection made by Donald Baan is elsewhere mentioned.

The Chiefs or principal persons of this Surname, as soon as the title of Thane came to be used, were among the first of our Nobility dignified therewith, by the title first of Thanes of the Isles, and afterwards Thanes of Argyle, upon account of that large tract of land possest by the Chiefs of that Surname, besides Kintyre and Knapdale, all along the Western sea-coasts of Argyle-shire. Of these were the two successive Sumerleds, mentioned in the reigns of King Malcolm IV. and King Alexander I. of Scotland. The last of these two Sumerled's successor was Reginald, or Rannald, mentioned in the records of the Abbey of Paisley, being founder of the Abbey of Sanda, Rannald's son was Donald, mentioned also in a mortification made by him to the Abbey of Paisley.

Donald had two fons, Angus or Æneas his fucceffor, and Alexander progenitor of the MacAllafters in Argyle-fhire. This Angus, upon account of a mortification made by him, is mentioned in the records of the Abbey of Paifley. Angus had alfo two fons, Alexander his fucceffor, and John anceftor of the MacEans of Ardnamurchan, now almoft extinct. To Alexander, mentioned in fome old records of Argyle, fucceeded Angus Moir or the Great, who with two thoufand men was with King Robert Bruce at the battle of Bannockburn. Angus's fucceffor was alfo called Angus, being married to a daughter of Okeyan Lord Dunfeverin in Ireland. His fucceffor was John, who very much aggrandized his family by marrying of Lady Margaret Stewart, daughter to King Robert II. as is evident by two charters by that King in his favour, by defignation of his beloved fon-in-law, of the lands of Moydert and Croydert. This John had four fons, Donald his fucceffor; John of Glins, anceftor of the Earl of Antrim in Ireland; Alexander, by fome faid to be anceftor of the MacDonalds of Keppoch, but both by what

I can find are errors; and Allan, who was anceftor of the Captain of Clanronald; whereas Keppoch's anceftor is reported to have been Rannald, fon to Alexander of Argyle and the Ifles, in the reign of King Alexander III.

Donald Lord of the Ifles married a daughter of Walter Lefley, who, in right of his wife daughter of William laft Earl of Rofs, was Earl of that eftate. He had one fon, who left only one dauhgter, heirefs to that Earldom; which daughter, having become a Nun, difponed her eftate to John Stewart Earl of Buchan, fecond fon to Robert Earl of Fife and Monteith, than Governor of Scotland. The Lord of the Ifles judging himfelf prejudged by the faid right, applied to the Governor for redrefs, but to no purpofe; whereupon refolving to affert his right by arms, he for that effect levied ten, or as moft affert, twelve thoufand men, and marching through Murray, was encountered with an army of equal number by Alexander Stewart Earl of Marr, the braveft General of his age, at a village called Harlaw in the year 1411; betwixt whom was fought the moft bloody conflict that for many ages had been obferved to have been fought betwixt native Scottifh men, till night parted them. Next morning obferving their mutual lofs, then marched off with the fmall remains of their feveral armies. However the Lord of the Ifles in a little time thereafter took poffeffion of the Earldom of Rofs, and left the fame to his fucceffor, Alexander defigned Earl of Rofs, Kintyre, and Inchegal, or Weft Ifles. He had alfo another fon Donald Balloch, or Spotted Donald, who, upon the acceffion of King James I. to the throne, and his depriving his brother Alexander Lord of the Ifles of the Earldom of Rofs, and imprifoning him, levied an army of ten thoufand men, and being engaged at Ennerlochy by the Stewarts Earls of Marr, and Caithnefs, their army was defeated by that of Balloch, with the death of the Earl of Caithnefs one of the generals: but upon the King's approach with another army, Donald Balloch was deferted by a great many of his forces, and was obliged to flee to Ireland, where at King James's defire he was executed.

Alexander Earl of Rofs and the Ifles was

married to the Earl of Huntley's daughter, of which marriage he had three fons; John his fucceffor; Hugh, firft of Slate, anceftor of Sir Donald MacDonald; and as moft affert, Alexander, anceftor of Glengairy. John Earl of Rofs married a daughter of James Lord Levingfton, by whom he had no iffue, and being deprived by forfaulture of the Earldom of Rofs, for fome difloyal practices in the minority of King James III. his other eftate was conveyed in favour of Donald, grandfon to this John by Angus his natural fon. This Donald alfo dying without iffue, King James V. took the eftate into his own hand; but this does not hold with the affertion of moft of the Seneciones, who record the affairs of this furname. They controvert the above account by afferting, that this Donald laft Lord of the Ifles died in the reign of King James VI. and leaving no iffue, the King took the eftate into his own hands, and afterwards difponed it to a brother of the Earl of Argyle, who dying without iffue, all thofe lands fell into the family of Argyle, as they yet continue. That which confirms this opinion is, that the Lord of the Ifles is mentioned in Knox's History to have received pay from Henry VIII. King of England, in the time of the Earl of Arran's Regency, which was after the death of King James V. It is also asserted, that the ancestor of MacDonald of Slate was son to Angus Lord of the Isles, and brother to that John who was married to a daughter of King Robert II. and that the ancestor of MacDonald of Lergie came off the family of MacDonald much about the same time. But seeing there are more who adhere to the first than the last account, I shall leave the same to be determined by those better seen in the concerns of that name; observing only, that MacDonald of Slate hath always been reputed the chief family of that surname, since the extinction of the Lords of the Isles, and as such is always designed by way of emimency MACONEL or MACDONALD, without any further distinction.

This surname was formerly, and at present divided into six different families, which retain the surname of MacDonald, and other six families which pass under other denominations, yet own their descent to be off the family of MacDonald.

The firſt of thoſe families who retain the Surname of MacDonald, is that of Slate, being not only the lateſt deſcended, but alſo poſſeſſed of the moſt plentiful eſtate of any other of that ſurname both in the Iſle of Sky, and the Weſtern Continent of Morvern and Croidert. The preſent MacDonald of Slate is a boy, being ſon to James MacDonald of Orinſay, ſecond brother to the late Sir Donald. The next principal man of that Family is William MacDonald, preſent tutor of Slate, and youngeſt brother to the ſaid Sir Donald. The principal reſidence of that family is the caſtle of Duntuilm, ſituated in the north part of the Iſle of Sky. They have alſo another place of reſidence, adorned with ſtately edifices, pleaſant gardens, and other regular polices, called Armodel upon the South coaſt of the ſame Iſle.

The ſecond Family of that Surname of moſt repute, next to that of Slate, in reſpect of eſtate and all other circumſtances, is that of Clanronald; the principal man of which is deſigned Captain of Clanronald, and in the Iriſh language Macmhicaillain, or the ſon of Allanſon; it ſeeming that his proper name who was progenitor of this Sept, and came firſt off the Family of MacDonald, was Allan. The whole tribe is alſo termed Siolaillain or the Progeny of Allan. The perſon of beſt repute of this Family, next to the Captain, is MacRonald of Bencula. This Family having an old quarrel with the Surname of Fraſer, determined the ſame by a formal conflict, in the time of the Regency of Queen Mary of Guiſe, mother to Queen Mary of Scotland, at the village of Harlaw, famous for the battle fought formerly thereat by Stewart Earl of Marr, and MacDonald Earl of Roſs. There were ſaid to be upwards of two thouſand men on both ſides, of which ſcarce a hundred are ſaid to have ſurvived that fatal conflict. The northern branch of the name of Fraſer was in a manner entirely cut off; but Providence favoured them ſo far, that eighty of their principal men left their wives with child, all of whom were delivered of ſons, who all came to age. The principal reſidence of the Captain of ClanRonald is Caſtletirim, in the Weſtern Continent of Moidert, where a good part of this Gentleman's eſtate lies, the other part lying in

North and South Uifts, in the firft of which Ifles the Captain ordinarly refides.

The third Family of beft repute of that Surname is MacDonald of Glengary. The next principal man of this Family to Glengary is Angus MacDonald, brother to the late Glengary, a Gentleman of good account and circumftances. Glengary's intereft lies moftly in that part of Lochaber within the fhire of Invernefs. Glengary in their native language is defigned Mac-Mhicallefter, or the Son of Alexander. This Gentleman's refidence is the Caftle of Innergray in Lochaber; but that Caftle not being now in repair, he refides in an Ifland in a Loch, called Locheawich, in the faid country.

The fourth principal Family of this Surname is that of Kepoch, ordinarily defigned MacHicraneill, or the Son of Ronaldfon. His refidence is in Kepoch in the lower part of Lochaber, which together with Glenroy, the property whereof belongs to the Laird of MacIntofh, being a large tract of land, is poffeffed by the prefent Kepoch, and hath been fo for divers ages by his anceftors, without any other acknowledgment to MacIntosh, than such a gratuity as they thought fit to give. The late Laird of MacIntosh in the year 1687 endeavouring to dispossess Kepock of these lands by force, raised twelve hundred of his own men, and obtained from the Government the concurrence of a company of the regular forces, under command of Captain MacKenzie of Suddey. Kepoch, with a few more than the half of that number, encountered with MacIntosh and his party, and entirely defeated the same, with the death of Captain MacKenzie, and a great many others, having taken MacIntosh prisoner, and obliged him to renounce his pretensions to those lands, for which Kepoch was denounced Rebel; but the Revolution coming on the subsequent year, he was not further prosecuted for that affair, and the present Laird of MacIntosh having given him a new grant of these lands, he continues in possession of the same. Next to this Family are, Ronald, Alexander, and Angus, brethren to the present Coll MacDonald of Kepoch.

The fifth principal Family of this Surname is that of Largy. This Gentleman's residence is in the South part of the Peninsula of Kintyre, within four miles of the Mule, or Cape of Kintyre. The next Man of account to this family is MacDonald of Sanda residing in the said country.

The sixth principal Family of this name is MacDonald of Glencoe, his residence being in Polliwiig in Glencoe. The next principal Man of this Family is MacDonald of Attriatain in the same country.

The first of those families of another denomination, which derive their origin from that of MacDonald, is that of MacCallaster, the principal man of which is MacCallaster of Loup, whose principal residence is in Airdpatrick upon the South side of the West Loch-Tarbit in Knapdale, in the shire of Argyle. The next principal man of this Family is MacCallaster of Tarbit in the same shire.

The second principal Family of those of another denomination, is that of MacNab, his principal residence being at Kinally in Braidalbin, in the shire of Perth. This Gentleman is recorded to be descended of a son of the first Abbot of Inchchaffery, whose surname was MacDonald, in the beginning of the reign of K. Alexander II. The Lairds of MacNab had of old a very good interest in those parts, but lost the greatest part thereof upon account of their assisting of MacDougal Lord of Lorn, against King Robert Bruce, at the conflict of Dalree. There are MacNabs of Incheun, and Acharn, with several other landed Gentlemen, besides the principal family in those parts. There is also a pretty numerous Sept of the MacNabs in the county of Dunegale in Ireland, who term themselves MacNabanies, but own their descent from the Scottish MacNabs, or Abbotsons.

The third Family of this kind, is that of the MacIntyres, the principal person of these being MacIntyre of Glennoe, in Glenorchy, in the shire of Perth. The other heritors of that name are the MacIntyres of Corries, and Cruachan.

The fourth Family of this kind is that of MacAphie, whose ancestors for many ages were Lairds of the Isle of Collinsay, which was violently wrested from that family in the beginning of the reign of King Charles I. by Coll Keitach MacDonald, who lost his life, and unjust purchase in the time of the civil wars: But the interest was never restored to MacAphie. The greatest part of that name reside in Lochaber, and Upper Lorn.

The fifth of these Families is that of MacKechoirn, whose principal residence is at Killellan, within two miles of the Cape of Kintyre. The sixth and last is that of the MacKechnies. The interest of the principal person of these was at Tangay in the South part of Kintyre.

Besides these mentioned, there are divers other small Clans, who tho' not descended from, yet of a long time have been dependants upon the MacDonalds; as the MacKinnings of the Isle of Sky, whose Chief is the Laird of MacKinney, a Gentleman of a good estate in that Isle, and in Mull, and depending on the family of Slate. The MacWalricks also, who derive their origin from one Ulrick Kennedy, a son of the family of Dunures, who for slaughter fled divers ages ago to Lochaber, his progeny from the proper name of their ancestor deriving their Surname of MacWalricks, the principal person of whom is MacWalrick of Linachan in Lochaber, who with his Sept are dependants of the family of Kepoch; as are the MacKenricks, being originally MacNauchtans, dependants on the family of Glencoe. The MacGillmories, and others, are dependants on the family of Glengary; as are the MacIlrevies on the family of Clanronald, with divers others, too numerous here to be mentioned.

The MacDonalds, in their atchievements or armorial bearings, have four several kinds of bearings; As 1st, Or, a Lyon, rampant, Azure, armed, and langued Gules. 2d, A Dexter Hand Coupee, holding a cross Croslet, fitchie Sable. 3d, Or, a Ship, with her sails furled salterwise, Sable. 4th, A Salmon naiant, proper, with a Chief waved, Argent.

An Account of the Surname of

MacDougal: Particularly of Lorn.

THE Surname of MacDougal, tho' now somewhat low, yet in respect of the ancient power, grandeur, and antiquity thereof, deserves in justice to be mentioned next to that of MacDonald; the Chiefs or principal men of that Surname being for some considerable time dignified with the title of Lords of Lorn, a country of a very large extent, and of old valued a 700 Merk land. These Lords of Lorn, from the beginning of the reign of King William the Lyon, till the reign of King Robert I. were of the greatest power of any other of the Highland Clans; the family of MacDonald being very much depressed in those times, by reason of the insurrections made against the Government by the two successive Sumerleds, Chiefs of that surname. It might be rationally presumed, that the MacDougals of Lorn are orignally descended of the family of MacDougal of Galloway, if not absolutely, at least among the most ancient families of Scotland; the armorial bearing of both these families, which is the most authentick document can be adduced in this case, differing very little in any material circumstance. Nevertheless the MacDougals of Lorn, for any thing I can find, refuse their descent to be from those of Galloway, making it from one of these Colls already mentioned in the genealogy of the MacDonalds, at least from the

Milesian race of the ancient Kings of Ireland, in common with some others of the most ancient Highland Clans.

The first to be met with on record of these Lords of Lorn, is Duncan, who, in the latter part of the reign of King William, founded the Priory of Ardchattan in Lorn, who had two sons, Alexander his successor, and Duncan. Alexander married a daughter of John Cummine Lord of Badenoch, Chief of that potent and numerous surname. Of this marriage he had John Bacah, or Halting, his successor. This John Lord of Lorn, upon King Robert I. his killing John Cummine Lord of Badenoch, Lorn's cousin, at Dumfries, became upon that account an inveterate enemy to that King and his interest, and as such used his utmost efforts in molesting Sir Neil Campbel of Lochow, the King's brother-in-law, and other Loyalists in those parts. For relief of whom the King, with a party of his friends, marched for Argyle-shire; but before he could join his friends there, the Lord of Lorn, with an army vastly superior to his, encountered him and his small party at Straithfillan upon a plain, called as yet from that event Dalree, or King's Plain, and did so far overpower the King's forces, that after a sharp conflict he entirely defeated the same. The King himself narrowly escaped being either killed or taken, one of Lorn's soldiers having taken hold of his scarf, worn bend-ways over his shoulder, and tho' the King knocked the soldier dead with a steel mace, yet he did not let go his hold till the King was obliged to loose the buckle which fastened the scarf, and to leave the same in the soldier's hands; which large silver buckle was of late extant in the hands of the Laird of MacDougal, if not as yet, as a Memorial or Trophy of that victory. The King was again assaulted by three robust fellows of Lorn's men, called MacAnorsoirs, who encountering him in a strait pass, one of them seized his bridle, and another his leg, and the third jumped on behind him; nevertheless such was the unparallelled valour and presence of mind of that Heroick Prince, that in the end he dispatched those three Ruffians, and escaped, but was necessitated to quit his horse, coming on foot for two miles of very bad way, to the upper end of Lochlomond, and for twelve miles more through woods and precipices all along the north side of that Loch, having lodged the night the battle was fought, in a Cave in Craigrostane in the Parish of Buchanan, called as yet the King's Cave, and as is asserted by tradition, having come next day to Maurice Laird of Buchanan, he conducted him to Malcolm Earl of Lennox, by whom he was preserved for some time, till he got to a place of safety.

This John Lord of Lorn, as soon as King Robert had obtained possession of his Kingdom, had his estate forfaulted, and given to Stewart of Innermeth, and Dining, a descendant of the family of Darnly, who, (as many of our Historians say) married a daughter of the Lorn of Lorn; which if he did, it was upon the same account that Levingstoun of that Ilk married a daughter of Patrick Lord of Callandar, forfaulted at the same time, both being done for the better securing of their rights to those estates, against the pretensions of the nearest of both those surnames to the same. This Lordship continued with the Stewarts for four descents, till in the reign of King James III.

the same was conveyed by marriage of the three co-heiresses of John last Lord Lorn, to the Earl of Argyle, and the Campbells of Glenorchy and Ottar.

There are none now remaining of the male issue of Stewart Lord Lorn, at least in those parts, except Stewart of Appin, whose ancestor was Dougal, son to Stewart second Lord Lorn, of which estate he got that of Appin, retained as yet by his representative, who with those of his family always associates with the other Clans. Next to Appin is Stewart of Ardsheal, who with a good number of gentlemen, and others of that family, reside in those parts.

The dependants on the surname of Mac-Dougal, are the MacOleas, MacAheirs, and others. The principal residence of John present Laird of MacDougal, is the Castle of Dunolich in Mid Lorn, being one of the ancient mansions of that family. The person of best account, next to the Laird of MacDougal, is MacDougal of Gallanach, there being divers other gentlemen of that name residing in those parts.

The Armorial bearing of MacDougal of Lorn is, Quarterly, 1st and 4th, in a Field

Azure, a Lyon rampant, Argent, for MacDougal. 2d and 3d, Or, a Lymphad Sable, with flames of fire issuing out of the topmast, proper for Lorn.

An Account of the Surname of

MACNEIL.

THIS Surname of MacNeil being one of the most ancient of our Scottish Clans, is originally descended from that once potent and flourishing Surname of the O'Neils of Ireland. These O'Neils were divided into two great Tribes, the one termed the Northern, and the other the Southern O'Neils. The first of these for a great many ages, untill the English Conquest, were Provincial Kings of North Ulster. After the English Conquest, the title of King being abrogated throughout that Kingdom, the successors of the Kings of Ulster were designed Earls of Tyrone, till in the reign of Queen Elizabeth, Shaan O'Neil Earl of Tyrone, with others of his country-men made an infurrection againft that Queen. But her better fortune prevailing, this family in a fhort time thereafter became extinct, the lineal reprefentative of it being now John O'Neil Efq; of Shaan-caftle in the county of Antrim, a gentleman of the Proteftant Religion, and of one of the moft confiderable fortunes in that Kingdom. He is manager to the Earl of Antrim's affairs, the Earl himfelf being Minor, who is a Nobleman of the greateft eftate of any of Scottifh defcent in that Kingdom, whofe anceftor was John, fecond fon to John Lord of the Ifles, by the Lady Margaret Stewart, daughter to King Robert the fecond of that name, and firft of the Stewarts. This John's lineal fucceffor was Sorely Buey, or Fair Sumerled MacDonald of Glins, who went to Ireland, as fome fay, in the reign of King Henry VII. of England, or as others more probably, in the reign of Queen Elizabeth, where he fo far fignalized himfelf in the Queen's fervice againft Tyrone, and others in arms againft her, that at the end of thofe wars, the Queen, in recompence of his fervices, gave him that eftate, of which his representative is yet in possession.

Ketine, and other Irish Historians, derive the origine of the O'Neils from Neil, son to Mileius King of Gallicia in Spain, who with Hiber, Erimon, and Ir, his three brethren, came with the first Gathelians, or Scots, who by conquest of Ecta, Ketur, and Tectius, Kings of the Dedannins, the ancient inhabitants of that Kingdom, obtained the Sovereign possession of the same. The MacNeils of Scotland, a Branch of those of Ireland, are reported to have come here with the First Scots, who from Ireland planted Argyle-shire, and the Western Isles, being for some ages bypast divided into two considerable families, these of Barra, and Taynish, who of a long time have contended for Chiefship, or Precedency; but the matter is generally determined in favour of MacNeil of Barra, who, of all other Highland Chiefs of Clans, retains most of the magnificence and customs of the ancient *Phylarchæ*. He is in possession of the Isle of Barra, which is of a pretty large extent, also of some small Isles round it. Mr Martin Composer of the Western Isles, asserts, that MacNeil of Barra can produce evidents for thirty-six descents, of his Family's possession of that Isle, besides a great many old Charters, most of which are not legible. However this be, he is accounted one of the most ancient Cheiftains of the Highland Clans. His principal residence is the Castle of Keismul, situated in a small Island of the same name, divided by a small Canal from Barra, and of no more extent than what the Castle, and a large Quadrangular area or closs round it occupieth. MacNeil of Taynish, the next principal person of this surname, resides in Knapdale in Argyle-shire, in which are also MacNeil of Galiachiol, and Tarbart. There is also another gentleman of that name, Laird of the Isle of Collinsay, once the property of the MacAphies. There are a good many more gentlemen of the surname in the Western Isles, and the Continents of Kintyre and Knapdale.

The Armorial Bearing of MacNeil of Barra is, Quarterly, 1st, Azure, or as others, Gules, a Lyon rampant, Argent. 2d, Or, a Hand coupee, fess-ways, Gules, holding a cross croslet, fitchee, in pale, Azure.

3d, Or, a Lymphad Sable. 4th, Parted per fess, Argent, and Vert, to represent the Sea, out of which issueth a Rock, Gules. Supporters, two large Fishes.

An ACCOUNT of the SURNAME of

MacLEAN or MacGILLEAN.

THIS brave and heroick Surname is originally descended from that of Fitz-girald in Ireland, being once the most potent Surname of any other of English extract in that Kingdom. Speed and other English Historians derive the Genealogy of the Fitz-giralds from Seignior Giraldo, a Principal Officer under William the Conqueror, at his conquest of England, anno 1066. This Giraldo got from the Conqueror the Lordship of Windsor, from which he was afterwards designed of Windsor, as were his posterity, from his proper name, Fitz-giralds or Giraldsons. Maurice Fitz-girald, grandchild to this first Girald, by orders of Strangbow Earl of Pembroke, with four hunderd and ninety men, in the year 1169, went in aid of Dermud Macmurcho, provincial King of Leinster to Ireland, being the first Englishman, who in a hostile manner invaded that Kingdom, whatever Atwood, and other obscure English writers assert to the contrary: The ground of Fitz-girald's invasion being briefly as follows:

In the reign of Roderick Oconer, last principal King of Ireland, the said Dermud took away by force Orork, provincial King of Meath's Lady, or Queen, which injury while Orork endeavoured to resent, he and his party were defeated by the Leinstrians; in which exigence having recourse to the principal King, he was so effectually assisted by him, as obliged Macmurcho, after some defeats to abandon Ireland, and betake himself to the Court of King Henry II. of England, to whom relating his misfortune, he implored his aid for recovering his principality, which upon being done he offered to resign in his favour. King Henry being a Prince who measured the justice of most causes, if in any way beneficial to him, by the length of his sword, would willingly have complied with Mac-Murcho's requeſt, had he not been engaged in a war with France. However he iſſued out proclamations authorizing any of his ſubjects that pleaſed, to adventure in behalf of that juſtly diſtreſſed Prince, promiſing to maintain them in poſſeſſion of what they could acquire in that Kingdom; Upon which Richard Strangbow Earl of Pembroke, a Nobleman no leſs powerful than popular in Wales, condeſcended to go to Ireland with Dermud, upon condition that upon recovery of Leinſter, he ſhould give him the ſame, and his only daughter in marriage, which being readily agreed to, Pembroke ſent firſt over Maurice Fitzgirald, as already mentioned, and went afterwards himſelf, with greater forces; and having defeated the Iriſh in a conflict, recovered Leinſter, and married MacMurcho's daughter. King Henry hearing of his ſubjects ſucceſs, patched up a peace with France, and in the year 1170, or as others 1171, went over into that Kingdom, with an army of twenty thouſand men, and by the aſſiſtance of the treacherous Leinſtrians, obtained a victory over Oconor the principal King, who in a short time thereafter died. After his death the King of England settled his conquest of that Kingdom, as the same has continued ever since, notwithstanding of the many efforts at divers junctures used by the native Irish for shaking off that yoke.

The Family of Strangbow in a little time became extinct, to which in grandeur succeeded that of Fitz-girald, being divided into two powerful families, the Earls of Desmond, and Kildare, concerning each of which two I shall relate a certain remarkable passage, 'ere I proceed to my designed subject. The first is in relation to that of Desmond, of which family were seven brethren in the beginning of the reign of Queen Elizabeth, or rather Queen Mary of England, who being accused of some practices against the Government, were by the Queen's orders carried into England, and relying either on their innocence, or the interposition of powerful friends, appeared very chearful for some hours after they went on board, till at length enquiring at the Captain the name of the ship, they were told it was named the Cow; upon hearing of which they all fell a weeping; the reason of which sudden change being demanded by the Captain, he was told there was an old prophecy among the Irish, that seven brethren, the most noble of the Kingdom, should be at once carried to England in the belly of a Cow, none of which should ever return, and now tho' the thing appeared very ridiculous, they were afraid that it would be accomplished; as accordingly it was, none of them having ever returned, some of them banished, others executed, and their estate forefaulted, so that in a short time that flourishing family was ruined. The other relating to Kildare is, that in the reign of King Henry VII. of England, that Earl was very ungovernable, against whom frequent complaints were made to the King, concluding with this, that all Ireland could not govern the Earl of Kildare. Then said the King, shall that Earl govern all Ireland. Upon which he sent him a commission for being Lieutenant of that Kingdom, which unexpected favour had such effect upon him, that he continued afterwards a very dutiful and loyal subject to that King.

There are divers other good Families of this Kingdom defcended of thofe two honourable Families, as the MacKenzies, of Colin Fitz-girald, fon to the fecond Earl of Defmond, who for his fervice at the battle of Largs againft the Danes, anno 1264, obtained from King Alexander III. the lands of Kintail, from whofe fon Kenneth the MacKenzies are denominated, by contraction inftead of Kennethfons. The Adairs, and divers others are alfo defcended of the Fitz-giralds; as are the MacLeans, fo termed contractedly, but more properly MacGilleans, Fitzgirald, brother, as fome fay, to Colin, anceftor of the MacKenzies. But others with more probability affert, this Gillean to have been a fon of the Earl of Kildare, and either at, or in a little time after his coufin's coming, to have come to Scotland, where falling into great favour with MacDonald Lord of the Ifles, he obtained from him the lands of Aros, afterwards in a fmall time the whole Ifles of Mull, Tyree, Coll, and others, being a very large eftate. While the family of MacDonald continued in grandeur, MacLean was always his Lieutenant in martial expeditions, as in the battle of Harlaw, in which MacLean, and Irwin of Drum, upon account of some ancient quarrel betwixt their families, and having no knowledge of one another till they had got it from their armorial bearings, or Coats of Arms, painted as was usual in those times upon their Shields, engaged hand to hand, and died both upon the spot.

MacLean, with his name and dependants, was at the battles of Flowdon, and Pinky, as was Hector MacLean, and his regiment, consisting of six hundred men, at the conflict of Innerkeithing, in the reign of King Charles II. in which he, and his regiment, after a valiant resistance, were killed by the English, few or none escaping. This surname has been known for some ages bygone in bravery and loyalty to be inferior to no other of this Kingdom. The Laird of MacLean's estate was evicted for debt by the present Duke of Argyle's grand-father, and is now in the Duke's hands. Hector, the present Laird, is abroad. The principal residence of the Lairds of MacLean, is the strong Castle of Dowart, situated upon the North Shore of the Isle of

Mull. There was another impregnable Fort belonging to this family, at a little diftance from Mull, called Kerniburg.

The next to the Laird of MacLean, is MacLean of Brolois. The perfon of beft eftate now of that name, is MacLean of Lochbuy, who hath a good Caftle and eftate in Mull. There is MacLean of Coll, being a confiderable ifland at fome leagues diftance from Mull. There is alfo upon the oppofite Continent to Mull a gentleman of good account, defigned MacLean of Ardgower. He is defigned ordinarily MacMhicewin or the Son of Hughfon, his anceftor, a fon of the Laird of MacLean, being properly named Hugh. There are alfo a great number of other gentlemen of that name in thofe parts. There is a gentleman termed MacGuire of Uluva, being a pretty large Ifle to the fouth weft of Mull, of which this gentleman is proprietor, and was a dependant upon the family of MacLean, while in a flourifhing condition, but fince the decline of that family, continues peaceable in his own Ifland, not much concerned with any affairs that occur in any other part of this Kingdom. There is in

Athole, and other Northern places, a Sept termed the MacOlays, some of which are in Stirling-shire, termed MacLays, descended also of the family of MacLean.

Divided by a small arm of the sea from the West Point of Mull, is the Isle Jona, or I-colm-kill, famous for the ancient Monastery and church situated therein, and no less so upon account of the Burial-place of forty-eight of our Scottish Kings, with divers of the Kings of Ireland and Norway, as also of most of the principal Families of our Highland Clans. The ruins of these once stately edifices and monuments evince their beauty when in repair. There are two singular kinds of stones to be found there, of which are a great many tombs, and crosses, and which composes the very mold round that church, and of which consists a great deal of the more ornamental parts of all these structures; the one of them being of a crimson red colour, the other white, the nature of which cannot be easily discovered. These stones in outward appearance resemble marble, but are much harder, and not so brittle, and are somewhat porous, and fully as light as any ivory or ebony. There is none of that kind of stone to be found in any other part of Britain or Ireland, but only in that Island, and in another little ruinous church dedicated to St. Colm, close by the Mule of Kintyre called Kilchollumkill.

The Laird of MacLean for Armorial bearing hath Four Coats, Quarterly. 1st, Argent a Rock Gules. 2d, Argent a dexter Hand fess-ways, couped Gules, holding a cross Croslet fitchee, in pale Azure. 3d, Or, a Lymphad, Sable. 4th, Argent, a Salmon naiant proper, in Chief, two Eagles Heads erased a fronte, Gules. Crest, a Tower embattelled, Argent. Motto, *Virtue mine Honour.* Supporters on a Compartment. Vert, two Selchs proper.

An Account of the Surname of

MACLEODS.

THE origin of the Surname of MacLeod is evidently found, and by that name always acknowledged to be Danish, one of the ancestors of the same in King William's reign, being the King of Denmark or

Norway's Vicegerent over the Isles belonging to that King along the coasts of Scotland, from whose proper name of Leodius, that Surname derived the denomination of MacLeods. From two sons of Leodius, called Torquil, and Norman, that surname was divided for a considerable time into two principal families of Siol Torquil and Siol Tormaild, or the progeny of Torquil, and Norman. The first of these was proprietor of Lewis, and the second of Harrise, from which two estates these families were designed. Which families, at the expulsion of the rest of their country-men by King Alexander III. were in such favour with the King, and some of his principal Nobility, that they were allowed to continue in possession of their large estates, and also obtained the benefit of being naturalized. After which they continued for divers ages in a flourishing condition, till in the reign of King James VI. that MacLeod of Lewis had the misfortune of falling into some disloyal practices, for which he was forfeited. King James having a design of civilizing and improving that large and fertile Island, thought that a fit opportunity of falling on that project, and in order thereto, gave a grant of the Lewis to certain gentlemen of the shire of Fife, for payment of a small sum of feu-duty, and some other casualties. MacLeod of Lewis dying, these gentlemen thought to get their design with all facility accomplished, but were very far disappointed; for notwithstanding that they built pretty good houses near one another, in the form of a village, for their mutual defence, yet Murdo MacLeod, bastard son to MacLeod of Lewis, with some of his father's tenants and dependants, assaulted the Fife Lairds in their village, and having fired their houses, obliged them all to become his prisoners, and for preservation of their lives, to swear, that with the utmost diligence they would abandon the Island, and never return, which was punctually performed. The King finding this method would not do, gave in a short time thereafter a grant of the Lewis to the Earl of Seafort, who with his Clan, residing upon the opposite Continent, obtained possession thereof, and the more easily, in regard the said Murdo MacLeod died about that time; after which for security of his possession,

Seafort, or as others say, one of his sons, married a daughter of the last MacLeod of Lewis, and retained possession of that estate in all time thereafter without disturbance. Since the extinction of the family of Lewis, the Principal person and Chief of that Surname, is MacLeod of Harrise, being a gentleman of the greatest estate of any of our Highland Clans; his principal residence is the strong Castle of Dunveggan in Sky, in which Isle the most part of his numerous Clan reside, of whom are a great number of gentlemen of good account.

The person of that name (for any thing I can find) next to MacLeod's family, is MacLeod of Tallisker. Those of other denominations descended of that surname, are the MacGillechollums, the Chief of which is MacGillechollum of Raarsa, a considerable Island near Sky. He hath a pretty numerous Clan, not only in those parts, but also in the Shires of Perth, and Argyle, tho' some in the last of these shires term themselves MacCallums, pretending to be Campbells; but it is generally thought these are led so to do, more by interest, than by justice, there being no satisfying reason given by them of their being of a different Stem from those others of that name, who own themselves to be MacLeods. The second Sept descended of the MacLeods, is the MacCriomans, whereof there are divers in the above mentioned two shires. The third Sept is that of the MacLewis, some of which are in the shire of Stirling.

MacLeod carries for Arms, Azure, a Castle triple towered, and embattelled, Argent, Masoned Sable, and illuminated Gules.

An Account of the

MACINTOSHES,

AND

MACPHERSONS.

THE Surname of MacIntosh, as a genealogical account thereof in my hands, and all other accounts of the same, assert, is descended of that Ancient and Heroick Family of MacDuff, Thane and afterwards Earl of Fife. The ancestor of that name, according to the above account was Sheagh, or Shaw MacDuff, second son to Constantine third Earl of Fife, and great grandchild to Duncan MacDuff, last Thane, and first Earl of Fife of that name. This Shaw MacDuff went with King Malcolm IV. as one of his Captains in that expedition he made against the rebellious Murrays, and other inhabitants of Murray-land, in the year 1163. After the suppression of that rebellion, Shaw MacDuff, in reward of his eminent service upon that occasion, obtained from the King the Constableship or Government of the Castle of Inverness, with a considerable interest in land in Peaty, Breachly, and other adjacent places to that Castle, with the Forrestry of the Forrest of Straithherin, all which formerly belonged to some of the rebels. The country people of those parts, upon notice of Shaw's descent, gave him the name of MacIntoshich or Thane's Son, the old title of Thane, by which his ancestors were so long designed, obtaining more among the vulgar than the new one of Earl, so lately brought into use.

So that he continued not only himself to be so denominated always thereafter, but transmitted the same as a Surname to his posterity, which is yet retained; tho' as it would seem, there was one of his sons, who instead of MacIntosh, chused rather to derive his surname from this Shaw's proper name, being ancestor of the Shaws of Rothemurchas in Badenoch, one of whose sons called Ferquhard Shaw, having settled in Marr, was ancestor of the Ferquhardsons there, the principal person of which is Ferquhardson of Innercauld, a gentleman of a good estate. There are also Ferquhardsons of Inverray, and a good many more gentlemen of that surname in those parts. These are termed in Irish MacKinlays from Finlay Moir, one of their ancestors, who bore the Royal Standard at the battle of Flowdon, or Pinky, in which he was killed. There are divers gentlemen, and others of the vulgar sort, in the Northern parts, who retain the surname of Shaw; so that its pretty clear our Southern Shaws, of which Shaw of Greenock is Chief, are of the same stem.

Angus, the fifth in defcent from Shaw MacDuff, married the only daughter and heirefs of Gilpatrick, fon of Dougal Dall, or Dougal the Blind, fon of Gilcattan in the year 1291. This Gilpatrick was Chief of the Tribe of Clan Chattan, whofe eftate and Chiefship by this marriage was conveyed to the family of MacIntofh, whence he was for a long time defigned Captain of the Clan Chattan. The principal perfon of that name, next to the Laird of MacIntofh, is Brigadier MacIntofh of Borlum. There are alfo MacIntofhes of Aberardor, Stron, Connidge, and a great many others of good account of that numerous furname. MacIntofh of Monnywaird, by this account, is reckoned the firft Cadet of the Family of MacIntofh, defcended of Edward fon to the fecond Laird of MacIntofh, about the year 1200; but Monnywaird refufes this, and differs, both in his Surname, and Armorial Bearing, from the other MacIntofhes, always defigning himfelf Tofhach, and afferting that his anceftor was a fon of the Earl of Fife.

The Clan Chattan derive their origin from the Chatti, a German Tribe, which is said to come here long before the expulsion of the Picts, there being no other ground for this allegation, than the affinity of the denomination of this surname to that Tribe. But the account of the family of MacIntosh, with more probability derives the origin of that name MacCattan or Gil-Chattan from Ireland, and so to be accounted an ancient Scottish name, that of Cathan being an ancient Scottish proper name; as for instance St. Cathan, one of our primitive Scottish Christians, or Saints, to whom was dedicated the Priory of Ardchattan in Lorn, and some others in this Kingdom, and from the proper name of this Saint was named Gillecattan, as Gillecollum and Gillepadrick were from the proper names of St. Colm, and St. Patrick, with a great many more of that kind.

The principal Person or Chief of the Clan Chattan in the reign of King David I. dying without male-issue, his brother Murdo, in Irish termed Muriach, Parson of the church of Kingusie in Badenoch, was assumed by the Clan for Captain or Chief, who had two sons; Gillecattan his succesfor; and Ewan Baan, or Hugh the Fair, his second son; who had three sons, Kenneth ancestor of the MacPhersons of Cluny, John ancestor of Pitmean, and Gilchrist ancestor of Inveressy. Some of this Ewan Baan's posterity assumed the surname of MacMurrichs, or Murdosons, from their ancestor's proper name; others of them MacPhersons, from his function; but both acknowledge one Chief, being MacPherson of Cluny, whose estate and residence, as also that of his Clan, is in Badenoch. The principal person of that Clan next to Cluny is MacPherson of Nuid. There are also MacPhersons of Inveressy, Pitmean, with a good many other gentlemen of both the above-mentioned Septs in Badenoch, and the adjacent places, being accounted so many of the best men of the Clans. The principal residence of the Laird of MacIntosh is in an Isle of a Loch upon the border of Lochaber, called Lochmoy, and thence the Isle of Moy. He hath another Castle called Delganross, upon the North side of the River of Spey, in the Head of Murray, or shire of Inverness.

The Laird of MacIntosh carries Quarterly, Or, a Lyon rampant, Gules, as Cadet of MacDuff. 2d, Argent, a Dexter Hand couped fess-ways, grasping a Man's heart, pale-ways, Gules. 3d, Azure, a Bear's head, couped, Or. 4th, Or, a Lymphad, her Oars erected in Saltyre, Sable, upon account of the marriage with the Heiress of Clan Chattan. Crest, A Cat faliant proper. Supporters, two Cats, as the former. Motto, *Touch not the Cat Gloveless.*

MacPherson of Cluny carries parted per fess, Or, and Azure, a Lymphad, or Galley, her Sails furled, her Oars in action of the first: In the dexter chief point a Hand coupée, grasping a Dagger pointing upward, Gules, for killing Cummine Lord Badenoch: In the sinister point, a cross Croslet, fitchee, Gules. Motto and Crest, the same with those of MacIntosh.

An Account of the

ROBERTSONS,

OR

CLAN DONNOCHIE.

THE Surname of ROBERTSON is descended of one Duncan Crosda, or Crossgrained, a son of MacDonald Lord of the Isles, about the Reign of King William the Lyon; but I did not enumerate this surname among the descendants of other denominations of that family, in regard that of Robertson hath for divers ages been reputed a distinct surname, and had no dependance upon that of MacDonald. So that altho' this above account be the most generally received in relation to the descent of that surname, I am not positive how far it is acquiesced in by those of the same. However this surname of Robertson hath been of good repute for some ages bygone; those of that surname are in Irish termed *Clan Donnochie*, or Duncansons, so denominated from the proper name of their anceſtor; but in Engliſh termed Robertſons, from one Robert, Chief of that name, who ſignalized himſelf very much in the reign of King James I. and apprehended Robert Graham one of that King's murderers.

The Surname of Skene are ſaid to be deſcended of the family of Strowan, and obtained the name of Skene, for killing a very big and fierce Wolf at a hunting, in company with the King in Stocket-Forreſt in Athole; having killed the Wolf with a Dagger, or Skene, as the Arms and Motto of that Surname pretty clearly evince. Alſo the Colliers are of this Surname, one of the ſame being cloſely purſued for ſlaughter, did hide himſelf in a Coal-pit, and ſo eſcaped. Of this are Collier Earl of Portmore, and divers others of good account in Holland. Robertſon of Strowan is Chief of that name. His reſidence is with moſt of his Clan in Athole, at Strowan-Caſtle.

His Arms are, Three Wolf Heads erazed, Gules, with a monſtrous Man in chains, for compartment, upon account of one of his anceſtor's ſeizing the above-mentioned Robert Graham.

An Account of the Surname of

MACFARLANE.

THE Laird of MacFarlane (whose ancestor Gilchrist, son to Aluin, and brother to Malduin, both Earls of Lennox, obtained the lands of Arrochar about the year 1200, in the reign of King William) being now reputed heir-male of that great and ancient Family, it will not be amiss, before I proceed to give an account of his family, to premise something concerning the antiquity and origin of the old Earls of Lennox, from whom he has the honour to be descended.

Peter Walsh, in his Animadversions on the history of Ireland, derives their descent from Mainus, son of Corus, provincial King of Leinster, who is said to have come to Scotland, in the reign of King Fincormachus, and to have married Mungenia, that King's daughter. This Mainus being surnamed Lemna, the estate he obtained from the said King was called Lemnich, or Lennox, which in after ages became a surname to his posterity: But this account seems too fabulous to deserve any credit.

Our own antiquaries with far greater probability, which is also confirmed by a constant and inviolable tradition, derive the origin of this ancient Family from Aluin, or Alcuin, a younger son of Kenneth III. King of Scotland, who died in the year 994. From this Aluin descended, in a direct male-line, Arkil, who was contemporary with King Edgar, and King Alexander I. and seems to have been a person of considerable note in both these reigns.

His son Aluin MacArkill, i. e. the Son of Arkill, as he is designed in old Charters, was a great favourite at Court, in the reigns of King David, and Malcolm IV. as is evident from his being so frequently witness to the grants and donations of both these Princes to Churches and Abbacys, particularly to the Church of Glasgow (*a*), and the Abbacy of Dunfermline. (*b*)

(*a*) Extract of the Register of Glasgow. (*b*) Chartulary of Dunfermline. See also Sir James Dalrymple's Historical Collections.

His son and successor called also Aluin, next Earl of Lennox, was, according to the devotion of those times, a liberal benefactor to the church, for he mortified the lands of Cochnach, Edinbarnet, Dalmenach, with a great deal of other lands, to the old Church of Kilpatrick, in honour of St. Patrick (c). Which mortification is on very good grounds supposed to have been made before the foundation of the Abbay of Paisly, anno 1160. This Earl Aluin left issue (besides others whose posterity is long since extinct) two sons, Maulduin his successor in the Earldom, and Gilchrist ancestor to the Laird of MacFarlane. Malduin was succeeded by his son Malcolm, and he again by his son of the same name, who was father to Donald the last Earl of Lennox of that family, whose only daughter Margaret was married to Walter Stewart of Faslane, son to Allan of Faslane, second son to Stewart Lord Darnly. The old family of Lennox being thus extinct for want of male-issue, and having produced no cadets since Gilchrist came off the same, it is pret-

---

(c) Register of Dunbarton

ty evident that the Laird of MacFarlane is latest cadet, and consequently heir-male of that ancient family. Having thus cleared my way, I proceed to the account of the Surname of MacFarlane.

Gilchrist ancestor to the Laird of Mac-Farlane, obtained by the grant of his brother Malduin Earl of Lennox, *Terras de superiori* Arrochar *de* Luss, very particularly bounded in the original charter, which is afterwards confirmed in the records of the Privy Seal (*d*). Which lands of Arrochar so bounded, have continued ever since with his posterity in a direct male-line to this day. This Gilchrist is witness in a great many charters granted by his brother Malduin the Earl of Lennox to his vassals, particularly to one granted by the said Earl of Lennox to Anselan Laird of Buchanan, of the Isle of Clareinch in Lochlomond, dated in the year 1225. As also to another granted by the said Earl of Lennox, to William son of Arthur Galbreath, of the two Carrucates of Badernock, dated at Fintry

---

(*d*) Charta in Rotulis Privati Sigilli.

anno 1238. In both which charters he is designed "Gilchrist Frater Comitis."

He left issue a son Duncan, designed in old charters "Duncan Filius Gilchrist, or "MacGilchrist," who had a charter from Malcolm Earl of Lennox, whereby the said Earl ratifies and confirms *Donationem illam quam* Malduinus, *Avus meus Comes de* Lennox, *fecit* Gilchrist *Fatri suo, de terris de superiori* Arrochar *de* Luss. This Duncan is witness in a charter by Malcolm Earl of Lennox to Michael MacKessan, of the lands of Garchel and Ballet. He married his own cousin Matilda, daughter to the Earl of Lennox, by whom he had Maldonich, or Malduin his successor, concerning whom there is little upon record.

Malduin's son and successor was Partholan, or Parlan, from whose proper name the family obtained the patronimical surname of MacPharlane, or Parlansons, being, as is asserted, for three descents before the assumption of this, surnamed MacGilchrists, from Gilchrist already mentioned. Some of these last have retained that surname as yet, who nevethelesss own themselves to be cadets of the family of MacFarlane.

Parlan was succeeded by his son Malcolm MacPharlane, who got a charter from Donald Earl of Lennox, upon the resignation of his father Parlan, son to Malduin (e), wherein he is confirmed by the said Earl in the lands of Arrochar, formerly called the Carrucate of MacGilchrist, together with four Isles in Lochlomond, called Island-vow, Island-vanow, Island-row-glass, and Clang, for four merks of feu-duty, and service to the King's Host. Altho' this charter, as many other ancient ones, wants a date, yet it is clearly evident, that it was prior to another granted by the same Earl to the said Malcolm Laird of MacFarlane, whereby the Earl discharges him and his heirs of the four merks of feu-duty payable by the former charter, both for by-gones, and for the time to come. This is dated at Bellach, May 4. 1354 (f).

To Malcolm succeeded his son Duncan, sixth Laird of MacFarlane, who obtained from Duncan Earl of Lennox, a charter of the said lands of Arrochar, in as ample manner as his predecessors held the same,

---

(e) Register of Dunbartoun.   (f) Ibidem.

which is dated at Inchmirin in the year 1395 (g). This Duncan Laird of MacFarlane was married to Christian Campbell, daughter to Sir Colin Campbell of Lochow, sister to Duncan first Lord Campbell, ancestor to the present Duke of Argyle. For clearing of this, there is still extant in the Register of Dunbartoun, a charter by Duncan Earl of Lennox, confirming a liferent charter, granted by Duncan Laird of MacFarlane, in favour of Christian Campbell daughter to Sir Colin Campbell of Lochow his wife, of the lands of Clanlochlong, Inverioch, Glenluin, Port-cable, &c. This charter is dated also in the year 1395.

For brevity's sake I omit giving an account of this Duncan's successors for several descents, it being sufficient for my present purpose to take notice, that in the reign of King James IV. Sir John MacFarlane of that Ilk married a daughter of the Lord Hamilton, by whom he had two sons; Andrew his successor; and Robert MacFarlane first of the branch of Inversnait. He married, secondly, a daughter of the Lord Her-

---

(g) Ibid.

ries, by whom he had Walter MacFarlane of Ardliesh, ancestor to the family of Gartartan. To Sir John MacFarlane of that Ilk succeeded Andrew his son, who married Lady Margaret Cunninghame, daughter to William Earl of Glencairn, who was Lord High Treasurer in the reign of King James V. By her he had issue, Duncan his successor.

This Duncan Laird of MacFarlane was one of the first of any account, who made open profession of the Christian religion in this Kingdom. He joined the Earls of Lennox and Glencairn at the fight in Glasgow-Moor anno 1544, against the Earl of Arran, who was Governor in the minority of Queen Mary. He was afterwards, together with severals of his name and followers, slain valiantly fighting for his country at the battle of Pinky, September 10. 1547, leaving by Anne his wife, daughter to Sir John Colquhoun of Luss, only one son, Andrew.

This Andrew Laird of MacFarlane inherited not only his father's estate, but also his zeal for the Protestant Religion, which he evidently shewed on several occasions;

particularly when Queen Mary, after her escape out of the Castle of Loch-Leven, endeavoured to re-establish Popery, and for that end had got together a great deal of forces: He hearing thereof, immediately raised no less than five hundred of his own name and dependants, with whom joining the Earl of Murray who was then Regent, they encountered Queen Mary's forces at the Village of Langside May 10. 1568, where the Laird of MacFarlane and his name behaved so valiantly, first galling and then putting to flight Queen Mary's Archers, that they were acknowledged by all to be the chief occasion of obtaining that glorious victory (*h*). In consideration of which signal piece of service in defending the Crown, he got, among other rewards, that Honourable Crest and Motto, which is still enjoyed by his posterity, viz. A Demi Savage proper, holding in his dexter hand a Shief of Arrows, and pointing with his Sinister to an Imperial Crown, Or, Motto, *This I'll Defend*. He married Ag-

---

(*h*) Petrie's Church History. Godscroft's History of the Douglasses.

nes Maxwell, daughter to Sir Patrick Maxwell of Newark, by whom he had three sons; John his successor; George MacFarlane of Mains, who got a disposition from his father to the Mains of Kilmaronock, but died without issue; and Humphrey MacFarlane of Bracheurn.

John next Laird of MacFarlane married, first, Susanna Buchannan, daughter to Sir George Buchanan of that Ilk, her mother being Mary Graham, daughter to the Earl of Monteith, by whom he had no issue. He married, secondly, Helen, daughter to Francis Steuart Earl of Bothwell, by Margaret Douglas his wife, daughter to the Earl of Angus, by whom he had Walter his successor. Thirdly, He married Elizabeth, daughter to the Earl of Argyle, by whom he had Andrew MacFarlane of Drumfad, John predecessor to George MacFarlane of Glenralach, and George ancestor to MacFarlane of Clachan. Fourthly, He married Margaret, daughter to James Murray of Strowan.

His son and successor Walter married Margaret, daughter to Sir James Semple of Beltrees, by whom he had two sons, John his fucceffor, and Andrew MacFarlane of Ardefs. Which John married Grizel, daughter to Sir Coll Lamond of that Ilk, by Barbara his wife, daughter to Robert Lord Semple. But having no male-iffue, he was fucceeded by his brother Andrew, next Laird of MacFarlane, who marrying Elizabeth, daughter to John Buchanan of Rofs, had by her two fons; John his fucceffor; and Walter, a youth of great hopes, who died unmarried. John late Laird of MacFarlane married, firft, Agnes daughter to Sir Hugh Wallace of Wolmet, by whom he had no furviving iffue: He married, fecondly, Lady Helen Arbuthnot daughter to Robert Lord Vifcount of Arbuthnot, by whom he had three fons, the prefent Laird of MacFarlane, William, and Alexander.

The other families of this furname are, Firft, The family of Clachbuy, feverals of which are difperfed through the Weftern-Iflands: Their anceftor was Thomas, fon to Duncan Laird of MacFarlane, in the reign of King Robert III. From whofe proper name they are frequently called MacCaufes or Thomas-fons. Secondly, The family of Kenmore, who are pretty numerous; their ancestor was John, a younger son of Duncan MacFarlane of that-Ilk, in the Reign of King James I. Of this Family is Robert MacFarlane of Achinvenalmore in Glenfroon, James MacFarlane of Muckroy, and Walter MacFarlane of Dunnamanich in the North of Ireland. Thirdly, MacFarlane of Tullichintaull, whose predecessor was Dugal, a younger son of Walter MacFarlane of that Ilk, in the reign of King James III. Of this family are descended John MacFarlane of Finnart, Malcolm MacFarlane of Gortan, and Mr Robert MacFarlane minister of the Gospel at Buchanan. Fourthly, MacFarlane of Gartartan, whose family is pretty numerous in the shire of Perth. His ancestor was Walter MacFarlane, eldest son of a second marriage to Sir John MacFarlane of that Ilk, by his wife a daughter of the Lord Herries, in the reign of King James IV. Of this family is John MacFarlane of Ballagan. Fifthly, MacFarlane of Kirktoun, in the Paroch of Campsy and shire of Stirling, whose ancestor was George MacFarlane of Merkinch, younger son to Andrew Laird of MacFarlane, in the reign of King

James V. Which George went afterwards and settled in the North, where his posterity continued till they bought the lands of Kirktoun. Sixthly, There is also one Parlane MacFarlane or MacWalter of little Auchinvenal, who pretends that his ancestor Walter was a natural son of one of the Earls of Lennox, a long time after MacFarlane came off that family. But this account is controverted by the Laird of MacFarlane, who asserts his predecessor to have been a cadet of his family, which is also owned by all the surname of MacWalter, Auchinvenal himself only excepted, who also never denied it till of late.

The surname of MacFarlane is very numerous both in the West and North Highlands, particularly in the shires of Dunbartoun, Perth, Stirling, and Argyle; as also in the shires of Inverness, and Murray, and the Western Isles; besides there is a great many of them in the North of Ireland. There is also a vast number of descendants from and dependants on this surname and family of other denominations, of which those of most account are a Sept termed Allans, or MacAllans, who are so called from Allan MacFarlane their predeceffor, a younger fon of one of the Lairds of Mac-Farlane, who went to the North, and settled there feveral Centuries ago. This Sept is not only very numerous, but alfo divers of them of very good account, fuch as the families of Auchorrachan, Balnengown, Drumminn, &c. They refide moftly in Marr, Strathdon, and other Northern Countries. There are alfo the MacNairs, Mac-Eoins, MacErrachers, MacWilliams, Mac-Aindras, MacNiters, MacInftalkers, Mac-Iocks, Parlans, Farlans, Gruamachs, Kinniefons, &c. All which Septs own themfelves to be MacFarlanes, together with certain particular Septs of MacNuyers, MacKinlays, MacRobbs, MacGreufichs, Smiths, Millers, Monachs, &c.

The Laird of MacFarlane had a very good old Caftle in an Ifland of Lochlomond, called Ifland-Rowglas, which was burnt by the Englifh during Cromwell's ufurpation, and never fince repaired. He has alfo another pretty good houfe and gadens in an Ifland of the fame Loch called Ifland-vow. But his principal refidence is at Inverioch or New Tarbet, which is a handfome houfe, beautified with pleasant gardens, situated in the Paroch of Arrochar, and shire of Dumbarton, near the head of that large Loch or arm of the Sea called Loch-long, where there is excellent fishing for herring, and all other sorts of sea-fish.

The Laird of MacFarlane's armorial bearing is, Argent, a Saltier engrail'd, cantoned with four Roses Gules, which is the arms of the old family of Lennox. Supporters, two Highland-men in their native garbs, arm'd with Broad Swords and Bows proper. Crest, a Demi Savage, holding a Sheaf of Arrows in his dexter hand, and pointing with his Sinister to an Imperial Crown Or. Motto, THIS I' LE DEFEND. And on a compartment, the word LOCH SLOY, which is the MacFarlane's Slughorn or CRIE DE GUERRE.

An Account of the Surname of

CAMERON.

THE most ordinary account delivered of the origin of the surname of CAMERON is, that in the latter part of the reign of King William, or the beginning of the reign of King Alexander II. a principal person of those Danes, or Norvegians, then in possession of most of our Northern Scottish Isles, named Cambro, did marry the daughter and heiress of MacMartin, proprietor of that part of Lochaber now possest by Locheal, Chief of that Surname of Cameron. And as MacIntosh did not change his surname upon his marrying the heiress of the principal person or Chief of the MacCattans, but instead thereof many of that surname went into that of MacIntosh; so also in this case the above-mentioned Cambro not only retained his own name, upon his marriage of the heiress of the principal person or chief of the MacMartins, a very old Clan in that Country, but also from his own proper name transmitted the surname of Cameron to his posterity, which in a short tract of time becoming the more powerful, the whole remains of the MacMartins went into that surname.

I find it asserted in the genealogical account of the Surname of Campbell, that Sir Neil Campbell, who flourished in a part of the reigns of King Alexander III. and King Robert I. for his second Lady, married a daughter of Sir John Cameron, Locheal's ancestor. But that account cannot hold, in regard Sir Neil was only married to Mary Bruce, sister to King Robert, who survived him, and was after his death married to Fraser Lord Lovat. But others with more probability assert, that Sir John Cameron's daughter was second Lady to Sir Colin, successor to Sir Neil. This Sir John Cameron upon very good grounds may be presumed to have been one and the same with him designed John de Cambron, or of Cameron, who was one of the subscribers of that letter sent by King Robert I. and his Nobles to the Pope anno 1320.

The Camerons, or Clan Chameron, seem to have been a name of considerable antiquity before the reign of King James I. in regard of the figure that Clan made in that King's reign; for being in conjunction with Donald Balloch brother to the Lord of the Isles, they with very considerable loss defeated an army sent against them by the King; but in a short time thereafter, the desertion of that Clan, with the Clan Chattan, so broke Balloch's measures, that he was obliged to disband his army, and flee to Ireland.

The Camerons, as most other neighbouring Clans, while the family of MacDonald continued in a flourishing condition, were dependants on the same: But after the extinction of that great family, each of these Clans came into an independant state, setting up upon all occasions for themselves, as at this present time. The Laird of Locheal in the latter part of the reign of King James VI. married Campbell of Glenorchy's daughter, aunt to the late Earl of Braidalbin. Of this marriage he had Sir Ewan, his successor, a very well accomplished gentleman, who performed a great many signal services against the English, in the reigns of King Charles I. and II. having defeated at one conflict, with very much loss to the enemy, a party of two hundred English, and at another wholly in a manner cut off a party of eighty, there escaping only two Centinels. In one of these adventures, a robust fellow of the enemy grappled with Sir Ewan, and trip't up his heels, and while the Englishman was searching for his dagger to stab him, Sir

Ewan got hold with his teeth of the Englishman's throat, and in a few minutes deprived him of his life. Upon the Restoration of King Charles II. he bestowed the honour of Knighthood upon that Gentleman, who always continued faithful to his interest. This Sir Ewan married the Laird of MacLean's daughter, by whom he had John, his successor. 2dly, He married Barclay of Urie's daughter, by whom he had also issue. John present Laird is abroad; he married Campbell of Lochnell's daughter, by whom he had Donald his son, and several other children. The nearest to that family is Captain Allan Cameron, brother to Locheal, who is also abroad. Locheal's principal residence is in Auchincarry in Lochaber, where he hath a large house, all built of Fir-planks, the handsomest of that kind in Britain. There are also the Camerons of Glendeshery, Kinlochlyon, and a good many more gentlemen of considerable estates, and a great many of the vulgar sort of this surname in Morvern and Lochaber.

The dependants on this surname are a Sept of the MacLauchlans, the MacGilveils, MacLonveis, MacPhails, and MacChlerichs or Clerks, who with the MacPhails or Pauls, are originally Camerons, with some others. There is also MacMartin of Letterfinlay, in Lochaber, being the principal person of the old Sept of the MacMartins, who with that whole Sept own themselves now to be Camerons. The Camerons also contend, that the surname of Chalmers is descended of a cadet of their surname, who having gone some years ago into the French service, assumed the name of Camerarius, or Chalmers, for that of Cameron, as more agreeable to the language of that country. One of this Chalmers's progeny having continued in France, was ancestor to the Lord of Tartas, and others of that name in that Kingdom: Another of that name having returned to Scotland, was ancestor to the Chalmers of the shire of Aberdeen, and other parts of this Kingdom.

The Camerons of old, as some Heralds record, carried for Arms, Or, Two Barrs Gules. But now, Argent, Three Pallets Gules. Or as some, Argent, pally barry Gules; as I have seen a seal of Locheall's cut.

An Account of the Surname of

MACLAUCHLAN.

THE Surname of MacLauchlan hath hath been of a long time reputed one of our ancient Clans, being originally descended of the Surname of the O'Lauchlans of Ireland, the principal person of whom, according to Mr Walsh, and other Irish Historians, was, in the second Century of the Christian Epocha, Provincial King of the Province of Meath, which dignity his successors enjoyed for many descents, till some little time before the English Conquest, the family of Orork obtained that Principality. This Surname is asserted to be of the Mileian Stem, or that of the ancient Kings of Ireland, and the progenitor thereof to have come to Scotland with the first who from Ireland planted Argyle-shire. I have heard some of this name affirm, that the Laird of MacLauchlan had a charter of his estate from King Congallus II. but cannot assent too far to any such assertion, there being no evidences of that antiquity as yet found out, at least any mention made of such in any place or Record of this Kingdom, tho' there may be a traditional account, that the above surname was in possession of their estate in that reign, or before the same, which is no way inconsistent with probability.

The Laird of MacLauchlan, Chief of that Surname's estate of Straithlauchlan, and principal residence being the large and ancient Castle of Castle-Lauchlan, are in the lower part of Upper Cowal, near the north side of Lochfine, in the shire of Argyle, in which most of his Clan reside. The next to that family is Colin MacLauchlan, the present Laird of MacLauchlan's uncle. There are also the MacLauchlans of Craigintairrow, Inchchonell, and divers other heritors of that surname in the said shire ; as also MacLauchlan of Auchintroig, in the shire of Stirling, in favour of Celestin MacLauchlan, one of whose ancestors, Duncan Earl of Lennox confirms a charter granted by Eugen MacKeffan of Garchels to one of the said Celestin's ancestors, which confirmation is dated in the year 1394, and eighth year of the reign of King Robert III. There is another numerous Sept of the MacLauchlans refiding in Morvern, and Lochaber, the principal perfon of thefe being MacLauchlan of Corryuanan in Lochaber. Of this family is MacLauchlan of Drumlane in Monteith, with others of that furname there. Thofe of this Sept refiding in Lochaber, depend upon the Laird of Locheal, as already mentioned.

MacLauchlan for Arms hath four Coats quarterly. 1ft, Or, or as fome, Argent, a Lyon rampant Gules. 2d, Argent, a Hand coupee fefs-ways, holding a crofs Croflet Fitchee, Gules. 3d, Or, a Galley, her oars in Saltyre, Sable, placed in a Sea, proper. 4th Argent, in a bafe undee, Vert, a Salmon naiant, proper. Supporters, Two Roe Bucks, proper. Motto, *Fortes et Fidus*.

An ACCOUNT of the SURNAME of

MACNAUCHTAN.

THE Surname of MacNauchtan, tho' now low, hath been a furname of very great antiquity, and for a long tract of time of much efteem, and poffeffed of a very confiderable eftate in Argyle-fhire. This Surname was fo denominated from the proper name of Nauchtan, being that of one of the progenitors of the fame, and an ancient Scottifh proper name. The anceftors or Chiefs of this furname are reported to be for fome ages defigned Thanes of Lochtay, and alfo to be poffeffed of a great eftate betwixt the fouth-fide of Lochfine and Lochow, parts of which are Glenera, Glenfhira, Glenfine, and others.

The firft of this name mentioned in our publick Hiftories, was Duncan Laird of MacNaughtan, an affiftant of MacDugal Lord of Lorn againft King Robert Bruce at the battle of Dalree, for which he loft a part of his eftate; but afterwards he, or rather his fon, was a loyal fubject to that King, and to King David II. his fucceffor. The prefent Laird of MacNauchtan's father, Sir Alexander MacNaughtan, was one of the braveft and beft accomplifhed Gentlemen of his age, and a very clofe adherent to the intereft of King Charles I. and II. in all their difficulties; fo that in recompence of that Gentleman's loyalty and fignal fervice, King Charles II. at his Restoration not only bestowed the honour of Knighthood upon him, but also a liberal pension during life, the latter part of which having spent at Court, he died at London.

There is a very considerable gentleman of this name in the county of Antrim in Ireland, whose ancestor was a son of the family of MacNauchtan. He hath a good estate called Benbardin, and a pretty Castle in which he resides, there being also divers of his name residing in his estate, and other parts of that country. Those of other denominations descended of this surname, are the MacKenricks, descended of one Henry MacNauchtan; a Sept of the MacNuyers, especially those of Glenfine; the MacNeits, MacEols, and others. It is a clear demonstration of the antiquity of a surname, that many branches, especially of other denominations, are descended off the same; it being evident, that in order of nature such things are not suddenly brought to any bearing, but gradually, and in a considerable progress of time.

The present Laird of MacNauchtan is in possession of no part of his estate, the same being evicted some years ago by creditors, for sums no way equivalent to the value thereof, and there being no diligence used for relief thereof, it went out of the hands of the family. MacNauchtan's eldest son, being a very fine Gentleman, was a Captain in the Scottish Foot-Guards, and was sometime ago killed in Spain; his only surviving son, John, being a Custom-House Officer upon the Eastern Coast. MacNauchtan's Estate, called MacNauchtan's-Letter, being a pretty good Estate, lyes upon the west-side of Lochfine, within a little way of that Loch, in the shire of Argyle. His principal Residence is the Castle of Dundaraw, situated upon a little rocky point, upon the west shore of Lochfine, contiguous to his own Estate.

The Armorial bearing of the Laird of MacNauchtan is, quarterly. 1st and 4th Argent, a Hand fessways coupee, proper, holding a cross Croslet fitchee, Azure. 2d and 3d Argent, a Tower embattelled, Gules, and a demy Tower for Crest. Motto, *I hope in GOD.*

An Account of the Surname of

MACGREGOR.

THE Surname of MacGregor, once a numerous name, and in poffeffion of divers confiderable eftates, hath of a long tract of time been accounted one of the ancient Scottifh Surnames, or Clans, being denominated from the proper name of Gregor, anceftor of that Surname, being a known ancient proper Scottifh name. Thofe of this Surname affert their progenitor to have been a fon of one of the Scottifh Kings of the Alpinian Race, more efpecially of King Gregory; But our Hiftorians are generally agreed that King Gregory never married, and was not known to have any iffue either legitimate, or illegitimate. However that be, that this furname is defcended from one properly fo called, a fon, or fome other defcendant of another of the Kings of the Alpinian Race, is no way inconfiftent with probability. But that Surname having loft their eftates at different junctures, and by various contingences, is a mean of the lofs alfo of any evidents relating to the manner and time of acquiring thofe eftates, and that were any way conducive for evincing the defcent of the Family: The beft document now extant in their cuftody, being their Armorial bearing, which infinuates pretty clearly, that the faid name was either defcended of fome of the Stem of the Scottifh Kings, or that they had done fome piece of fignal fervice for fome one of the Kings, and Kingdom, tho' the circumftances of either of thefe cannot at this diftance be fully cleared. I find in the genealogical account of the furname of Campbell, that Sir Colin Campbell of Lochow, who had divers great offices from King Malcolm II. had a daughter married to MacGregor laird of Glenurchy, and that of this marriage was Sir John MacGregor of Glenurchy, a perfon of very good account in the reign of King Malcolm III. The Chief of that name is very well known to have been for many generations Lairds of Glenurchy; and to have built the Caftle of Balloch, or Taymouth, at least to have had their Residence there, and also to have built Castle Caolcbuirn, in the west part of that country. How this Estate was lost is not very evident; but it is probable, that the name of MacGregor, being so near neighbours, might be induced or obliged to join MacDugal Lord of Lorn, against King Robert I. and upon that account lost a good part of their estate; as the MacNauchtans, and MacNabs lost a part of theirs for the same cause. However the first of the name of Campbell who got that estate of Glenurchy, was Black Sir Colin Campbell, second son to Sir Colin Campbell of Lochow, in the latter part of the reign of King James II. or in the beginning of the reign of King James III. being ancestor of the present Earl of Braidalbin. Besides the chief family of Glenurchy, there was also MacGregor of Glenlyon, who, having no issue, nor near relation, disponed his estate to a second son of Sir Duncan Campbell of Glenurchy, being ancestor of Campbell of Glenurchy, in the beginning of the reign of King James VI. There was also MacGregor of Glenfre, who was forfeited in the same reign, the Laird of MacGregor having also near the same time sold the last lands that family had in those parts, called Stronmiolchon; so that since that time, viz. the latter part of the reign of King James VI. the Lairds of MacGregor had no estate, till the principal branch of that family became extinct in the reign of King Charles II. the chief-ship devolving upon Malcolm MacGregor, descended of a collateral branch of the chief family, whose son Gregor MacGregor, in the reign of King William, dying without issue, was succeeded by Archibald Mac-Gregor of Kilmanan, whose male-issue being all dead, and those few who pretend nearest relation to him being of mean repute and circumstances, made (as is reported) a formal renounciation of the Chief-ship in favour of Gregor MacGregor of Glengyle, who is lineally descended from a son of the Laird of MacGregor.

This surname is now divided into four principal families. The first is that of the Laird of MacGregor, being in a manner extinct, there being few or none of any account of the same. The next family to that of MacGregor is Dugal Keir's family, so named from their anceftor Dugal Keir, a fon of the Laird of MacGregor; the principal perfon of that family is MacGregor of Glengyle, whofe refidence and intereft is at the head of Lochcattern, in the parifh of Callander, in the fhire of Perth. The third family is that of Rora, the principal perfon of which is MacGregor of Rora in Rannach, in the fhire of Perth. The fourth family is that of Brackley, fo denominated from Brackley, of which the principal perfon of that family was not long ago proprietor.

Thofe of other denominations defcended of this furname, are the MacKinnins, being a pretty numerous Clan in the Ifle of Sky; the principal perfon of that Clan hath a pretty good eftate in the Ifles of Sky and Mull. How far this pretenfion is acquiefced in, I cannot determine; but am confident, that gentleman's Armorial bearing differs very much from that of the furname of MacGregor. Another branch of another denomination is that of MacCarras, a pretty numerous Sept in the North parts of Perthfhire. There are alfo the MacLeifters, MacChoiters, and divers others defcended of that Surname; of which the Armorial Bearing is,

Argent, a Fir-Tree, growing out of a Mount in base Vert, surmounted of a Sword bend-ways, supporting on its point an Imperial Crown, in Dexter chief Canton proper, importing the descent of that Surname from one of our Kings, or the same having done some signal service to the Crown. Motto, *Undoe and spare not.*

An Account of the Surname of

COLQUHOUN:

And the ancient LAIRDS of LUSS, before the assumption of that Surname.

THE ancestor of the Surname of COLQUHOUN was Humphrey Kilpatrick, in whose favour Malduin Earl of Lennox grants charter of the lands of Colquhoun in the reign of King Alexander II. That of Kirkpatrick, or Kilpatrick, always reputed the place in which St Patrick the Apostle of Ireland was born, is presumed to have obtained that Denomination in very ancient times; as is evident by a Charter by Aluin Earl of Lennox, mortifying some Lands to the old church of Kilpatrick, before the foundation of the Abbey of Pailley, anno 1160. that being then, and as it would seem for a long time before, so designed: From which, and the adjoining village of the same denomination, was an ancient Surname in those parts denominated, of which was that Humphrey, who first acquired the lands of Colquhoun, which lands were so named before he acquired the same: The import of which denomination being a Sea-coasting Corner or Point, to which the former situation of those lands, especially of that now termed Dunglass, the ancient Mansion-House thereof, very well agrees; rather than to that from Connaucht in Ireland, or any other to that purpose pretended for the Denomination of that Surname. The first who assumed the Surname of Colquhoun, was Ingram the above Humphrey's Successor, being so designed in the Charter of Luss by Malcolm Earl of Lennox, to Malcolm Laird of Luss, confirming John

Laird of Luſs his Charter to his ſon of thoſe lands in the Beginning of the Reign of King Robert I. This Ingram's Succeſſor was Robert of Colquhoun, who is mentioned, as alſo his ſucceſſor of the ſame name, in divers charters by Malcolm the ſecond, and Donald, Earls of Lennox.

To Robert the ſecond of that name of Colquhoun, ſucceeded Humphrey of Colquhoun, who, in the year 1394, and fourth year of the reign of King Robert III. married the daughter and heireſs of Godfrey Laird of Luſs; however otherwiſe aſſerted, that at that time the Laird of Luſs married the heireſs of Colquhoun, it being evident that the family of Luſs of that Ilk, or as others, Lennox of Luſs, was the greater family, both in reſpect of antiquity and eſtate than that of Colquhoun; ſo that being the greater, it cannot be preſumed he would have quitted his ſurname, and aſſumed that of the leſſer upon his marriage with the heireſs thereof: As for inſtance, MacIntoſh, Locheall, and Shaw of Greenock, with many others, whoſe anceſtors, tho' married to heireſſes equal to themſelves, retained their ſurnames: And ſo it may be thought would

Luss upon marrying the heiress of Colquhoun. For further illustration of this matter, Godfrey Laird of Luss is witness to a charter granted by Duncan Earl of Lennox in the year 1349; As also Humphrey of Colquhoun is witness in another charter of the same date, by the same Earl; And in the charter of Camstroddan, confirmed by the same Earl, in the year 1395, being the very next year, the same Humphrey Colquhoun is designed " of Luss," and Robert, Camstroddan's ancestor, is designed " Robert Colquhoun, his brother": So that by the above charters the time and manner of the marriage of the Laird of Colquhoun with the heiress of Luss is fully illustrated.

The most ancient charter now extant of the Lands of Luss, is a charter by Malduin, Earl of Lennox to Gilmore, son of Muldonich, of the lands of Luss. This Muldonich, or another of Gilmore's ancestors, is upon very good grounds asserted to be a son of the Earl of Lennox, and to have retained the surname of Lennox, or, as others, assumed that of Luss, and retained the same till the marriage of the Heiress with Colquhoun. The above charter was in the Reign of King

T

Alexander II. but it is thought the Estate was given off to one of the Ancestors of that family before that charter, tho' the same be the oldest now extant in their hands. To Gilmore succeeded Maurice, being only mentioned witness by designation of Luss in a charter by the Earl to Maurice Galbraith, of the lands of Auchincloich. Maurice's successor was Sir John of Luss, in whose favour Malcolm Earl of Lennox grants charter of the lands of Luss, and superiority of Banra, and the adjacent Isles belonging in property to Gilmichal, Gilmartin, and Gillecondad, surnamed Galbraiths. To Sir John succeeded Malcolm, in whose favour Malcolm second son of that name Earl of Lennox grants charter of confirmation of Luss, with the property of Easter Glinn, in the reign of King Robert I. Malcolm's successor was Duncan, in whose favour Donald Earl of Lennox grants charter, and he is a frequent witness in others of that Earl's charters. The last Laird of Luss was Godfrey already mentioned.

Humphrey Colquhoun, first of that name Laird of Luss, granted charter of the lands of Camstroddan and Auchigavin, to Robert Colquhoun his brother, and his heirs male, which failing to another Robert, and Patrick, his other brethren; which charter was written at Luss, and subscribed by the Laird, and confirmed by Duncan Earl of Lennox, at Inchmirrin, his Mansion-house, upon the 4th day of July 1395, being the fifth of the reign of King Robert III.

To Humphrey succeeded Sir John, who was married to the Lord Erskine's daughter. He was first Governor of Dunbarton-castle, afterwards of the Castle of Inchmirrin, and being enticed under a shew of friendly conference, or parley, to come out of his garrison, by means of Lauchlan MacLean, and Murdo Gibson, comanders of an Army of Isles-men, who harrassed Lennox in the minority of King James II. was by an ambush planted for that purpose treacherously slain, with 120 of his men. I have seen this Sir John designed in an old Scotish chronicle in manuscript, " Sir John Colquhoun of Luss and Sauchy," the lands of Sauchy and Glyn being reported to be given to Malcolm laird of Luss, by King Robert I. for his service at the battel of Bannockburn.

Sir John's succeſſor was called Sir John who was married to the Lord Boyd's daughter. He was for some time treaſurer to King James III. His succeſſor was Sir Humphrey mairred to the Laird of Houſtoun's daughter. His ſecond ſon was Patrick of Glyn, who had a daughter married to Murray of Tullibairn, who had to him ſeventeen ſons. To Humphrey ſucceeded John, who married the Earl of Lennox's daughter, by whom he had John his ſucceſſor, and James anceſtor of Colquhoun of Kilmardinny, of which family is Colquhoun of Craigtoun; and two daughters married to the lairds of Houſtoun and Kilbirny. John fourth of that name laird of Luſs, was married to the Earl of Monteath's daughter, by whom he had Sir Humphrey his ſucceſſor, Alexander, afterwards laird of Luſs, and John. Sir Humphrey was married to the Lord Hamilton's daughter, by whom he had one daughter, married to Campbell of Carrick. This Sir Humphrey fought the conflict of Glenfroon, againſt the MacGregors, and was afterwards killed in Benachra-caſtle by the MacFarlanes, thro' influence of a certain Nobleman whom Luſs had diſobliged. He was succeeded by Alexander his brother, who married Helen, daughter to the Laird of Buchanan, by whom he had five sons, Sir James his successor; Sir Humphrey of Balvey, Alexander of Glins, Walter and George. Sir Humphrey, Walter, and George died without issue.

Sir James of Luss married the Earl of Montrose's daughter, and had by her Sir John his successor, Sir James of Corky, and Alexander of Tullichewn. Sir John married Baillie heiress of Lochend, by whom he had three sons, who died all unmarried, and eight daughters, three of which only had issue, being Lilias the eldest married to Stirling of Keir, Christian to Cunningham of Craigends, and Helen to Dickson of Invereſk.

To Sir James succeeded his brother, Sir James of Corky, who was married to Cunningham of Bellyechan's daughter, by whom he had Sir Humphrey, his successor, and James. Sir Humphrey was married to the Laird of Houstoun's daughter, by whom he had no children that came to age, but one daughter, Anne, who being heiress of that estate, was married to James Grant of Pluſcarden, second son to Grant of that Ilk, who, upon the death of Sir Humphrey, succeeded to the estate of Luss, and in a little time thereafter, through decease of Brigadier Alexander Grant, his elder brother, without issue, succeeded also to the estate of Grant, being now in possession of both those great and ancient estates, designing his eldest son for Laird of Grant, and his second son for Laird of Luss. The principal residence of the Lairds of Luss is Rosdoc, pleasantly situated in a little peninsula, upon the south shore of Lochlomond, in the parish of Luss, and shire of Dunbarton.

The next to the family of Luss of that name in this Kingdom is Colquhoun of Tullichewn. There is also in the parish of Luss Colquhoun of Camstroddan, descended of a son of the said family in the reign of King James V. There is Colquhoun of Garscaddan in the parish of Kilpatrick, descended from the family of Camstroddan in the minority of Queen Mary. There is also Colquhoun of Craigtoun, a cadet of the family of Kilmardinny, as already mentioned. Those of other denominations descended of this Surname are the Cowans, pretty numerous in the shire of Fife, and in the East parts of the shire of Stirling. The chief person of that name is Cowan of Corstoun, in Fife. Also the MacMainesses, who are not very numerous. There is also a Sept of this surname very numerous in Appin, and other places of Upper Lorn, called MacAchounichs.

The Armorial Bearing of Colquhoun of Luss is, Argent, a Saltyre engrailed, Sable. Supporters, Two Hounds Sable, collared Argent. Crest, a Hart's Head coupee, Gules. Motto, *Si Je Puis*.

An ACCOUNT of the SURNAME of

LAMOND.

THE Surname of LAMOND did not upon most occasions associate with most others of the more remote Clans: Nevertheless upon very solid grounds it hath been always accounted a surname of great antiquity and esteem; the same for divers ages being in possession, and the Chiefs thereof Lairds or rather Lords of all Lower Cowal, a very fertile country, and of a large extent, tho' moſt part thereof at ſeveral junctures and occaſions (of which the circumſtances cannot in this age be diſcovered) was wreſted out of their hands. The name itſelf did alſo ſuſtain very great loſs or diminution in the time of the Civil Wars, in the reign of King Charles I. having joined with the Marquis of Montroſe's party, who ſtood for the King's intereſt. Upon the defeat of the Marquis at Philiphaugh, and ſuppreſſion of that party, the Lamonds for ſome time defended themſelves in their Chief's Caſtle of Towart; but being beſieged by a party of the Parliament's Forces, were obliged to yield themſelves priſoners of war, and as ſoon as they came into the enemies hands were all put to the ſword; as were alſo near the ſame time a great number of the MacDougals, and MacNeils, who defended themſelves for ſome time in the Fort of Dunabarty in Kintyre, againſt Lieutenant General Leſley, after the defeat of Alexander MacDonald's Army at Largy: Leſley having given quarters to a party of Iriſh, who with the above Clans defended that Fort, did put all the Scots without diſtinction to the ſword, of which the moſt part were of thoſe mentioned with ſome MacDonalds, after they had ſurrendered at diſcretion; ſo that none of theſe ſurnames are any thing ſo numerous ever ſince as formerly.

The ſurname of Lamond is aſſerted to be deſcended of Lamond O'Neil, a ſon of the great O'Neil, provincial King of North Ulſter. The Chiefs of this ſurname were allied with very honourable families both in Scotland and Ireland; as with the families of Argyle, MacDonald, Luſs, Buchanan, Okyan, Lord Dunſeverin, and other families in Ireland. I find Duncan MacLamond, who ſeems to have been Laird of Lamond, mentioned witneſs in a charter granted by Duncan Earl of Lennox in the reign of King Robert III. This ſurname is always in Iriſh termed, MacLamonds or Clan Lamond.

Archibald late Laird of Lamond married Margaret daughter to Colonel Hurry, by whom he had no iſſue; ſo that the eſtate went to Dugal Lamond of Stiolaig, as being neareſt heir-male: He married Margaret ſiſter to James Earl of Bute, by whom he had five daughters, the eldeſt whereof,

Margaret, is married to John Lamond of Kilfinan, whose eldest son is to succeed to the estate of Lamond. There are of other denominations descended of this surname, the MacLucases or Lukes, MacInturners, or Turners, MacAlduies, or Blacks, MacIlwhoms, and Towarts. The Laird of Lamond, since the demolition of his Castle of Towart, by the above-mentioned siege, resides in Ardlamond, in Upper Cowal. The principal Gentlemen of that name are the Lamonds of Silvercraig, Lamond of Willowfield, who with some other gentlemen, and most others of that Surname, reside in Lower Cowal. There is also descended of a son of the Laird of Lamond, Burdon of Fedale, in Straithern, with others of that name there, having got that estate by marriage of the heiress thereof some ages ago.

There is also in Argyle-shire a Gentleman of a small estate designed MacOrquodale of Faintislands. His interest lyes upon the south-side of Lochow, and he is accounted one of the most ancient Gentlemen of his own station in that shire, or probably of any other in this Kingdom, it being with assurance asserted that the cause of his ancestor's getting that estate was for taking down the head of Alpin, King of the Scots, by night off the walls of the Capital City of the Picts, where these had affixed it, and upon bringing the same to King Kenneth the Great, he was for that service recompenced with that estate possessed by his successor as yet; and that there was a charter granted of the said estate by King Kenneth, which is reported to have been sent upon his earnest request to Sir George MacKenzie to be perused by him, some little time before the Revolution, and that the same was not got back. However this be, that Gentleman is reputed to be of very great antiquity by all in these parts; but I could not obtain any distinct account of the same, or of his Armorial Bearing.

There was also a Gentleman of a good estate in Kintyre, designed MacKay of Ogendale, which family continued in a very good repute for a good many ages. The principal family is lately extinct. There continues a considerable number of that Surname as yet in Kintyre, and the North of Ireland; so that I am very apt to think that the ancestor of the Northern MacKays, of which the Lord Rae is Chief, was descended off this ancient Family of that name in Kintyre, rather than from one Forbes a son of Forbes of Ochanochar, as is asserted by some modern writers.

Lamond for Armorial Bearing carried sometimes Azure, a Mond, or Globe Argent; But the most ancient and more ordinary Bearing of that Family is Azure, a Lyon Rampant, Argent. Crest, a Hand coupee proper. Motto, *Ne pereas nec spernas.*

An ACCOUNT of the SURNAME of

MACAULAY.

AS divers of the most ancient Surnames in the Western parts of the Lennox derive their origin from the Family of Lennox; so also the surname of MacAulay may upon good grounds be presumed to be descended off that ancient family. For confirmation of this allegation, in a charter by Malduin Earl of Lennox to Sir Patrick Graham, of the Carrucate of Muckraw, one of the witnesses is Aulay the Earl's brother: As also in another charter by the same Earl to William, son of Arthur Galbreath, of the two Carrucates of Bathernock, and Carrucate of Kincruich, now Culcruich, the witnesses are, Duncan and Aulay, the Earl's brethren. This Aulay is mentioned in divers other charters of the said Earl; as also the said Aulay's son, and successor, designed Duncan, son of Aulay, or MacAulay, Knight, is inserted in a charter by the said Earl to Walter Spreul, of the lands of Dalquhern, and in a great many others. I find no mention of this Duncan's successor. The next to be met with, and to be presumed of that family, is Arthur, designed of Arncaple, being witness in a charter by Duncan Earl of Lennox to Murdac son of Arthur Dinin; of the lands of Drumfad, and Kirkmichal; so that this Arthur might be grandchild to Sir Duncan last mentioned. There is a current tradition that this family or surname was designed " Arncaples of that Ilk" for some time, until from one of the Chiefs of that family, properly called Aulay, the whole surname was so denominated. But there is much more ground for the first, than the last of these suppositions, in regard of the small interval betwixt the time of the above

Sir Duncan MacAulay, and that surname's being found upon record to be so denominated as it continues to this present time.

The next of that name to the family of Arncaple, is the representative of Major Robert MacAulay, a Gentleman of a good estate in Glenerm, in the county of Antrim in Ireland, in which county a great many of that surname reside. There is also a numerous Sept of that surname in Caithness, and Sutherland, who own their descent off the family of Arncaple, and that Gentleman to be their Chief. The MacPheidirans of Argyle-shire own themselves to be originally of this surname. The principal residence of the Laird of Arncaple is the Castle of Ardincaple, in the shire of Dunbarton, situated upon the north-side of the Frith of Clyde, opposite to the Town of Greenock.

The Armorial Bearing of MacAulay of Arncaple is, Gules, Two Darts their points conjoined in Base, in form of a Cheveron reversed Argent, surmounted of a fess Checky of the 2d and 1st. Crest, a Boot coupee at the Ancle, with a Spur thereon proper. Motto, *Dulce Periculum.*

AN HISTORICAL AND GENEALOGICAL ESSAY

UPON THE FAMILY AND SURNAME OF BUCHANAN.

By WILLIAM BUCHANAN of AUCHMAR.

[FIRST PUBLISHED IN THE YEAR 1723.]

EDINBURGH:

PRINTED AND SOLD BY WILLIAM AULD,
TURK'S CLOSE, LAWN-MARKET.

M,DCC,LXXV.

An ACCOUNT

Of the Family and Surname

OF

BUCHANAN.

I may upon very solid grounds presume, that any one who offers to treat of the Genealogy of any Scottish Surnames, which can lay any just claim to considerable antiquity, especially such as are planted in, or near the more remote or Highland parts of this Kingdom, cannot in reason be supposed to have Records, or written Documents, upon which any thing that ordinarily is, or rationally may be advanced upon such a subject, can be founded; there being for the most part little diligence used by these Surnames or Clans in obtaining, and tho' obtained, in preserving any such documents; as is evidently instanced by the deportment of the Nobility and Barons to King Robert I. upon his requiring them to produce their evidents; There being also many contingencies, particularly the feuds so frequent betwixt Families of these Clans, carried on to such a degree of violence and animosity, and so detrimental to the private affairs of all concerned therein. Besides, the publick commotions affecting the Nation in general, may in reason be imagined a palpable means of the loss of many private evidents in custody of those, subject in a greater measure to such inconveniencies, than were many other surnames planted in the more inland places. Tho' indeed some who treat of the origin even of some of those last mentioned, are obliged to found their allegations in relation to the origin of these surnames, of which they treat, upon probable and solid tradition. As for instance, that exquisite Historian of the celebrated Surname of *Douglas;* also the Historian of the Surname of *Lesley*; as indeed in general, all who treat of that subject use the same method in relation to the more ancient surnames. The reason being obvious which obliges them so to do, if that allegation be as generally allowed, as the same is asserted by the greatest part of our modern writers, that there can be no written Record or evident evinced to have existed, or at least be produced of a more ancient date than the reign of King David the I. which commenced in the year 1124. So that in that case, all those surnames, whose origin is asserted to be more ancient than the commencement of that reign, must of necessity be founded upon tradition. Upon which account, and more especially that of the practice of the above-mentioned Historians, I judge it cannot be esteemed any disparagement to me, or to the subject I resolve to treat of, to be obliged to found the account of the origin of the Surname of BUCHANAN in general, and of six of the first principal men of that Family successively in particular, upon probable and uncontroverted tradition. In regard, conform to the more modern method used in genealogizing that Surname, the origin of the same is extended to a more ancient date than the reign already mentioned. Tho' mean while, I am much more inclinable to join sentiments with those of the more ancient Seneciones, or Genealogists, who, upon very solid grounds, contend the generality of our Clans, and more ancient Surnames, whose origin is truly Scottish, to be the real and genuine progeny of the Gathellan, or Scottish Collonies, which in the several junctures before and afterwards, under the conduct of the two Kings Fergus I. and II. came from Ireland, and planted Scotland. And for confirmation of this supposition, these demonstrate, that many of the most potent and ancient surnames in Ireland are of the same denomination, (except what must be allowed to some little difference of the dialect and accent of the Irish language used in both Nations) with a great many of the most ancient and modern of our Highland Clans; as the O'Donels and O'Neils with our MacDonalds and MacNeils; MacCuſtulas, almoſt the ſame with MacAuſlan, the ancient denomination of the now Surname of Buchanan, with divers others. A good many of the Clans do as yet cloſely adhere to this ancient kind of Genealogy. Some others of them are induced to adhere to a newer form, compoſed by a ſett of men ſome ages ago, come in place of the ancient Seneciones, which arrogate to themſelves the title of *Antiquaries*. Theſe rejecting the ancient method, as too general, and inconſiſtent with the notions of theſe more modern ages, have compoſed Genealogies in their opinion more exact and circumſtantiate than the former, by fixing, upon certain periods of time, the manner and other circumſtances relating to the Families or Clans of whom they treat. But all their allegations being founded upon tradition, and the matters they treat of being generally of more ancient date than the ages of theſe Antiquaries, they are ſubject to the ſame inconveniences, and, in my opinion, can be allowed only the ſame meaſure of Hiſtorical credit due to the moſt ancient of the traditions delivered by the former, if equally ſolid and probable. However, in regard this laſt method is that more generally received by, and moſt agreeable to the taſte and ſentiments of the greater part of thoſe of the preſent, and ſome bygone ages, I ſhall conform myſelf thereto as to what I am to offer in relation to the origin, and other concerns of the Surname of Buchanan. And in regard thefe latter Antiquaries do derive the Genealogy of fome of our Scottifh Clans, upon very good grounds, from the Danes, rather induced thereto by the fame acquired by the Danes by their martial atchievements for fome ages in Britain and Ireland, than upon any other folid ground, or fhew of truth; and more efpecially, feeing the progenitor of the Surname of Buchanan (according to the above Antiquaries) was obliged to abandon Ireland, thro' tyranny of the fame Danes, then domineering over that Kingdom, I prefume it will not be efteemed too incoherent with the enfuing fubject, nor unacceptable to thofe who fhall have occafion of perufing the fame, that I fhould briefly glance at the origin of that people, and fome few of thefe furprifing atchievements managed by them in Britain and Ireland, and fome other parts, as a native introduction to the account of the time, manner, and caufe of the Buchanans their anceftor his abandoning Ireland.

The Danes, according to their own and divers other Hiftorians, are the native progeny of the ancient Cimbrians; who, as Puffendorff relates, had Kings for fome ages before our Saviour's Nativity, having dominion over Denmark, Norway, Sweden, and fome other Northern Regions. That people was of fuch a gigantick ftature and unparalled fiercenefs, as gave occafion to Livy, Prince of the Roman Historians, to relate them to be framed by nature for the terror and destruction of other mortals. These Cimbrians in the third Consulship of the Famous Caius Marius (then the glory, tho' afterwards the scourge, of his native country) to the number of 400,000 fighting men, with their wives and children, went to invade Italy, which put the Romans in no small consternation, concluding their State in a manner lost; and probably it would have been so, had not, as Livy observes, such a brave and politick Captain as Marius been their General at that juncture, who by divers stratagems weakened the power, and broke the fierceness of these Barbarians, and in conclusion engaged their army, and entirely defeated the same, with the slaughter of 140,000 of them. Their wives and children during the battle being placed in waggons, on both wings of their army, greatly molested the Romans with slings, and other missive weapons; but at last observing the defeat, they in the first place killed their children, and lastly themselves; the women as well as men partaking in a great measure of that fierceness natural to their nation. This fatal defeat struck such a terror to the Cimbrians, as for some ages thereafter deterred them from encroaching upon the Roman territories; till in the middle of the Fifth Century of the Christian Epocha, having some ages before that, changed the name of Cimbrians into that of

Danes, they made up a part of that formidable army with which Attila the Great King of the Huns, attempted to subvert the Roman Empire in the reign of the Emperor Valentinian the third, and year 451. And in regard these were the two most formidable armies that ever invaded the Roman State and Empire, and contributed very much towards subverting the same, I shall briefly recount the manner and success of this expedition of Attila, in which the Danes were concerned, and shall then proceed to narrate some of the most considerable actions performed by them in Britain and Ireland.

Attila was King of the Huns, now Hungarians, and did by his courage and conduct bring under his subjection most part of all these Nations betwixt the Euxene and Baltick Seas, entitling himself " Attila the Great, King of the Huns, of the Medes, Goths, Vandals, Gepidæ and Danes, the scourge of GOD, and terror of the world." This magnanimous and ambitious Prince resolved to subdue the Roman Empire, then in the decline, and in order thereto levied an army of 500,000 chosen men, which, the quality of General and Soldiers duly considered, was not only of power to subdue the Roman Empire, but, as it might seem, the whole known world. Etius, who indeed may be accounted the last of the Roman Heroes, being General of the Roman Army in Gaul, and being informed of the march of this army towards that Country, not only muſtered all the forces the Roman Empire could raiſe, but alſo thoſe of the Viſi-Goths, and Alans of Spain, Franks and Burgundians of France, all at that time in confederacy with the Romans; by which means he made up an army equal to that of Attilla, and engaged in battle with him in the large plains of Chalons, near the City of Lyons in France. This battle laſted a whole day, with the loſs in end of 180,000 of Attilas's army, and 100,000 of that of Etius. The ſlaughter was ſo prodigious, that the waters of a rivulet which traverſed the plains where the battle was fought, were ſo increaſed with blood, as carried many dead bodies divers miles with the current thereof. Attila being in a manner defeated, and not in condition to make a ſafe retreat, cauſed fortify his Camp with waggons in the night-time, and ordered his army to defend the ſame to the utmoſt. Mean while having cauſed a large pile of combuſtible matter to be erected in the middle of his Camp, he ordered, if the enemy ſhould enter his camp per-force, that fire ſhould be put to the pile, and his body burnt therein, to prevent the enemy from triumphing over the ſame. Etius next morning obſerving Attila's army in a poſture of defence, and conſidering the loſs his own had ſuſtained, thought not fit to aſſault ſuch a number of deſperate men;

therefore he drew off his army, and by that means gave opportunity to Attila to march away with his.

The Danes, with their neighbours the Saxons, for some considerable time before, but in far greater number after this expedition of Attila, having fitted out a great many long small vessels, by them termed *Kiuls*, and having put a great many of their people on board the same, grievously infested the Coasts of Britain, France and Ireland, and the Netherlands with their Piracies; but in a greater measure the Coasts of England and Ireland. For no sooner had the Saxons wrested the Sovereignty of England from the Britons, than the Danes began their attempts upon the Saxons by frequent depredations and rapine committed upon the sea-coasts of their dominions; till in the year 858, and reign of Ethelred the first of that name, and fourth Monarch of the Saxons, or Englishmen, the Danish King, being influenced by Biorn a discontented Saxon Nobleman, sent a numerous army under command of Hubba his son, and Hungar a Danish Nobleman, in order to invade England, who, having first landed in Scotland, judging by the easy conquest thereof, to open their way into England, were herein disappointed, being engaged by Constantine, the Scottish King, at Leven-Water in Fife, and the one half of their army commanded by Huba defeated; but being relieved by the other part, the Danes, in the night-time, marched in all haste to Crail, where their ships road at anchor, and embarking their army with all diligence, sailed for England, in which arriving, they engaged with Edmund and Ofbright, tributary Kings of the East Angles and Northumberland, killed these two Princes in battle, and possessed most part of their dominions. And not only so, but in a short time obliged the Saxon Kings of England to pay them a vast tribute yearly, which they augmented at pleasure upon every advantage they obtained, till in the end it became so insupportable, as to put Ethelred the second of that name King of England, upon a very tragical method of redressing the same, by giving private orders to his subjects to assassinate all the Danes throughout England in one night; which was punctually performed upon the eleventh of November 1013. But this massacre was not attended with the projected success; for Sueno King of Denmark, informed of his country-mens fate, arrived next year with a potent army in England, and having defeated Ethelred in divers battles, obliged him in the end to abandon his dominions, and fly to Normandy; Sueno meantime taking possession of the whole Kingdom, and retaining possession thereof till his death, as did Canutus his son, Harold, and Hardiknout his grand-children, for the space of twenty-six years, with greater authority than any ever did that Kingdom. And if the Royal Line of their Kings at that period of time had not failed, and their native country Denmark been harraſſed with Civil Wars, in all human probability England might have continued for a much longer time, if not as yet, under the dominion of the Danes.

English Hiſtorians aſſert their country-men to be brought to the utmoſt degree of ſlavery, during the Danes their government; there being a Dane quartered in each Engliſhman's houſe, and the Engliſhman being upon all occaſions neceſſitated to ſhew a deal of reverence and reſpect towards his gueſt, and to addreſs him always by the title of Lord, which gave a riſe to the term of *Lurdan* given in after ages to idle uſeleſs fellows. Yea the Engliſh were brought to that pitch of dejection and ſervile adulation, as to urge their Daniſh King Canutus to receive divine adoration or honour from them. For which purpoſe, a vaſt confluence of his ſubjects attending that King near Southampton, he ordered his throne to be placed within the ſea-mark, and being ſet thereon at the ſeaſon the tide flowed, he commanded the waters to keep back and not to approach him; but the ſea diſobeying his orders, he was obliged to retire therefrom; upon which he cauſed proclaim aloud, that none ſhould preſume to give divine adoration to any, but to ſuch as the sea and all other created beings behoved to obey. These, and divers such stories English writers relate concerning the servitude imposed upon them by the Danes, whose avarice and ambition was not satiated with the Conquest of England, but they did also invade France under the conduct of a Noble Dane, named Rollo. And tho' that Nation was then governed by Charles the Bald, a very martial Prince, yet after a tedious and bloody war, he was obliged to yield to Rollo the Province of Neustria to be possessed by him and his army, the name of which, after obtaining, he changed into Normandy, anno 866. The seventh in descent from Rollo was Duke William of Normandy, who, in the year 1066, with a potent army invaded England, and at Hastings engaged in battle with the English King Harold, who, with 56,653 of his English soldiers, was killed: And Duke William, by that one battle, having entirely conquered England, was afterwards termed William the Conqueror.

The Danes being desirous to try their fortune once more in Scotland, to retrive the loss lately sustained by them therein, invaded that Kingdom the second time, under the Command of Hago and Helricus, in the reign of King Indulfus; but with no better success than at first, being beat back into their ships, and obliged to sail off for England. Notwithstanding of these reiterated losses, they with a more numerous army than in any former time, invaded Scotland the third time, in the reign of King Kenneth III. and year 988. The Scottish King with his Army engaged in battle with the Danes at Lancarty, within a few miles of Perth, in which the left wing of the Scottish army was defeated; which one Hay, with his two sons observing, who were ploughing at the time near the place of battle, pulled the beams off their Ploughs, and entered a strait pass thro' which the Scots were flying, and beat down promiscuously all who came within their reach. The Danes, amazed at the sudden change, retired to the body of their own army; as did the flying Scots, not a little encouraged, with all speed join theirs: And by a miracle of Divine Providence, within a few hours, obtained a glorious victory, by the assistance of these three Heroick Persons, being Progenitors of the Noble and Ancient name of HAY.

The Danes, by these repeated defeats, being rather incensed, than dejected, with a greater army and more resolute than ever, invaded Scotland the fourth time, under command of Ollaus Viceroy of Norway, and Enecus Governor of Denmark, in the year 1010, and sixth of the reign of King Malcolm II.; who with his Army engaged in battle with the Danes at Mortlich, and after a bloody and obstinate battle, defeated that potent army, with the death of one of their Generals Enecus. Sueno the Danish King, governing then in England, sent an army, under command of Camus, to reinforce the remainder of the Danish troops in Scotland; which being done, King Malcolm defeated that army. Also at Balbride the Danish General Camus being slain by a Scottish Gentleman called KEITH, ancestor of that Honourable Family, Sueno irritated to a degree, upon intelligence of the late defeat, sent the most potent Danish army that any age invaded Scotland, under command of his son Camutus. King Malcolm, notwithstanding of the vast loss he had sustained in the two former engagements, did, with unparallelled resolution and bravery, engage in battle with this army also, which continued till night separated them. The Scots keeping the field, were reputed victors, and as such, were addressed next day for peace by the Danes, which was concluded upon very honourable terms to the Scots.

It is recorded, that for a long time after the battle of Lancarty, all Danes and Norvegians, who received the honour of Knighthood, were solemnly sworn upon all occasions to revenge their Country-mens blood upon the Scots: But that after this last battle fought by King Malcolm, there was a curse imprecated upon all such of those Nations as should attempt to invade the cursed Scots;

which imprecation, it seems, took effect in the Danes their two last invasions of Scotland, by Sueno, and Acho, Kings of Norway, in the reign of King Duncan I. and Alexander II. of Scotland: The first of these Norvegian Kings getting off only so many as manned one ship, and the other scarcely what could mann four, of their two numerous armies. So that the Danes, who were a terror and scourge to most of the neighbouring Nations, reaped no other advantage by their frequent invasions of Scotland, than that the same, upon very good grounds, should be termed *Danorum Tumulus*, The Grave of the Danes.

The reason which partly induced me to insist at such a length upon the Danes their wars in Scotland, and conquests in other parts, was, to illustrate the S c o т s their Heroick Valour and Bravery, so conspicuously superior to that of any of their neighbouring Nations of these times, to the conviction of all, who industriously, if not maliciously, endeavour to derogate in any degree therefrom. For tho' the reason why the Scots, after divers attempts for that effect, continued unconquered by the Romans, be imputed to the inaccessibleness of their Country, by which means they were defended, rather than by force of arms; yet no such reason can hold, in the Danes their frequent invasions of them; all that war being managed in the open fields, with plain force, and fair play, as the Proverb runs. While at the same time, moft other nations, with whom they had dealings, were either obliged to fubmit to their yoke, or allow them very advantageous conditions, as is evident by what is already mentioned, and no lefs fo by what follows.

In relation to Ireland, the Hiftorians of that Nation affert the Danes to have begun their defcents and depredations in the begining of the fourth Century, upon the fea-coafts of that Kingdom; which obliged Cormackulfada, then King of Ireland, to employ 3000, or, as others fay, 9000 of the choice men of the Kingdom; which number he appointed as a ftanding army, for oppofing the infults, and reftraining the rapines of thefe Danifh Pirates. Thefe forces were termed *of Feans*, being the ancient Irifh term for Giants; and their General was termed *King of Feans*, than which the Irifh ufe no other term as yet in their own language for a General. About the middle of the fifth Century, the Irifh, with fome of our Scottifh Hiftorians, affert Finmacoel to be General of thefe Irifh forces; whofe huge ftature and actions againft the Danes, and others, are fomewhat above meafure extolled in divers rude rhimes, in their own language, retained as yet by the Irifh, and by fome of our Scottifh Highlanders. However this General, with thefe under his command, gave fo many checks to the

Danes, as obliged them for some time to desist from infesting his native country. But he was badly rewarded for his good service by his ungrateful country-men, who esteeming those forces useless in time of peace, and desirous to be free of some little tax of cloaths, arms and provision, ordinarily paid them, upon their refusing to disband, by the permission, or rather contrivance of Corbred the Irish King, Fean with all his forces were assassinated in one night. Which inhuman action was not long unpunished: The Danes within few years thereafter, having with greater numbers and violence than at any former time, infested the coasts of that Kingdom, and finding the same destitute of the disciplined troops, which were in use to oppose their insolencies, were thereby encouraged to march a good way into the inland country; which having done with little or no opposition, they fortified themselves in a convenient place, and sending some of their number to Denmark for more forces, which they obtained in a short space, subdued a good part of the Kingdom; having fortified and garrisoned a good many of the sea-port towns thereof, and also built throughout the Kingdom, forts at convenient distances, termed in Irish *Raes*, or Wheels, in regard their form was round like that of a wheel. These forts were ordinarily built upon eminencies, the inside thereof raised with stone, and the outside faced with square turf, of a considerable height and breadth, that four men might walk a-breast round the same. The buildings were joined round the inside with sloping roofs. There were also two, sometimes more ports, or entries, with stairs mounting to the battlement, and a draw-well or spring within each. The Garrisons kept in these, with the others in the fortified towns, so over-awed the Irish, that they durst not fall upon any means, or so much as think of regaining their liberty; altho' they had always elective Kings of their own natives, not always of the old line of their Kings, but more often of other stems, the state of the country obliging them to chuse men of valour and conduct, without much regard had to their pedigree. These elective Kings were rather Kings in name, than effect, being in condition for a long time of doing no other service in behalf of their Country, than to keep themselves with such as adhered to them in woods, mountains, and other inaccessible places, being intent upon all occasions to cut off such small parties of the Danes, as they found either robbing or purchasing provisions in the country.

Things continued in this state till the year 998. in which the Irish elected a valiant Nobleman, and eminently expert in martial fates, for their King, called Brian MacKennedy: Who entering upon the government, and pondering with himſelf what inſuperable difficulties he was to grapple with, in ſupporting the burden of ſuch a diſordered ſtate, did fall upon the moſt effectual methods he could in prudence imagine, for remedy of the preſent inconveniencies; and for that effect having called his whole ſubjects to a general Randevouſe, he elected out of them 9000 men which number he kept as a ſtanding army in place of the old Feans, terming this new army *Dalgheaſs*. For the ſubſiſtence of theſe, he impoſed upon that part of the Kingdom ſubject to him, a tax in money, which ſeems the firſt of that nature impoſed there. This King upon that account was termed *Brianboray*, or the Taxer, who, with his ſelect band of the Dalgheaſs, with other forces, proſecuted the war ſo ſucceſsfully againſt the Danes, that he not only defeated them in divers battles, but alſo obliged them to abandon their whole Forts, or Raes, throughout the Kingdom; and in fine, immured them within the four ſtrong towns of Dublin, Limerick, Cork, and Kingſaile. Theſe being ſupplied by the Daniſh Pirates at ſea, King Brian reſolved to deprive them of that advantage, by ordering a certain number of ſhips to be rigged out for clearing the coaſts of theſe Daniſh Pirates. For this purpoſe, he ordered the Provincial Kings, and other Nobility, to convey certain quantities of timber to the next adjacent ſea-ports, and amongst others, Mallmoro MacMurcho Provincial King of Lienster, whose sister was King Brian's Queen. MacMurcho designing to visit King Brian residing then at Fara, went in company with his servants, who had the care of conveying his share of the timber, of which a large mast, in carrying thro' a rugged way, stuck betwixt two rocks, so as neither force of horse nor servants could disengage the same, till at length MacMurcho himself was obliged to dismount, and assist his servants: In which business a silver clasp which he wore in the breast of his purple mantle, was almost torn off; which not regarding, he proceeded on his journey, and arriving at Fara, after some conference with the King, went to visit the Queen his sister, who, noticing his mantle, asked, how it came to be so: he telling plainly the manner, the Queen desired a sight of it, which so soon as she obtained, she threw it into a fire which was in the room; withal reproaching her brother, in most bitter terms, that he and his predecessors being Provincial Kings, he should so far degenerate, as to become in a manner a slave to her husband, whose ancestors never exceeded the character of Noblemen. MacMurcho's choler, as well as ambition, sufficiently inflamed by these speeches, and some others which past betwixt him and Prince Murcho King Brian's eldest son, left Court in a great rage, and posted to the Danish garrison in Dublin, using what arguments he could with them, to use all diligence in getting supplies of men from the King of Denmark, promising, upon their so doing, to join them with all the forces of Lienster. The Danes being now in desperate circumstances, gladly accepted of his proposals, and dispatching a message to the Danish King importuned him earnestly, that he should not neglect to send a competent army to their assistance; for that then, or never, the affairs of Ireland were to be retrieved. The King of Denmark, being that Sueno who afterwards conquered England, glad of this opportunity, dispatched an army of 15,000 men for Ireland, under command of Carolus Knutus his brother, and Andreas a Danish Nobleman, with all the Danish Pirates, and others in garison in Ireland to join this army. Which being done, and MacMurcho joining also with his Lienster men, made up altogegether an army of 60,000 men. Of all which King Brian getting intelligence, levied an army of 50,000 men to oppose these invaders, whom he found encamped in the plain of Clantarf, within two miles of Dublin. These two grand armies drawing near one another, neither did, nor could defer joining battle; which was begun, and maintained with equal valour and obstinacy for most part of the day, till towards evening, the left wing of the Irish army began to give ground, which brave Prince Murcho obferving, (King Brian his father, by reafon of his great age, being left in the camp) caufed a regiment left there for guard of the old King to be haftily brought out, with which he fo vigoroufly charged the right wing of the enemies army, commanded by Carolus, as wholly difordered the fame, and caufed the death of Carolus their General; at whofe fall the Danes were fo difcouraged, that they wholly abandoned the field, flying towards Dublin, the Leinftrians bearing them company, whofe perfidious King was alfo killed, as the juft reward of his perfidious rebellion. Prince Murcho, with his own guards, too refolutely purfuing a part of the Danifh army which went off in a body, was unfortunately killed, being a Prince of the greateft expectation of any ever born in that country. The old King was alfo killed by a party of Danes, which accidentally fled near by the camp, and obferving the fame without any guards, entered it, as alfo the King's tent, and killing all they found therein, thereafter efcaped. There are reported to be flain in this fatal battle 70,000 men, with all the perfons of diftinction on both fides. The circumftances of this memorable battle are not only related by the Irifh, but alfo by Marianus Scotus, an unexceptionable Hiftorian. The Irifh never fully retrieved the lofs fuftained in this battle; but in the end, by the means of Dermud Mac-

Murcho, lineal successor of the former, the Irish nation was brought under subjection to the English in the year 1171.

After this fatal disaster, for want of a more sufficient, the Irish were necessitated to elect Maolseachluin for King, whom they had formerly deposed upon account of his incapacity to govern, and he behoved to be much more so at this time, in regard of his great age. This old King could do little good for repairing of the disordered state of this country, the remnant of the Danes having secured themselves in their garrisons, and being reinforced with new supplies from England, over which Sueno the Danish King, or as others say Canutus his son, had then the sovereignty. So that by these joint Danish forces, Ireland was reduced to its former state of servitude, till in some time an occasion was presented to the Irish King of doing service to his country.

Sueno, or Canutus, at this time King of England, and Denmark, his birth-day approaching, which all the Danish officers and soldiers in Ireland resolved to solemnize with great jolity, Turgesius, the Danish General, sent orders to all the Danish officers in Ireland to repair to Limerick, being their principal garrison and his residence, to assist at the solemnity, fearing nothing that the Irish would or could do in such low circumstances. The General at the same time sent orders to the Irish Noblility and Gentry, to send to Limerick against the King's birth-day a 1000, or as others say, 2000 of the most beautiful of their daughters, to dally with the Danish officers at the festival. Of this the Irish King getting intelligence, resolved to send the desired number of the most clear complexioned youths who could be found, cloathed in womens habit with long Irish skiens, or daggers below their cloaths, with orders, that so soon as they went to bed with their several paramours, being generally drunk on such occasions, they should stab them with these concealed daggers, and afterwards seize upon their guard-house, where their arms were laid by, and if matters succeeded, to give a signal by kindling a large fire upon the town-wall; the Irish King with a small party being absconded in a wood near by, in expectation of the event. These Irish Viragoes put their orders in execution to the utmost, and having given the concerted signal to the King, introduced him and his party to the town; who, without any mercy or resistance, killed all the Danes in the garrison, being destitute of sense, officers, and arms; reserving their General Turgesius for further punishment, which was inflicted upon him by drowning, which then, and as yet is reputed the most ignominious death among the Irish. Most of all the other Danes throughout the Kingdom were shortly after cut off.

This massacre was a kind of parallel to another of that nature committed on the Danes in England some little time before this, by command of Ethelred the English King. But as that, so also this, fell short of the success projected thereby. For no sooner was the Danish King of England informed of his country-men's disaster, than he sent a powerful army into Ireland, which with the utmost rigour did prosecute all who had any hand in this late tragedy; so that most of them fell victims to the rage of their inveterate enemies, and those who did not, were necessitated to abandon their native country. Among the number of these was

ANSELAN BUEY, or FAIR, OKYAN, son to *Okyan* Provincial King of the south part of Ulster, being one of the youths concerned in the above-mentioned massacre. These Okyans, with some others of the most ancient and reputed Irish surnames, are asserted to be of the Mileian Stem or Lineage; as are also the MacDonalds, and some others of our Scottish Clans. These Mileians are reputed the progeny of the sons of Mileius Gathelian King of Gallicia in Spain, under whose conduct the Gathelians or Scots were first brought to, and planted in Ireland: So that all surnames in Ireland, or Scotland, descended of these, term themselves in their native language, *Clanna Miley*, or the Mileian progeny.

The time of this Anselan Okyan his leaving Ireland is generally computed to be in the year 1016, and twelfth year of King Malcolm II. his reign. He having landed with some attendants upon the Northern coast of Argyle-shire, near the Lennox, was, by a Nobleman, who had a considerable interest in those parts, and in the King's favour, introduced to the King, who took him into his service against the Danes; in which service, upon several occasions, particularly those two last battles fought by that King against Camus and Canutus, Okyan so signalized himself, that he obtained in recompence of his service several lands in the North part of Scotland, of which the lands of Pitwhonidy Strathyre may upon good grounds be presumed a part; which in due place shall be more particularly observed.

Not only the Okyans of the South part, but also the O'Neils of the North part, with all the other provincial Kings, who enjoyed that title in the Kingdom of Ireland, upon the English Conquest of that Kingdom, were not only obliged to quit their title of Kingship, but also a great part of the territories enjoyed by them formerly, and to content themselves with the title of Noblemen. The O'Niels, formerly Kings of the North part of Ulster, were after that Conquest entitled Earls of Tyrone; as were the Okyans, Provincial Kings of the South part, entitled

Lords of Dunseverin: With which family the Lord MacDonald of the Isles, the Laird of Lamond, and other principal families of the Highland Clans, have been allied. The circumstances of the O'Kyans in the Kingdom of Ireland are at present somewhat low; however upon all occasions wherein they have business or converse with any of the name of Buchanan in that Kingdom, they adhere closely to them upon account of the ancient relation. This Anselan O'Kyan, and some of his ancestors called by that name, are in old Charters termed *Absalon*; which difference is not material, in regard the writers of these Charters (as it would seem) were not acquainted with the orthography of ancient Irish names, and therefore exprest those which were better known, and could best be rendered in Latin. As is evident by a Charter relating to the family of MacPharlane, wherein the progenitor of that surname is termed *Bertholoneus*; whereas by the manner that name both write, and in an ordinary way of speaking express themselves, their progenitor's proper name behoved to have been Partholanus, or Partholan, a known ancient Irish name: As is also that of Anselan, ancestor of the MacAuslans, now Buchanan. So that the manner the clerks of these more ancient times exprest these names, is not to be too much criticised, nor relied upon.

There is a current tradition or account, that this Anselan O'Kyan married one Dennieſtoun, heireſs of a part, if not the whole, of the eſtate of Buchanan. But this account is not too generally adhered to, becauſe that heireſs of the name of Dennieſtoun, whom that Anſelan married, is only reputed to have had ſome little part of the eſtate of Buchanan, with Drumquhuaſſils and other lands on the water of Ainrick; and becauſe the greater part of the eſtate of Buchanan was given to the ſame Anſelan, by King Malcolm, with other lands, in reward of his ſervice againſt the Danes. Tho' indeed the name of Dennieſtoun was a very ancient and honourable name in the Lennox, and continued to be ſo for divers ages; Hugh Lord of Dennieſtoun, being witneſs to a Charter granted by Malcolm the firſt of that name, Earl of Lennox, to John Laird of Luſs, in the reign of King Alexander III. As alſo Robert Lord Dennieſtoun is recorded to be ſheriff of Dunbartoun-ſhire in the reign of King Robert I. The male-iſſue of this family failed in the reign of King Robert III. The Lord Dennieſtoun his two daughters being then married, the eldeſt to Cunninghame of Kilmaurs, and the ſecond to Maxwell of Calderwood. Dennieſtoun of Colgrain is now the Repreſentative of that ancient family.

Anſelan O'Kyan not only was recompenced for this ſervice by King Malcolm with lands of confiderable value, but alfo with very fplendid arms; as the fame King is recorded to have done to the anceftor of the Keiths, upon his killing of Camus the Danifh General, and to others upon the like accounts. The Arms affigned by that King to this Anfelan upon account of his defcent, and more especially upon account of his heroick atchievements, are, In a Field, Or, a Lyon rampant Sable, armed, and Languid Gules, holding in his dexter paw a Sabre, or crooked Sword, proper. Which arms that furname retained always without the leaft addition or variation, untill that addition obtained upon a very honourable occafion, at the battle of Bauge, as in due place fhall be obferved. Notwithftanding of the entire affection of that family for feveral ages to, and dependance upon the family of Lennox, yet the family of Buchanan did never, by way of conceffion, or pratronage, affume any part of that honourable family their Armorial Bearing; albeit it is evident that moft other ordinary names of this Kingdom, at fome time or occafion, affumed fome one part or other of their patron or fuperior's Armorial Bearing, in conjunction with their own. As for inftance, moft furnames of Teviot-dale and Douglas-dale, affume a part of the Douglaffes arms; and thofe of Murray-land, the arms of the Murrays. So that few of an equal character with that of Buchanan, reserved their arms so free of any addition or mixture as that surname did; which is no small argument, not only of the honour of the family, but also of the cause and reason of the first granting of these Arms.

This Anselan O'Kyan, agreeable to the most ordinary and received Genealogy of that surname, is reputed the progenitor of that surname, and first Laird of Buchanan. His son and successor was called

JOHN, In whose favours (as I have been informed by gentlemen of very much integrity, who asserted, they had seen the same in custody of the late Laird of Buchanan) there was a Charter granted by *Alcuin*, (as it would seem) first Laird of Lennox, in the reign of King Malcolm III. of the Wester Mains of Buchanan. But the Laird of Buchanan, in the decline of his age and jugdment, having conveyed his estate to strangers, by that means, many of his ancient evidents, as not conductive to the purpose then in hand, are lost, and probably this Charter among others. And therefore not having seen the same, I cannot positively determine thereanent; but will only place this John, agreeable to the traditional account delivered of him, as a son and successor to the first Anselan, and consequently second Laird of Buchanan. John, his son, and successor, conform to the same manner of account, was called

Anselan, the second of that name, and third Laird of Buchanan; whose son and successor is reported to be

Walter, the first of that name, being fourth Laird of Buchanan. This Walter's son and successor is reported to be

Girald, or as others say, and that with most probability, Bernard, being fifth Laird of Buchanan. I have been credibly informed, that these three last mentioned Lairds are recorded as witnesses in a mortification granted by Aluin Earl of Lennox, of the lands of Cochnach, and others, to the old church of Kilpatrick, before the foundation of the monastery of Paisley; and I have seen myself a Charter, by which that church and lands mortified thereto, by the same Aluin, or an Earl of that name his successor, are disponed to that Abbacy, some little time after the foundation thereof. But not having seen this other Charter, in which these three Lairds of Buchanan are inserted, I leave what concerns the same undetermined. Bernard, the last mentioned Laird of Buchanan, his son and successor was called

MacBeath, being sixth Laird of Buchanan. And this proper name was very ordinary to the MacCauslans, before the assumption of the surname of Buchanan, as also to that Sept of that surname, who after assumption of Buchanan have retained as yet the ancient denomination; as for instance, one Mac-

Beath MacCauflan, proprietor of that little intereſt called the Baronry of MacCauflan, in the Lennox, who lived in the reign of King Robert III. and of whoſe uncommon ſtature and ſtrength ſome accounts are retained to this very time. MacBeath Laird of Buchanan's age is evinced by the record after ſpecified in favours of his ſon and ſucceſſor

Anselan, the third of that name, and ſeventh Laird of Buchanan; who is ordinarily termed, in any record in which he is mentioned, " Anſelan ſon of MacBeath, and Se-" neſcallus, or Chamberlain to the Earl of Len-" nox," in written mortifications in the Chartulary of the Abbacy of Paiſley. This Anſelan the third, with Gilbert, and Methlen his two ſons, are inſerted witneſſes in a Charter granted by Malduin Earl of Lennox, to Gilmore, ſon of Maoldonich, of the lands of Luſs, in the beginning of the reign of King Alexander II. and they are deſigned in that Charter, The Earl's clients, or vaſſals. This Anſelan the third, beſides Gilbert his eldeſt ſon and ſucceſſor, who firſt aſſumed the ſurname of Buchanan, and Methlin his ſecond ſon, anceſtor of the MacMillans, had a third ſon, called Colman, anceſtor of the MacColmans, as ſhall be elſewhere more fully illuſtrated.

Anſelan third of that name, and ſeventh Laird of Buchanan, having ſucceeded his father MacBeath, as is already said, obtained from Malduin Earl of Lennox a Charter of an island in Lochlomond, called Clareinch, dated in the year 1225. Witnesses, Dougal, Gilchrist, and Amelyn, the Earl's brethren. The same Anselan is also mentioned as witness in a charter granted by the Earl of Lennox, of the lands of Dalmanoch, in mortification to the old church of Kilpatrick, by the designation of Absalon de Buchanan; Absalon being the same name with Anselan, as has been already observed. Tho' that of Clareinch is the most ancient can be found in this age, in relation to the family of Buchanan; nevertheless, it is very presumeable, there were other charters of greater antiquity belonging to that family, the first of them found upon record being of such repute, and charters having become customary so long before that time; as is partly instanced by the original charter of Luss, which was of an anterior date to this of Clareinch; yet the same Anselan with two of his sons Gilbert, and Methlen, are designed the Earl's clients or vassals therein. I have been also informed by some of very good judgment, who went through the late Buchanan's evidences, when entire, that they observed one little charter, being the original, of as great antiquity as any other in the Kingdom, being reckoned to be granted in, or about the reign of King David the I. which with other of these evidences, having since gone through so many hands, may upon very good grounds be presumed to be neglected, or rather lost.

The Isle of Clareinch was the Slughorn, or Call of War proper to the family of Buchanan; such like being usual in all other families in these times, and for some following ages. So soon as this Call was raised upon any alarm, the word Clareinch was sounded aloud from one to another, in a very little time, throughout the whole country; upon hearing of which, all effective men belonging to the Laird of Buchanan, with the utmost diligence repaired well armed to the ordinary place of Randezvouz, which, when the Lairds resided in that Island, was upon a ground upon the shore opposite thereto. That which in these modern times came in place of the Slughorn was the Firecross, being a little Stick with a Cross on one end of it, the extremities of which were burnt, or made black by fire. This Cross being once set a-going, was carried through with such dispatch, as in a few hours would alarm the people of a vast extent of ground.

GILBERT his son, being first of that name, and eight Laird, and who first, by any thing can be collected, assumed the surname of Buchanan, was Seneschal, or Chamberlain to the Earl of Lennox, which office his father Anselan enjoyed for some time. There is a charter of confirmation of that of Clareinch, and some other lands of Buchanan, granted in favour of this Gilbert, by King Alexander II. in the seventeenth year of his reign, and of our Lord 1231 (*a*). The same Gilbert is also inserted witness in a charter granted by Malcolm Earl of Lennox, discharging the Abbot and Monks of Paisly of all service and duties prestable by them to the Earl, for any lands mortified by him or his ancestors to that Abbacy; which charter is dated at Renfrew in the year 1274 (*b*). To Gilbert succeeded his son

Sir Maurice, first of that name, and ninth Laird of Buchanan, as is evident by a charter of confirmation by Malcolm Earl of Lennox, in favours of Malcolm MacEdolf, son to Gilmichal MacEdolf of West Cameron, of the lands of Gartachorrans, dated at Bellach in the year 1274. Witnesses to the said charter, Patrick Graham, Maurice of Buchanan, and Duncan son of Aulay, Knights (*c*). Sir Maurice had three sons, Maurice his successor, Allan who first married the heiress of Lenny, and John always reputed ancestor of Buchanan of Auchneiven. He was succeeded by his son

Sir Maurice, second of that name, being tenth Laird of Buchanan, as is clear by a

---

(*a*) Charter among Buchanan's old evidences.
(*b*) Chartulary of Dunbarton-shire.
(*c*) Chartulary of Dunbarton-shire.

charter by Donald Earl of Lennox to Maurice of Buchanan, son and heir to Sir Maurice of Buchanan, of the lands of Sallochy, with confirmation of the upper part of the Carrucate of Buchanan (*d*). This charter, as do many others granted in these times, wants a date; but by the subsequent service, the time in which this Maurice lived is plainly made appear, he being one of the members of an Inquest by Malcolm Earl of Lennox, for serving of Mathild, Elizabeth, and Forveleth Learmonths heirs-portioners to Thomas Learmonth of Cremennan, their father; the said inquest being at the kirk of Killearn in the year 1320, and fourteenth year of the reign of King Robert I. (*e*) The other members thereof, besides Buchanan, were Duncan MacEdolf, Eugen MacKessan of Garchell, Malcolm MacMurdac, Kessan Innes of Finicktenent, Gillespie MacSawel of Ledlewan, John MacGilchrist, Malise MacAlbaine of West Finnick, Gilchrist MacKessan, Gilbert MacPaddo, Gilchrist MacGilbert, and Padmund MacCeggo. All which gentlemen may, upon good grounds, be supposed to have been of most considerable interest and repute of any others in that country, and age: Yet in this there in ot

---

(*d*) Charter among Dunbarton's old evidences.
(*e*) Extract of the above service from the Chartulary of Dunbarton-shire.

the least memory of any of them extant, except that of Buchanan:—A very remarkable instance of that vast alteration and decay, surnames and other affairs frequently meet with in an ordinary tract of time.

As his father Sir Maurice had, so did also this brave gentleman adhere to the cause and interest of his Prince and Country, with much resolution, constancy and valour, to the evident hazard of his life and fortune, in imitation of his brave patron, that eminent patriot, Malcolm Earl of Lennox: Who, with the Lairds of Buchanan, and Luss, the first the greatest Nobleman, the others the best Gentlemen, and of best repute and circumstances of any others in these parts of this Kingdom, could never, by any artifice used by the Kings of England, be induced to do any action prejudicial to their own honour, or the interest of their native country; as is demonstrable by their refusing to sign the Ragman-Roll, which few others, or rather none of any tolerable repute or circumstances either durst, or did decline. There is a traditional account, that King Robert Bruce, after his defeat at Dalree, near Straithfillan, by MacDougal Lord of Lorn and his adherents, came all alone on foot, along the north side of Lochlomond, (being the most rugged way of any other of this Kingdom) the day after that battle, to the Castle of Buchanan; where being joyfully received, and for some days entertained, he was secretly conveyed by the Earl of Lennox, and Buchanan to a place of safety. This report is the more probable, in regard there is a Cave near the shore of Lochlomond, in Buchanan parish, termed the King's-Cave; being reported, that King Robert lay over night in that Cave in his journey towards Buchanan.

This Maurice lived to a considerable age, having obtained a charter of the lands of Buchanan from King David Bruce, in the beginning of his reign. He is also witness in the same reign, in a charter by Donald Earl Lennox to Finlay Campsy, of a part of the lands of Campsy, being designed in that charter Maurice MacCausland, Dominus, or Laird of Buchanan: Whence it is pretty plain, that tho' the surname of Buchanan was assumed by Gilbert this Maurice his grandfather, yet he and some of his successors, seem to have used their ancient surname, as their humours or inclination led them. Maurice the second his successor was

Sir Walter, second also of that name, and eleventh Laird. He seems to have been a very active gentleman, and made a very bright figure in his time; having made a very considerable addition to his old estate, by the purchase of a great many other lands. There is a charter of confirmation of some of his lands of Buchanan, granted in his favours by King Robert II. in which he is designed the King's Consanguineus or Cousin, upon resignation of William Boyd of Auchmar in the hands of Walter of Faslane Lord of Lennox, of the lands of Cameron, Drumfad, and divers other lands *(f)*. Sir Walter lived to a great age, having only one son,

JOHN, who married the heiress of Lenny, and died before his father, and was never entered to the estate of Buchanan. However seeing this John had issue, which continued or carried on the line of the family, I shall mention him in order as his father Walter's successor. The clearest document can be found in relation to him is, a charter granted by King Robert III. in favours of John Buchanan, and Janet Lenny his spouse, in life-rent, and to their heirs in fee, of the Baronry of Pitwhonydy, in the year 1363 *(g)*. Whether the Baronry of Pitwhonydy belonged formerly to the family of Lenny, or was part of that which belonged to the family of Buchanan, and was at this juncture given off by this John to that of Lenny, cannot be clearly determined, this being the most ancient charter relating to that, or any other lands in hands of the present Lenny. Nor is there so much as a tradition, that the family of Lenny had any lands before this

---

(f) Charter among Buchanan's old evidences.
(g) Ch. penes Buchanan de Lenny.

marriage, except those possest by Keir, and Lenny, and, as is thought, some part of these lands so designed in Mid Lothian.

This John, twelfth Laird of Buchanan, is the first mentioned in the Genealogical Tree of Buchanan, there being a part of that tree cut away, the actor, as well as design of that action, being unknown. John Laird of Buchanan and Lenny had three sons, who came to age; the eldest, Sir Alexander, who killed the Duke of Clarence at the battle of Bauge, was also himself afterwards killed at the battle of Vernoil anno 1424, being never married. The second was Sir Walter, who succeeded to the estate of Buchanan; and the third John, during his father's lifetime, designed of Ballachondachy, and who did, after his father's death, succeed to the estate of Lenny, as the Tree of Buchanan, and some other evidents among those of Buchanan testify, as shall be in due place observed. I will elsewhere briefly recount some of the heroick atchievements of that gallant gentleman, Sir Alexander, eldest son to John Laird of Buchanan, who acquired an addition to the Armorial bearing, and a much greater to the honour of his family; and will endeavour to remove some little mistake our Historians are in concerning his surname; and mean while proceed to the account of

Sir Walter, third of that name, and thirteenth Laird of Buchanan, who upon the death of Sir Alexander, fucceeded to his father John, Laird of Buchanan and Lenny. There is a charter granted by Duncan Earl Lennox to Walter Laird of Buchanan, of the lands of Ledlewan; and he is witnefs to a charter by the fame Earl to John Hamilton, fon and heir to John Hamilton of Bardowie, of the lands of Bathernock; moft of his evidents in relation to the eftate of Buchanan being by fome contingency or other loft. However he is mentioned by the Genealogical Tree of the Family, and is thereby afferted to be married to Ifobel Stewart, daughter to Murdoch Stewart Duke of Albany, and Governor of Scotland, and to Ifobel, heirefs of Lennox his lady. This marriage is further made appear by a charter in the hands of Buchanan of Drumikill, granted by Ifobel Duchefs of Albany, and Countefs of Lennox, to one Donald Patrick, of a tenement of houfes and land next adjacent to the north-fide of the church-yard of Drymen, dated in the year 1443. Witneffes being Andrew and Murdoch, the Dutchefs's nephews, and Walter Laird of Buchanan, her fon-in-law, Knight, with divers others. Sir Walter had three fons, Patrick his fucceffor; and Maurice, who was Treafurer to Lady Margaret, daughter to King James I. and Dauphinefs of France; having gone to that Kingdom with her, there is no further account of him. His third fon was Thomas, Carbeth's anceftor. Sir Walter had a daughter married to Gray of Foulis, the Lord Gray his anceftor. To Sir Walter fucceeded his fon

PATRICK, firft of that name, and fourteenth Laird of Buchanan. He acquired a part of Strathyre from David O'Quahuanan heritor thereof, in the year 1455, being the date of the charter thereof, confirmed by charter under the Great Seal in the year 1458, as is alfo a charter in his favour under the Great Seal, of his eftate of Buchanan dated in the year 1460. He purchafed the lands of Eafter Balleun; and in the year 1414, refigned the lands of Drumfad, and Kirkmicheal, in favour of Walter Buchanan, his fon and heir, which this Walter fold to the Laird of Ardkindlafs in the year 1513. Patrick Laird of Buchanan, and Andrew Laird of Lenny made in the year 1455, mutual tailzies of their eftates in favour of one another, and the heirs of their own bodies, and paft fome of their brethren of either fide; by which it is pretty clear, they have been no further removed in kindred than coufin-germans: So that the genealogy of both families, as already afferted, will hold good. He was married to one Galbraith, heirefs of Killearn, Bamoir, and Auchinreoch, and had with her two fons, Walter his fucceffor; and Thomas anceftor of Drumikill; and a daughter Anabella, married to her coufin, James

Stewart of Baldorrans, grand-child to Murdoch Duke of Albany. He had also an illegitimate son, Patrick, of whose issue there is no account.

The last mentioned Laird of Buchanan, being married to an heiress of the name of Galbraith, and the circumstances of that name being now parallel to that of Buchanan, mutual sympathy in a manner obliges me to digress a little, in giving a brief account of that name.

The name of Galbraith is evidently an ancient Scottish surname, the denomination of that name importing in Irish A brave Stranger. The first I find upon record of this name was Gillespie, or Archibald Galbraith, being inserted witness in a charter by Malduin Earl of Lennox to Humphrey Kirkpatrick, of the lands of Colquhoun in the reign of King Alexander II. This Gillespie's son was Maurice, as evinces a charter in his favour of Cartonbenach, now Bathernock, by the above Malduin Earl of Lennox, in the forecited reign. Maurice's son was Arthur, in whose favour there is a charter of Auchincloich and Bathernock, with power to seize and condemn malefactors, with this proviso, that those so condemned be hanged upon the Earl's gallows. This charter is of date in the year 1238. Witnesses, David Lindesay, David Graham, William Douglas Malcolm, Thane of Calentyr, Maurice Galbraith, Auleth, the Earl's brother, and Maurice Parson of Drymen. Arthur's sons were William, ancestor of Culcruich, as testifies a charter in his favour by Malcolm Earl of Lennox of these lands, and the ancestors of the Galbraiths of Greenock and Killearn: The heiress of the principal family of Bathernock having married a son of the Lord Hamilton, the present Bardowie's ancestor; as did the heiress of Greenock a son of Shaw of Sauchy, Shaw of Greenock's ancestor; and the heiress of Killearn was married to the Laird of Buchanan. The only remaining family of that name being Balgair, Galbraith Laird thereof fell into such bad circumstances in King Charles I. his time, as obliged him to pass his estate, and go to Ireland, where his posterity are in very good circumstances. Galbraith of Balgair is now Representative, the family of Culcruich's ancestor being a son of that family.

To Patrick Laird of Buchanan succeeded his son

WALTER, fourth of that name, and fifteenth Laird of Buchanan, as is clear by the charter of resignation in his favour, by Patrick his father, in the year 1474. He married the Lord Graham's daughter, whose mother was the Earl of Angus's daughter. Of this marriage he had Patrick his successor, who, as is confidently asserted, was with a great many of his name killed at the battle of Flowdon in the year 1513. And John of Auchmar, afterwards Arnpryor and Gartartan; and two daughters, one of them married to the Laird of Lamond, the other to the Laird of Ardkinglafs.

PATRICK, the fecond of that name, albeit his father outlived him many years, yet as in the Tree of the Family, fo alfo in this place, he may be accounted the fixteenth Laird. He was married to the Earl of Argyle his daughter, her mother being the Earl of Huntley's daughter. He had of this marriage two fons, and two daughters, that came to age. His eldeft fon, was George, his fucceffor, his fecond Walter, Spittle's anceftor. His two daughters were married to the Lairds of Auchinbreck, and Calder. He had alfo an illegitimate fon called Robert. Patrick's fucceffor was

GEORGE, firft of that name, and feventeenth Laird of Buchanan, as is clear by charter under the Great Seal in his favour of the lands of Buchanan, in the year 1530. He purchafed the lands of Duchray, and others, as evinces charter thereof, anno 1532. He was made fheriff principal of Dunbartonfhire, anno 1561. He was firft married to Margaret Edmonftone, daughter to the Laird of Duntreath, her mother being Shaw of Sauchy's daughter. He had of this marriage John, his fucceffor, He married for his fecond Lady Janet Cunninghame, daughter to Cunninghame of Craigens, being firft married to the Laird of Houftoun. He had with his fecond Lady William, anceftor of Buchanan of Auchmar, in whofe favour his father grants charter of the thirteen merkland of Straithyre, in the year 1556. He had alfo of this marriage one daughter, Margaret, firft married to Cunninghame of Robertland, fecondly, to Stirling of Glorat, and laftly, to Douglas of Maines. George was fucceeded by

JOHN, fecond of that name, and eighteenth Laird of Buchanan. His father grants charter in his favour, in the year 1552. He died before his father, and was twice married, firft to the Lord Levingftone's daughter, her mother being daughter to the Earl of Morton, which marriage was confummated by virtue of a difpenfation, in regard of propinquity of blood. There was of this marriage one fon George, who came to age. He married fecondly a daughter of one Chifholm, brother to the Bifhop of Dumblane, and had with her one daughter, married to Mr Thomas Buchanan of Ibert, Lord Privy Seal. To John fucceeded his fon

SIR GEORGE, fecond of that name, and nineteenth Laird of Buchanan, as is clear by charter in his favour, by King Henry and Queen Mary, of the lands of Buchanan, Ifles of Clareinch, and Kepinch, with bell and alms of St Keſſog, dated in the year 1564. This George was married to Mary Graham, daughter to the Earl of Monteith, her mother being the Lord Seaton's daughter. Of this marriage he had one ſon Sir John, and two daughters, Helen married to Alexander Colquhoun of Luſs, and Suſanna, firſt married to Andrew MacFarlane of Arrochar, ſecondly to Campbell of Craigniſh. Sir George's ſucceſſor was

SIR JOHN, third of that name, and twentieth Laird of Buchanan, as appears by charter in his favour, by King James VI. of the lands of Buchanan, in the year 1618. This Sir John mortified ſix thouſand pounds Scots to the univerſity of Edinburgh, for maintaining three Burſers at the ſtudy of Theology there; and an equal ſum to the former to the Univerſity of St Andrews, for maintaining, upon the intereſt thereof, three Burſers at the ſtudy of Philoſophy there: And conſtituted the Magiſtrates of Edinburgh Managers or Patrons of both mortifications, as the one double of the contract betwixt the ſaid Sir John and the Magiſtrates of Edinburgh, in the hands of the Duke of Montroſe, among the late Buchanan's evidents, does teſtify. Sir John married Anabella Erſkine, daughter to Adam Commendator, or Lord Cambuſkenneth, being ſon to the Maſter of Mar, her mother Drummond of Carnock's daughter. He had with her one ſon, George, his successor, and a daughter married to Campbell of Rahein. Sir John's successor was

Sir George, third of that name, and one and twentieth Laird of Buchanan. He married Elizabeth Preston, daughter to Preston of Craigmillar, her mother being Ballenden of Broughton's daughter. Sir George, being Colonel of Stirling-shire regiment, lost a great many of his regiment and kinsmen at the fatal conflict of Ennerkeithing, in which being taken prisoner, he died in that state in the latter part of the year 1651, having left one son, John his successor, and three daughters, Helen, married to Sir John Rollo of Bannockburn, Agnes, married to Stewart of Rossyth, and Jean to Lecky of that Ilk.

John, third of that name, the two and twentieth, and last Laird of Buchanan, succeeded to his father Sir George. He was first married to Mary Erskine, daughter to Henry Lord Cardross, her mother being Lord Colville's daughter. With her he had one daughter Elizabeth, married to James Stewart of Ardvorlich. He secondly married Jean Pringle, daughter to Mr Andrew Pringle, a minister. With her he had one daughter, Janet, married to Henry Buchanan of Lenny. John last Laird died in December 1682.

Having thus given a Genealogical account of the Family of Buchanan, it may not be improper to enquire how their estate came family. Not to go any further back, it is fit to know, that Sir John Buchanan, grandfather to the laft Laird, by his frequent travels into foreign nations, and other extravagancies, had involved his eftate in fuch an immenfe debt, that his grand-fon found it inconvenient for him to enter as heir, till he had caufed David Lord Cardrofs, his brother-in-law, to compound with the moft preferable of his creditors, and upon that compofition to apprize the eftate: Upon which acquifition of Cardrofs, he entered upon the eftate as fingular fucceffor; nor did he feek for any new right during the life of the Lady Mary Erfkine his firft Lady, who at her death left only one daughter. Some few years after which, he entertained fome thoughts of a fecond marriage, and for that purpofe addreffed himfelf to a daughter of Sir John Colquhoun of Lufs; between which family and that of Buchanan there had been fuch frequent alliances, and communication of mutual good offices, as rendered the propofal very agreeable to Sir John. The only obftruction that offered, fprung from the mutual tailzies betwixt the families of Buchanan and Auchmar, whereby both interefts were fettled upon heirs-male. Buchanan, in order to remove this difficulty, went to London, and obtained a new charter of his eftate upon the right already mentioned, acquired by him from the Lord Cardrofs; and further procured an additional clause in it, impowering him to dispone his estate to heirs whatsoever, and to whom he pleased. By this means Buchanan of Auchmar, nearest heir-male annexed in succession by the tailzie, was wholly excluded, and his pretensions cut off. Buchanan's design however was wholly defeated; the young lady having, much against his expectation, married the Laird of Keir, before his return. This disappointment had such effects upon his high spirit, as in a little time threw him into a palsie, and prejudiced him in his judgement, in which unhappy circumstances he continued till his death. A little time before this misfortune befell him, John Buchanan of Arnpryor, then a widower, having come into Buchanan's family, gained such an influence over him, as to be entrusted with the whole management of his affairs. Arnpryor was not wanting to improve such an opportunity for the promoting his own interest, and found means to prevail on the Laird to agree to a match between his daughter and Arnpryor's son, then a student of the Civil Law, that by this means the estate might be kept in the name, failing other heirs of Buchanan. The proposal would have certainly taken place, had not the young lady interposed, by refusing her consent; upon which her father, then very much declined in his judgement, conceived so much displeasure against her as to make a disposition of his estate in favour of Arnpryor, and in prejudice of her right. However keeping this paper in his own custody, and happening to go to the Bath for recovery of his health, he in his return fell in love with Mrs Jean Pringle, and married her, and upon her arrival at Buchanan, caused the disposition in favour of Arnpryor to be cancelled, which gave rise to an inveterate animosity, which continued ever after between him and Arnpryor.

In a little time after this marriage, Buchanan, for reasons we cannot account for, disponed his estate to an old comrade of his, Major George Grant, Governor of Dunbarton-castle, with this provision, that the Major should marry his eldest daughter, and assume the name and arms of Buchanan; reserving his own life-rent and his Lady's jointure, and settling the estate so as to return to Buchanan's heirs-male, and failing heirs of Grant's own body to Buchanan's heirs whatsoever. Agreeable to this disposition, Grant made his addresses to the young Lady, but was rejected by her with the utmost indignation. The late Lady Buchanan has been blamed, as promoting this disposition in favour of Grant; but I have received such information, from people well versed in Buchan's affairs, as fully justifies her. Sometime after this, there was a project formed by Buchanan and Grant, of selling so much of the Highland lands of the eftate of Buchanan, as might, together with the price of fome woods lately fold, and Buchanan's other moveables, clear the whole debts affecting the Lower Barony, or remainder of that eftate. Thefe Highland lands accordingly were fold to the Marquis of Montrofe, who; for fecurity of that part fold to him, got infeftment of real warrandice upon the Lower Barony. This bargain being compleated, it was fuggefted to the Marquis, that he could not be fully fecured in thofe lands, lately purchafed by him, till well informed of the extent of Buchanan's debts, and other circumftances of his affairs. For this purpofe, Arnpryor, who of all others beft knew thofe affairs, was prevailed upon to make a difcovery of them to the Marquis, having for his fervice therein, and his affiftance in evicting the whole eftate, obtained the fourth part thereof, burdened with a proportionable part of the debts. Thus, there having been a debt due by Buchanan to Sir James Dick of Prieftfield, for which all legal diligence was ufed, infomuch that the Laird, with Drumikill, and fome other cautioners, were denounced, and continued more than a year unrelaxed; and Arnpryor, while manager for Buchanan, having been ordered to clear this debt, it was accordingly paid, and difcharge and relaxation procured for the cautioners, but the principal unhappily was left unrelaxed,

This secret once devulged, there was a gift obtained of Buchanan's life-rent, and moveable escheat; by which his whole moveables being exhausted, there was room left for wresting the estate out of his hands, by procuring rights to those debts, for payment whereof these moveables were allotted. This project was the effectual means of ruining that estate; for divers adjudications being led in Arnpryor's name, then principal manager for my Lord Marquis, (the Marquis himself, as it seems, being passive in it) Buchanan's eldest daughter found herself obliged to resign her pretensions for a sum of money to his Lordship; and Major Grant having a little before his death given up all Buchanan's evidences, both the rights and the fortune became to be entirely transferred.

This estate, as all others, was sometimes increased, or diminished, as it fell into the hands of good or bad managers. The Lairds of Buchanan had, besides their old estate, several lands in the parishes of Killearn, Strablane, and others in Lennox. The most flourishing condition it has been in for divers ages was upon the last Laird's accession to it. For his old estate, which together with Strathyre, Brachern, and some superiorities, was worth thirteen thousand merks of yearly rent, most of the same arising from steelbow horses, cows, corn, and red-land, besides casualties, and woods, computed in this age to be worth two thousand pounds sterling each cutting. Besides this he had the whole estate of Badindalloch, amounting to six thousand merks per annum, which was acquired by Sir John, the late Laird's grand-father, for money he was engaged in for Cunninghame of Glengarnock, proprietor thereof; as also he had the estate of Craigmillar in Mid-Lothian, being ten thousand merks per annum, acquired by his father. So that from these three estates the family had near thirty-thousand merks of yearly rent. But Buchanan having sold Badendalloch, and Craigmillar, when in health, and that of Buchanan going off in the manner we have already mentioned, after having continued six hundred and sixty-five years in that name, and in an uninterrupted succession of twenty-two Lairds; by this mismanagement, and want of proper advice from his friends, this flourishing fortune has been destroyed, and the family itself extinguished.

The Paternal ARMS of the FAMILY of BUCHANAN.

Or, a Lion Rampant Sable, Arm'd and Langu'd Gules, within a double Tressure, flower'd and counterflower'd with *Flower-de-luces* of the 2d. Crest, a Hand coupee holding up a Ducal Cap or Duke's Coronet proper, with two Laurel Branches wreathed surrounding the Crest, disposed Orle-ways proper; supported by two Falcons garnished Or. Ancient Motto above the Crest, *Audaces Juvo*. Modern Motto in compartment, *Clarior Hinc Honos*.

AN
Account of the Family of
AUCHMAR.

IN giving an exact account of these cadets, now become Families, which came immediately off that of Buchanan, and retain that Surname, I shall begin with that Family last came off the principal one, and consequently next to the same, and shall mention each of the rest in order, according to the times of their several descents off the Chief Family. In prosecution of this method I shall begin with the Family of AUCHMAR, which by the original charter thereof, as also by the Genealogical Account or Tree of the Family of Buchanan, is not only clearly evinced to be descended of a son of the Laird of Buchanan, but also to be the latest cadet of that family. Though the principal Family continued in being for the space of 135 years after the Family came off the same, nevertheless the few second sons, or cadets, which descended of Buchanan since that of Auchmar came off, left no male-issue; so that by this means Auchmar continued to be the latest cadet of that ancient family.

The interest of Auchmar was for sometime tanistrie, or appenage-lands, being always given off to a second son of the family of Buchanan for patrimony, or rather aliment during life, and at his death, returning to the family of Buchanan. These lands were in some time after disponed irreversibly to the ancestor of the present family of Auchmar, and his heirs. The first of which was WILLIAM BUCHANAN, first son of the second marriage to George Buchanan of that Ilk, and Janet Cunninghame daughter to Cunninghame (for any thing I can find) first Laird of Craigens, who was son to the Earl of Glencairn. This Lady was first married to Patrick Laird of Houston, Director of the Chancery in the reign of King James V. Houston, with divers other good and loyal patriots, having joined that brave Nobleman, John Earl of Lennox, in order to liberate their Sovereign from the restraint put upon him by the Earls of Arran, and Angus, with their associates; and Lennox having engaged with the Earl of Arran's army at Linlithgow, or Evanbridge, was there slain together with Houston, and a great many others of his party. Buchanan, after Houston's death, having married his relict, granted charter in favour of William Buchanan, his first son of this second marriage, and his heirs, of the lands of Auchmar, dated the 3d of January 1547 years. Nor did Buchanan's indulgence and liberality to this his son stop here, but he did also in the year 1556, grant charter in his favour of the thirteen merk-land of Straithyre, with real warrandice for the same in the Easter Mains of Buchanan, being the best portion any second son of that family had got of a long time, or rather at any time before that. After what manner this family lost possession of the lands of Sraithyre is not very evident; the most common account however of that event is this, that in the time of the Civil Wars in the reign of King Charles I. particularly in the year 1645, the lands of Buchanan being at that time very sadly harrassed, and most of the houses burnt, George Buchanan of Auchmar lost upon that occasion the evidents of Straithyre, and as is also apprehended the double, lodged in that Family's hands, of the mutual tailzie betwixt them and the Family of Buchanan. After which Sir John Laird of Buchanan did in an unjust and oppressive manner, dispossess the said George of those lands, and would have done the same to him in relation to the lands of Auchmar also, had not the evidents thereof been at that time providentially in the Laird of Craigens's custody, which was the only means of their preservation. This with some other hard usage given by Sir John, created such animosity betwixt these two families as could scarcely be fully extinguished: The said Sir John being accounted the worst, if not the only bad one of all the Lairds of Buchanan, and the greatest oppressor of his name and neighbours; whereas the other Lairds generally taken, are reported to have been the most discreet neighbourly gentlemen of any in these parts of this Kingdom.

William, the first of Auchmar was married to Elizabeth Hamilton daughter to the Laird of Inchmachan, (or as I find him sometimes designed of Eglismachan) this family having become extinct in the reign of King Charles II. any little remains of that interest fell into Hamilton of Aitkenhead, as nearest heir to Hamilton of Inchmachan. Of this marriage betwixt Auchmar and Inchmachan's daughter, three sons and two daughters came to maturity. The eldest of the sons was Patrick, the second George, and the third Mr William. Margaret the eldest daughter was married to Cunninghame of Blairwhoish; the second to James Colquhoun merchant in Glasgow.

Patrick the eldest son succeeded to his

father William in the lands of Auchmar, and Straithrye. He married Helen Buchanan heiress of Ibert, daughter to Mr Thomas Buchanan of Ibert, nephew to the great Mr George Buchanan, which Thomas became Lord Privy Seal by resignation of that office in his favour by Mr George his uncle. Mr Thomas's wife was a daughter of John Laird of Buchanan. Patrick above-mentioned died within a few years of his marriage, his children having not long survived him; so that his interest devolved to George his second brother, as is evident by precept of Clare Constat, and charter thereupon in his favour by John Laird of Buchanan, of the lands of Auchmar dated in the year 1606.

This George in his eldest brother's lifetime married Janet Stewart, daughter to Andrew Stewart, who had a beneficial tack (esteemed in these times equivalent to heritage) of the lands of Blairgarie, and some other lands, from the Earl of Murray in Straithgartney, and the parish of Callender. He was also the Earl's baillie in those parts. That family is now represented by Alexander Stewart of Gartnafuaroe in Balquhidder parish; and is with the families of Ardvorlich and Glenbucky, (from which three are sprung most of the Stewarts in the southern parts of Perth-shire) lineally descended of James Beg, or Little James, son to James Stewart, youngest son to Murdoch Duke of

Albany, and Governor of Scotland. James Beg was married to Annabella Buchanan, daughter to Patrick Laird of Buchanan, as testifies a charter in his, and the said Annabella's favour of the lands of Baldorrans in Stirling-shire, in the reign of King James II. I find also this James witness in a charter by Isobel, Dutchess of Albany and Countess of Lennox, of a tenement of land in Drymen in the year 1443, being designed in that charter the Dutchess's nephew. James's successor was Walter Stewart of Baldorrans, as is clear by charter in his favour by Janet O'Quhanan of a wadset-right the said Janet had upon a part of the lands of Straithyre, of date in the year 1528, from three sons of this Walter, or according to their own traditional account, from a son of Walter called William, are descended the three families above-mentioned.

George Buchanan of Auchmar had seven sons; Patrick his successor, John, Andrew, Mr Maurice, William, Robert, and George. He had also two daughters; the eldest married to Colquhoun of Camstrodan, the second to Captain Pettigroe.

To George succeeded his eldest son Patrick, as is clear by charter in his favour of the lands of Auchmar dated in the year 1662. He married Agnes Buchanan, daughter to William Buchanan of Ross. He had by her one son, John, who had issue, and five daughters, Janet, married to Buchanan of Cameron, Mary, to Thomas Anderson, Elizabeth, to Walter MacPharlan, Agnes to Galbraith of Armfinlay, and Jean, to Nairn of Baturich. He had also an illegitimate son, John, who went to Ireland.

To Patrick Buchanan of Auchmar succeeded his son JOHN. He married Anna Graham, daughter to John Graham of Duchray. He had by her two sons, and four daughters. The eldest of these daughters was married to Robert Graham of Glenny. The second daughter was first married to George Buchanan, son to Arthur Buchanan of Auchlessy, and afterwards to Andrew Stewart of Townhead of Drymen. The third daughter was married to Robert Stewart of Cailliemore. The fourth to George MacPharlan merchant.

John Buchanan of Auchmar was succeeded by WILLIAM, his son. He married Jean Buchanan, daughter to John Buchanan of Carbeth. Colin, second son to the said John, married Anna Hamilton, daughter to James Hamilton of Aitkenhead.

The first cadet of the Family of Auchmar was Mr William Buchanan, third son to William the first of Auchmar. This Mr William went to Ireland, and became manager or factor for the estate of the family of Hamilton, then Lords of Clandeboys, and afterwards Earls of Clanbrazel in the county of Down, which family is now extinct. He married in that country, and had one son, Major William Buchanan, a very brave gentleman, who was Major to George Laird of Buchanan's Regiment at the fatal conflict betwixt the Scots and English at Inverkeithing. The Major, upon defeat of the Scottish army, being well mounted, made his way thro' a party of English horse-men, and tho' pursued for some miles, came off safe, having killed divers of the pursuers. He went afterwards to Ireland, and purchased an estate there, called Scrabohill, near Newton Clandeboys in the county of Down. He had two sons, the eldest continued in Ireland, and the younger went abroad. He had also two daughters, both married in that country.

William of Auchmar had an illegitimate son, called George, whose son John had a wadset upon the lands of Blairluisk in Kilmaronock-parish, which having sold, he went to Ireland, where divers of his progeny reside near the village called St Johnstoun, in the county of Derry; from whence one of them having come to the Paroch of Bonneil, had two sons, Archibald, at present in Bonneil, who hath three sons, George, a trader at sea, William, a residenter in London, and James residing near Glasgow. Another Archibald, being also descended of the said George, resides in Inverary, in Argyle-shire.

The second cadet of the family of Auchmar was Mr Maurice Buchanan, fourth son to George Buchanan of Auchmar. He was a preacher in the county of Tyrone, and had one son, James, who had only one son, Captain Maurice, who resides near Dublin.

George of Auchmar's fifth son was William, who was a Captain in the Swedish service in Germany. He was upon account of his valour, conduct, and other laudable qualities, very much esteemed; having signalized himself upon divers occasions, particularly in vanquishing an Italian, who in most countries of Europe had acquired very much fame by his martial atchievements, and dexterity in performing divers feats of arms, having always carried the prize in all places he went to, till at last he was overcome by this Captain William, no less to his honour than to the Italian's disgrace. Upon account of this action he obtained a Major's commission, but was within few days thereafter killed in the said service. He was married to Anna Pennel an English-woman. His children and their posterity have continued in Germany.

George of Auchmar's seventh and youngest son, George, had one son, William, who married at London, having left a son, James, who is a merchant in that city. John, Andrew, and Robert, George's other sons, their issue is wholly extinct.

Patrick Buchanan of Auchmar, besides

John his fucceffor, had an illegitimate fon, called alfo John, who went to Ireland. He had two fons, Patrick, who went to the Weft-Indies, and is in very good circumftances in that country; and John, who refides near Newton-ftewart in the county of Tyrone, and hath three fons. He had alfo an illegitimate fon, Samuel, who refides in Laggan of Tyrconnel.

The laft cadet of Auchmar is Colin Buchanan, brother to the prefent William Buchanan of Auchmar, who for Armorial bearing, carries the paternal arms of the family of Buchanan, as already blazoned, without any manner of diftinction.

I am hopeful, by clear and authentick documents to have demonftrated this family laft mentioned to be the lateft in defcent from that of Buchanan, notwithftanding that Mr Nifbet, in his late book of Heraldry and Genealogy, hath afferted the contrary, by giving it to a certain gentleman who is among the remoteft cadets of the family of Buchanan. I am furprized he fhould have fallen into fuch a miftake, efpecially after having had much better information conveyed to his hands by the author of thefe papers. But I am confident, his accounts of the matter will not make the leaft impreffion on any judicious reader, that fhall well weigh what he has only barely afferted, and compare it with the authentick account I have given.

AN

Account of the Family of

SPITTEL.

THE case of the Family of Spittel seems to be much the same with that of divers other families of that name, they having been in possession of several lands at some little time after they came off the family of Buchanan, a great part of which lands are since gone from it, as from other families, by ways and means not easy to be discovered at this distance of time.

The ancestor of the present family of Spittel, and who first obtained these lands, was Walter Buchanan, son to Patrick the second of that name, Laird of Buchanan. This Walter, and his successor John, their charters of these lands, by bad keeping in turbulent times, are so effaced, and the writing thereof so obliterated, as renders the same in a great measure illegible. However it is very presumeable, that the Laird of Buchanan gave the lands of Spittel to his son Walter for patrimony, when he came off the family, notwithstanding of the above inconveniency, that the two first, or original charters of that family labour under. But for further proof of this family's defcent off Buchanan, there being divers of our Kings Reigns Records of Jufticiary, by which all Chiefs of Clans were obliged for the good and peaceable behaviour of their name, or Clan, it is remarkable, that in one of thefe Records in the latter part of King James V. his reign, Walter Buchanan of Spittel is defigned brother-german to George Buchanan of that Ilk: Alfo in a feafin by the fame Laird of the lands of Auchmar anno 1547. John Buchanan, fon and heir to the deceaft Walter Buchanan of Spittel, the Laird's brother, is one of the witneffes. So that George Laird of Buchanan being well known to have been eldeft fon, and fucceffor to Patrick Laird of Buchanan, and by thefe two documents, Walter Buchanan of Spittel being defigned brother to the faid George, the defcent of this family is cleared beyond all controverfy, however little their orginal writings conduce to that purpofe. Walter Buchanan firft of Spittel was married to Ifobel Cunninghame, afferted to have been daughter to the Earl of Glencairn. There is a charter by Andrew Cunninghame of Blairwhoifh, with confent of Walter Stirling of Ballagan, his curator, in favour of Walter Buchanan of Spittel, and Ifobel Cunninghame his fpoufe, of the lands of Blairvocky, dated in the year 1535. There is alfo another charter in favour of the fame

Walter by Alexander, Master of Glencairn, of the lands of Arrochymore, dated in the year 1530. Which lands seem to be given in portion to him with Glencairn's daughter. Walter left one son John, his successor, and a daughter, married to Walter Buchanan of Drumikill.

He was succeed by his son JOHN, who married Elizabeth Cunninghame, daughter to Cunninghame, Laird of Drumquhuassle, as is evident by an heritable right by Alexander Earl of Glencairn to Elizabeth Cunninghame, spouse to John Buchanan of Spittel, in life-rent, and Edward Buchanan her son, in fee of the lands of Merkinch, dated in the year 1553.

EDWARD first of that name succeeded to his father John. He married Christian Galbraith, daughter to the Laird of Culcruich, as testifies a charter in his and his said spouse's favour under the Privy Seal, dated in the year 1555. He had two sons, Robert his successor; and George.

To Edward of Spittel succeeded his son ROBERT. He married Lawson of Boghall's daughter, and had by her two sons, Walter his successor, and Andrew. There is a charter under the Privy Seal in favour of this Robert, in the latter part of Queen Mary's reign.

To Robert succeeded his son WALTER. He married Galbraith of Balgair's daughter, and had with her two sons, that came to maturity, Edward, and Walter.

Eeward second of that name succeeded to Walter his father. He was first married to Edmonstone of Balleun's daughter. With her he had James, his successor, and John, a Captain in George Laird of Buchanan's Regiment, who was killed at the fatal conflict betwixt the Scots and English at Innerkeithing. He was secondly married to John Buchanan of Ross's daughter, and had with her Robert Buchanan Baker in Glasgow, and Edward, who was a man of great learning, and died while at the study of Divinity in the College of Edingburgh; and one daughter married to Cunninghame of Trinbeg.

James succeeded to his father Edward. He married a daughter of John Buchanan of Cashlie, and had with her five sons, Edward, Captain John, Captain Archibald, Andrew and Walter.

To James succeeded Edward third of that name. He married Christian Mitchell, daughter to Mr Thomas Mitchell, Minister of Kilmaronock, and had with her two sons, John, and Thomas; and two daughters.

John, eldest son to Edward Buchanan of Spittel, married Margaret Muirhead, daughter to Muirhead of Rashiehill, relict of Mr Robert Buchanan of Arnpryor. Thomas his brother was married to Napier of Ballachairn's daughter.

The first cadet of Spittel's family was GEORGE, second son to Edward first of that name, and third of Spittel. George had one son, William, who obtained a beneficial tack of Arrachybeg in Buchanan-parish. William had also one son, Donald, who had four sons, William, Duncan, Robert, and Walter. Of these William had one son, Donald, lately in Arrachybeg, who left issue. Duncan had one son, John, who has also one son, Duncan in the Foot-Guards. Robert was killed in the year 1645, and had only one daughter, married to James MacGown in Catter. Walter, who mostly resided in Cashill in Buchanan-parish, had two sons, John and William, both whereof have male-issue. The said Donald had another son called Walter, Malt-man in Glasgow, father to Margaret Buchanan, who married James Couper merchant in Port-Glasgow; whose only daughter Agnes is married to Andrew Crawford merchant in Port-Glasgow. The progeny of the above-mentioned George are ordinarily termed Buchanans of Arrachybeg, or Donald MacWilliam's race.

The second cadet of the family of Spittel was Andrew, son to Robert Buchanan of Spittel, this Andrew seems to have been a a man of education, and was factor to part of the Earl of Mar's estate for sometime. He bought Blairvocky from Spittel, and having never married, disponed that interest to Walter Buchanan his nephew, anceftor to the Buchanans of Blairvocky, as fhall be hereafter obferved. Andrew had one illegitimate fon, Robert, who refided for the moft part in Arrachymore, in Buchanan-parifh. Robert had four fons, Andrew, James, Robert, and Alexander. Andrew had no male-iffue. Robert had one fon, who left no iffue. James had one fon, Andrew, lately in Auchingyle in Buchanan-parifh, who had four fons. Two of thefe refided in Buchanan-parifh, one in the parifh of Lufs, and another in that of Kilmaronock. Alexander had two fons, John in the parifh of Killearn, and Andrew, merchant-taylor in Glafgow; father to James Buchanan, merchant in the Tron-gate there.

The third cadet of the family of Spittel was WALTER the firft of Blairvocky, fecond fon to Walter Buchanan of Spittel. There is a contract of wadfet for the fum of one thoufand merks Scots, upon the lands of Sallochy by John Buchanan of that Ilk, in favour of this Walter, dated in the year 1618. Walter of Blairvocky had one fon, Alexander, who had four fons, Walter, Alexander, William, and George. Walter's progeny is extinct. Alexander left only one daughter. George the youngeft went abroad. William the third brother, having obtained the intereft of Blairvocky, fold the fame to John Buchanan younger of Spittel. William the laft of Blairvocky refided moftly in Ireland.

He had four sons, Alexander, William, Walter, and Henry. Alexander the eldest resides in Glendermon, within two miles of Derry, being in very good repute and circumstances. William, Walter, and Henry reside near Omagh in the county of Tyrone and Kingdom of Ireland.

The fourth cadet of Spittel's family was ROBERT BUCHANAN, late Deacon of the Bakers of Glasgow, being one of the sons of the 2d marriage of Edward Buchanan second of that name of Spittel, and Buchanan of Ross's daughter. His son Robert Buchanan writer in Glasgow, married Buchanan of Drumhead's daughter. He had also two daughters, one married to Mr Neil Snodgrafs, writer in Paisly, who left one son, John Snodgrafs, their former children being dead; she was afterwards married to Alexander Wallace writer in Paisly: The other was married to John Buchanan elder, merchant in Glasgow.

The next cadets of this family are the present Edward Buchanan of Spittel's brethren. The first of these, Captain John was Captain in the Dutch and English service, during the whole time of the wars betwixt the French, English and Dutch, with their other confederates, from the year 1690, till the last peace; and was also an officer in the service of the Dutch, and some other states of Europe, a good many years before the commencement of thefe wars. The next brother was Captain Archibald, who for divers years before his death was one of the Captains of the King's horfe-guards, being a gentleman inferior to none of his age and ftation in all valuable qualities. Andrew and Walter the other two brethren died both unmarried.

The laft cadet of this family is Thomas Buchanan, Chirurgion in Glafgow, fecond fon to Edward Buchanan elder of Spittel.

This family came off Buchanan immediately before that of Auchmar, Walter of Spittel being uncle to William the firft of Auchmar.

It has appeared a little furprizing to fome, that the family of Buchanan fhould have run through twenty-two generations in fo fhort a time as 695 years; and yet here we fee in this family of Spittel no lefs than ten generations in the fpace of about 223 years, which is a great deal more in proportion than in the former cafe; and I doubt not but frequent obfervations of this nature might be made in many other families.

AN ACCOUNT of the OLD FAMILY of ARNPRYOR.

THIS of Arnpryor having been for a considerable tract of time one of the most reputed Families of the name of Buchanan, both upon account of the estate possest by them, being pretty considerable, as also in regard these gentlemen themselves were for the most part among the best accomplished of that name. Nevertheless since the middle of the last age, or some little time before, this family is so much decayed, that there can be very little said concerning the same, more than to give some account of what it hath been, and of some few cadets now extant thereof, and who represent the same. The oldest writs of this family being either carried off when the last Laird of Arnpryor went to Ireland, or some other way lost, the manner of the descent thereof off the family of Buchanan cannot be so clearly illustrated as otherwise it might. The most clear document for that purpose is the Genealogical Tree of the Family of Buchanan, which positively asserts John Buchanan first of Arnpryor to have been second son to

Wlter, fourth of that name, Laird of Buchnan, and of the Lord Graham's daughter: Which Tree being compofed, anno 1600, the compofers thereof might have lived in or near the latter part of this gentleman's life-time, fo that the account given thereby may fully fatisfy all fuch as are not too much addicted to criticifm or needlefs fcrupulofity. The portion this gentleman obtained from his father, the Laird of Buchanan, was the lands of Auchmar, which at his death returned to the family of Buchanan, as the cuftom was of Appenage, or Taniftry-Lands. The manner of his obtaining of the lands of Arnpryor was pretty fingular, being this.

In the Reign of King James IV. And for divers ages before, the Meinziefes were proprietors of a great part of the parifh of Kippen, and fome of the parifh of Killearn, tho' fcarce any memory of that name remains in either of thofe parifhes in this age. A Gentleman of that name being Laird of Arnpryor, at the above mentioned juncture, who had no children of his own, nor any of his name in thefe parts, that could pretend any relation to him, was for fometime at variance with one Forrefter of Carden, a very toping gentleman of Arnpryor's neighbourhood, who, upon account of his neighbour Arnpryor's circumftances, fent a menacing kind of meffage to him either to difpone his eftate in his favour voluntarily, otherwife he would dispossess him of it by force. Arnpryor not being of power to oppose Carden, and being loath to give his estate by compulsion to his enemy, judged it the more proper, as well as honourable method, to dispone his estate to some other gentleman who would counterballance Carden, and would maintain the rightful owner in possession thereof during his life. In this exigency he had recourse to the Laird of Buchanan, offering to dispone his estate to one of Buchanan's sons, if he would defend him from any violence offered by Carden. Buchanan readily accepted of the offer, and so far undervalued Carden, that he sent his second son, then only a child, without any other guard, than his dry-nurse, to over-see him, along with Arnpryor, to be kept by him as his heir. Upon notice hereof, Carden came to Arnpryor's house with a resolution to kill him, or oblige him to send back Buchanan's son, and grant his former demands. Arnpryor having gone out of the way, Carden very imperiously ordered the woman who attended Buchanan's child, to carry him back forthwith whence he came, otherwise he would burn Arnpryor's house, and them together. The woman replied, that she would not desert the house for any thing he durst do, telling him withal, if he offered the least violence, it would be revenged to his cost. This stout reply was somewhat damping to

Carden, who at the fame time reflecting, that he would not only be obnoxious to the laws for any violent meafures he fhould take, but alfo to emnity with Buchanan, which he was by no means able to fupport, therefore followed the fafeft courfe, by defifting for the future either to moleft Arnpryor, or fruftrate his deftination, fo that his adopted heir enjoyed his eftate, without the leaft impediment, after his death.

This John Buchanan of Auchmar and Arnpryor, was afterwards termed King of Kippen, upon the following account. King James V. a very fociable debonair Prince, refiding at Stirling, in Buchanan of Arnpryor's time, carriers were very frequently paffing along the common road, being near Arnpryor's houfe, with neceffaries for the ufe of the King's Family, and he having fome extraordinary occafion, ordered one of thefe carriers to leave his load at his houfe and he would pay him for it; which the carrier refufed to do, telling him he was the King's carrier, and his load for his Majefty's ufe, to which Arnpryor feemed to have fmall regard, compelling the carrier in the end to leave his load, telling him, if King James was King of Scotland, he was King of Kippen, fo that it was reafonable he fhould fhare with his neighbour King in fome of thefe loads, fo frequently carried that road. The carrier reprefenting this ufage, and telling the story as Arnpryor spoke it, to some of the King's servants, it came at length to his Majesty's ears, who shortly thereafter with a few attendants came to visit his neighbour King, who was in the meantime at dinner. King James having sent a servant to demand access, was denied the same by a tall fellow, with a battle-ax, who stood Porter at the gate, telling, there could be no access till dinner was over. This answer not satisfying the King, he sent to demand access a second time; upon which he was desired by the Porter to desist, otherwise he would find cause to repent his rudeness. His Majesty finding this method would not do, desired the Porter to tell his Master that the Good-man of Ballageigh desired to speak with the King of Kippen. The Porter telling Arnpryor so much, he in all humble manner came and received the King, and having entertained him with much sumptuousness and jollity, became so agreeable to King James, that he allowed him to take so much of any provision he found carrying that road, as he had occasion for; and seeing he made the first visit, desired Arnpryor in a few days to return him a second at Stirling, which he performed, and continued in very much favour with the King, always thereafter being termed King of Kippen while he lived.

Arnpryor had also the lands of Gartartan,

by which he was sometimes designed, particularly he is so designed in a charter in his favour by John Commendator of Inchmahomo, of certain lands called Hornhaugh. He obtained charter of the lands of Brachern from John MacNair, heritor thereof, dated in the year 1530. There is a certain traditional account, that the lands of Brachern, after Arnpryor obtained right thereto, were violently possessed by one MacTormad, Captain of a Company of outlaws, who with his associates, in number twenty-four, coming to a Tavern in Drymen-parish, at a place called Chappellairoch; Arnpryor upon notice thereof, came in the night-time to the Tavern, accompanied with some few horse-men, and finding these outlaws overcome with liquor and sleep, made fast the door of the house where they lay, and then set fire to it, all therein being either burnt, or killed. He afterwards gave the lands of Brachern, with those of Cashly, to one of his sons. This brave Gentleman, with divers others of his name, being killed at the battle of Pinky, in Queen Mary's minority, he was succeeded by

ANDREW, his eldest son, as is clear by charter in his favour, and of John Buchanan, his son and apparent heir, of the lands of Arnpryor, dated in the year 1560. There is also a charter by Bartholomew Bane, in favour of the said Andrew, of the Miln-town of Bochlyvie, dated in the year 1557. Andrew had two sons, John, his successor, and Walter, to whom his father disponed the Miln-town, or as others write Hiltown of Bochlyvie.

There is little account to be had of John third Laird of Arnpryor, or his successors for two descents, upon account of the loss of the principal writs of that family. The last of these who was in possession of Arnpryor, was John, who sold those lands to Sir John, Laird of Buchanan, and were by him disponed to John Buchanan of Mochastel, of Lenny's family, and grandfather to Francis Buchanan, now of Arnpryor.

John Buchanan, who sold Arnpryor, having gone to Ireland, was killed by the Irish in the year 1641. He had two sons, William, and David, who both died without issue. He had also three daughters; Dorothy, first married to Robert Buchanan, one of King Charles I. his Butlers. To him she had two daughters, both married in Ireland. She was afterwards married to Colonel Hublethorn, an Englishman, Governor of Watterford. She had to him one son, Captain Hublethorn and some daughters. Arnpryor's second daughter was Alice, married to Cunninghame of Trinbeg. The third, Anna, married to Cunninghame of Finnick.

This last Arnpryor had two brethren. Mr David, a Gentleman of great learning, of whom I shall speak afterwards. And Captain William, a Gentleman of very much courage, and of the greatest art and dexterity in managing a sword of any of his time. He killed an Italian in Dublin, in presence of the Lord Lieutenant, and other Nobility of that Kingdom; the same Italian having gone through most nations in Europe, always having had the victory of all he encountered with. Captain William, being one of Buchanans Captains at Innerkeithing, a certain English officer, when the two armies advanced near to one another, stept forth, and challenged any of the Scottish army to exchange some few blows with him. The challenge was accepted by Captain William, who tho' a very little man of person, did in a trice kill that English Champion. This Captain William resided mostly in Ireland, in which Kingdom his progeny continued.

The first cadet of the family of Arnpryor was DUNCAN, second son to John Buchanan first of Arnpryor, in whose favour his father disponed the lands of Brachern, in Buchanan-parish. He was succeeded by Duncan, his son, who purchased from James Drummond of Innerpafray, the lands of Carshly, and Gartinstarry, as is clear by charter of these lands in his favour, dated in the year 1468. Duncan's daughter, and heiress, Margaret, married her cousin John Buchanan of Hiltown, or Miln-town of Bochlyvie, to whom she conveyed all her father's interest.

The second cadet of the family was WALTER, second son to Andrew Buchanan, the second of Arnpryor, to whom his father disponed the Miln-town of Bochlyvie. His son John married the heiress of Cashly and Brachern, as already mentioned. He was killed at the conflict of Glenfroon, betwixt Luss and the MacGrigors. He left two sons, John, and Andrew. John the second of Bochlyvie and Cashly, sold the lands of Brachern to one Duncan MacPharlan. This John had two sons, Duncan, who sold the lands of Cashly, except Gartinstarry; and Andrew, who purchased the lands of Ballachneck. Duncan had two sons, John, late Gartinstarry, who had two sons, James, now of Gartinstarry, Rrepresenter of the family of Arnpryor, and John, Malt-man in Glasgow. Andrew of Ballachneck, had two sons, John father to Moses Buchanan of Ballachneck, and George at present in Ballachneck. Andrew, second brother to John late Gartinstarry, purchased the lands of Nenbolg and Provanstoun, being designed by the latter. Andrew, second son to John first of Cashly, who went to Ireland was ancestor to John, Andrew, and William, with others residing near Dungivan in the county of Derry. There are also descended of this family Andrew Buchanan, merchant in Borrowſtounneſs; James Buchanan, Wright in Edinburgh; and John Buchanan, Merchant in England, with Robert Buchanan, Cordiner in Glaſgow, and the progeny of Duncan Buchanan, Notar in Arnmoir, and others in Kippen-pariſh.

AN

Account of the Family of

DRUMIKILL.

THE eſtate of Drumikill, with a great many other lands in the eaſt parts of the Paroch of Drymen, (as far as a traditional account may be relied on) did of old belong to the name of Arral, which name, in the minority of King David Bruce, having aſſociated with the enemies of their Prince, and country, they, upon the reduction of their adherents, not only continued obſtinate in their rebellion, but in further aggravation of their guilt, committed divers other inſolencies, which in the end gave juſt cauſe for their whole lands being forfeited, and letters of fire and ſword being directed againſt them. The execution of these letters being committed to the Laird of Buchanan, he did, with no small difficulty and blood-shed, bring the surviving remainder of these Arrals to justice. Among the number of these was Thomas Arral of Drumikill, commonly termed *Taus na Dunnach*, or Thomas the Mischievous. The King is said to have offered this Gentleman a pardon at the place of execution, which he refused, disdaining to live after so many of his name, who had lost their lives through his influence, and in his quarrel. After the subversion of these Arrals, Buchanan in reward of his service against them, obtained Drumikill, Easter and Wester Ballats, and some other parts of their lands, lying most contiguous to his own estate, which the Lairds of Buchanan retained in their own hands, till the one half of Drumikill, with Easter Ballat, was given to Carbeth's ancestor, as the other half, with Wester Ballat, was given to Drumikill's, at the times the ancestors of these two families came off that of Buchanan.

There is a current tradition, that the Laird of Buchanan gave the half of the estate of Drumikill, with Wester Ballat, and some other lands, formerly belonging to the Arrals, to one of his sons long before the ancestor of the present family of Drumikill came off Buchanan's family, and that Thomas the first of this present race for his first Lady married the heiress of the principal person of the old Family. And that which favours somewhat this account, is, that the ancestors of the Buchanans of Drumhead, and Wester Ballat, though always reputed cadets of Drumikill, can produce some evidents of their lands of a date not long posterior to the most ancient now in custody of Drumikill. But having found no document either among the late Buchanan's or Drumikill's evidences that can in any measure clear this allegation, I must leave it undetermined, though it be no way improbable, if there had been any such evidences, the same might by some contingency or other be lost, as are a great many of these of Buchanan, and the whole of Baron MacAuslan's most ancient writs. However this be.

The first of the present Family of Drumikill, that is recorded by the Genealogical Tree of Buchanan, and evidences of Drumikill, is Thomas Buchanan, son to Patrick, first of that name Laird of Buchanan, and of Galbraith, heiress of Killearn, Bamoir, and Auchinreoch, his Lady. The first document relating to this Thomas, is a disposition to him, by Finnoyse MacAulay, heiress of a little tenement in Drymen, called Croftewer; in which disposition he is designed, An Honourable Person, Thomas Buchanan, brother-german to Walter Buchanan of that Ilk; the said disposition being dated in the year

1482. There is a resignation by John Blair of Adamtoun, in the hands of William Lord Graham, of the lands of Middle Ledlewan, now Moss, for new infeftment to be given of these lands to Thomas Buchanan of Balleun, brother-german to Walter Buchanan of that Ilk, dated in the year 1484. Procurators to the resignation are Walter Buchanan of that Ilk, Patrick Colquhoun of Glyn, and John Nenbolg of that Ilk. There is a charter also of Balleun, by Walter Laird of Buchanan in favour of this Thomas, some little time before this of Moss, in the same year. There is also charter by Matthew Earl of Lennox in favour of this Thomas, designed of Balleun, of that part of the half lands of Drumikill not formerly disponed, called Browster-Croft, of date 1491. The same Thomas grants charter of the half-lands of Drumikill to Robert Buchanan his son in fee, with reservation of his own, and Geils Cunninghame, his Spouse's life-rents, dated in the year 1495. This Thomas, upon the death of Thomas Buchanan of Carbeth, his uncle, obtained the lands Gartincaber, which he and his successors retained possession of until Carbeth sold his half of Drumikill to the proprietor of the other half of that estate; upon which occasion Carbeth re-obtained the beneficial tack of Gartincaber, of which a cadet of his family is now in possession. And this seems to be the ground of the error into which some have run, concerning the ancestors of these two families being the same, in regard two Thomas's, whose age differed so little, were proprietors of Gartincaber, and sometimes designed thereby. Thomas Buchanan of Carbeth's resignation of the half-lands of Drumikill, in the hands of James Halden of Glenegeis, superior thereof, and Glenegeis's confirmation of these lands in favour of Robert Buchanan, are dated in the year 1565. Thomas Buchanan first of Drumikill was married to Geils Cunninghame, daughter to Cunninghame of Drumquhassil; and by her as far as can be collected, he had four sons, that came to age; Robert his successor; Thomas, afterwards of Moss; William of Baturrich, now Drumhead; and John of Drumdash, afterwards of Camochoill and Wester-Ballat.

To Thomas first of Drumikill succeeded his son, ROBERT, as is evident by the charters in his favour of the lands of Drumikill; as also by charter in his favour of Spittel of Finnick, with Boat and Boatland of Catter, by Matthew Earl of Lennox, dated at the Earl's ancient Mansion-House of Middle-Catter, in the year 1505. This Robert was married to Margaret Hay, of what Family not mentioned; and by her had two sons, Thomas his eldest, who, by any thing can be found, was married to Logy of that Ilk's daughter;

This Thomas was not entered to any of his father's estate, having died young, and long before his father, he being only mentioned as Procurator in a seasin of Robert his father, by designation of Thomas Buchanan, Premogenitus, or eldest son of Robert Buchanan of Drumikill. Robert's second son was John, ancestor of Buchanan in Wester-Cameron. Thomas, last mentioned, left two sons, Robert and Walter.

Robert, eldest son to the said Thomas, was served heir to his grandfather, Robert Buchanan of Drumikill, by designation of his nephew, and apparent heir, in the year 1518. He died unmarried, at least without issue, and was succeeded by his brother Walter, as testifies a precept of Clare Constat and charter thereon, in favour of him, and Janet Buchanan, his spouse, in life-rent, and Thomas Buchanan, their son, in fee of the lands of Drumikill, dated 1536. I find this Walter mentioned in a bond of an hundred merks due to John Lennox of Branshogle, by Graham of Fintry, Cunninghame of Glengarnock, and Galbraith of Balgair, Principals, Earl of Glencairn, Cunninghame of Drumquhassile, and Walter Buchanan of Drumikill, Cautioners, all in one bond, and subscribed by two Nottars, in regard none of all the Principals, or Cautioners could write, except Fintry, and Drumikill. This bond was dated in the year 1537, which being in the time when Popery prevailed in this Nation, and a confummate ignorance of all manner of learning, it is not to be wondered at, that fo many Laicks fhould not be able to write, when I have even heard from a gentleman of very good repute, that he had perufed a writ of date near that time, in which two of the Monks of Paifly were inferted witnesses, for whom the Nottar was obliged to fign, in regard thefe two clergymen were ignorant of letters. Walter Buchanan of Drumikill was firft married to Janet Buchanan, daughter to Walter Buchanan of Spittel, by whom he had Thomas, his fucceffor. He had for fecond Lady a daughter of Kinrofs of Kippenrofs, and had by her William, afterward of Rofs.

To Walter fucceeded his fon THOMAS, as is clear by the charter already mentioned, with divers others. He was firft married to Logan of Balvey's daughter, fecondly to Stirling of Glorat's daughter. Of thefe marriages he had three fons, William, his fucceffor, Walter of Conachra, and James who went to Ireland.

Thomas was fucceeded by his fon WILLIAM, who married Semple of Fulwood's daughter, by whom he had three fons, Walter, his fucceffor, Thomas, and George; which laft two went to Ireland, where divers of their progeny live in good circumstances. He had also one daughter, married to Kincaid of Auchinreoch.

Walter succeeded his father William, and was married to Hamilton of Kinglaffy's daughter. By her he had two sons, William, first of Craigievairn, and Dugal of Gartincaber.

To Walter succeeded his son William, who was married to Cunninghame of Boquhan's daughter. He had with her three sons, John, William, and Walter. The two last left no issue. This William sold the estate of Drumikill to his cousin, Captain William Buchanan, second son to William Buchanan, first of Ross, and afterwards purchased from my Lord Napier the lands of Craigievairn, by which he, and his successors were afterwards designed.

To William, first designed Craigievairn, succeeded his son, John, who married Cunninghame of Trinbeg's daughter, and had by her one son, William, his successor, and one daughter, married to Lieutenant James Hamilton, brother to Hamilton of Bardowie.

William present Craigievairn, married Hamilton of Bardowie's daughter, and hath by her a numerous issue.

The first cadet of the family of Drumikill was Thomas Buchanan, second son to Thomas Buchanan, first of Drumikill, who obtained the lands of Moss. He married Agnes Herriot, daughter to Herriot of Trabrown, and had by her three sons. Of these was Patrick, sent to the King of Denmark, to require that Hepburn Earl of Bothwell, then prisoner in that Kingdom, should be sent to Scotland, in order to be punished for Darnly's murder. This Patrick had no male-issue; so that the Moss, by virtue of some certain clause in his father Patrick's charter of the same, returned to the Laird of Drumikill, or was purchased by him. Thomas of Moss's other two sons were Alexander Buchanan of Ibert, and the Great Mr GEORGE BUCHANAN.

There are some of opinion, that Patrick, Alexander, and Mr GEORGE were sons of Thomas, eldest son to Robert, second Drumikill. But this supposition is clearly overthrown by a charter among Drumikill's evidences, lately perused by me, which had escaped me upon my first perusal of them, being a charter by William Earl of Montrose, to Thomas Buchanan, brother-german to Robert Buchanan of Drumikill, as nearest heir to Thomas Buchanan, his Pupillus, that is, as I take it, his nephew, or brother's son, of the lands of Moss. So that the Moss being then the Appenage, or second son's portion of the family of Drumikill, and this Thomas being the only second son existing at that time, obtained these lands, at least during his own life-time, as the custom of such lands was then, and for a long time thereafter. For further illuftration of this matter, I have feen in the hands of George Buchanan of Bellachruin, lineal fucceffor of Alexander Buchanan of Ibert, and confequently Reprefenter of the family of Mofs, a difcharge by Walter Buchanan of Drumikill, to Alexander Buchanan of Ibert, his Coufin, and Emm, difcharging his intromiffion for fome years with the rents of a part of the eftate of Drumikill. Which Walter by authentick documents already mentioned is found to be fon to Thomas younger of Drumikill, and grand-child to Robert. And Alexander of Ibert, by the evidences of Gartcalderland, and others, is known to be fon to Buchanan of Mofs, and brother to Mr GEORGE. Whereas if he, and Mr GEORGE, had been fons to Thomas younger of Drumikill, they had undoubtedly been defigned brethren to Walter of Drumikill, granter of the faid difcharge, and the term of Coufin, and Emm, had been utterably unfuitable and nonfenfical, the word Emm importing an Uncle, or Grand-uncle's fon, which was the real relation of thefe two gentlemen to the faid Walter Buchanan of Drumikill.

Thomas of Mofs's fecond fon was ALEXANDER BUCHANAN of Ibert, who had two fons, the eldeft of whom was Mr Thomas Buchanan, as is clear by charter of Ibert in his favour, by Mr Thomas Archibald, Vicar of Drymen, of date 1567 years. He became

Lord Privy Seal 1578, upon demiffion of that office by his uncle, Mr GEORGE. He married a daughter of the fecond marriage, of John, Laird of Buchanan, by whom he had two daughters, the eldeft married to Patrick Buchanan of Auchmar, the fecond to Captain Henry Cunninghame. John fecond fon to Alexander of Ibert, acquired the lands of Ballachcruin, being anceftor to George Buchanan of Ballachruin, whofe brethren were Mofes Buchanan, Merchant, and Arthur, Wright in Glafgow, and William; who left one fon George, who went abroad. There are alfo defcended off this family, Buchanan lately of Harperftoun, Buchanan Portioner of Clober, with fome others.

Thomas of Mofs's third fon was the faid Mr GEORGE BUCHANAN; of whom being an honour to our Name and Nation, I fhall give a large account, after having finifhed my account of the family of Drumikill.

The next cadet of the family of Drumikill to that of Mofs, was William Buchanan of Baturrich, third fon to Thomas Buchanan of Drumikill. The firft lands obtained after he came off that family, were thofe of Meikle Baturrich in Kilmaronock-parifh. He married one of the name of MacAulay, heirefs of Blairhenachan, now Drumhead, in the parifh of Cardrofs, and fhire of Dunbarton, as appears by charter in favour of the faid William Buchanan, dated in the year 1530.

The Genealogical Tree of the family of Buchanan afferts this William to have been married to Arncaple's daughter; but it feems this MacAulay of Blairhenachan, whofe heirefs he married, was a fon of the family of Arncaple, fo that the error is not very confiderable. William firft of Blairhenachan's fucceffor was Robert, who obtained a charter of thefe lands from Alexander MacAulay of Arncaple, dated in the year 1552. This Robert made an excambion with Haldan of Glenegeis of the lands of Baturrich with thofe of Blairwhoifh, in poffeffion of which Drumhead continues. Robert above-mentioned, had three fons; Robert his fucceffor, Mungo firft of Tullicheun; and John, or as others fay with no lefs probability, Thomas firft of Drumfad.

Robert fecond Blairhenachan was fucceeded by his fon of the fame name who had two fons, Archibald his fucceffor; and Robert, who went to Ireland, and refided in Glenmaqueen in the county of Derry. He had two fons, Archibald, and George. Archibald, the eldeft of thefe fons, married his coufin-german, heirefs of Blairhenachan, the title of which he changed into that of Drumhead, yet retained. He was married to Anderfon of Stobcrofs's daughter, by whom he hath three fons, and two daughters. His eldeft fon, Archibald Buchanan younger of Drumhead, is married to Gilbert Buchanan of Bankel's daughter. James and George, his other two sons, both Merchants in Glasgow, are unmarried. His eldest daughter is married to Robert Buchanan Writer in Glasgow. His other daughter is unmarried. Drumhead had two sisters, the eldest married to Napier of Ballikinrain, the youngest to Buchanan of Balfunning.

The first cadet of Drumhead's family is Buchanan of Tullichewn. Mungo Buchanan, second son to Robert second Blairhenachan, who purchased the Spittels of Creitingaws from the Dennistouns, co-heiresses of these Spittels; the one part thereof from the one of these, with consent of Thomas Buchanan, her husband, who seems to be brother to the said Mungo, in the year 1603, the other half of these Spittels from the other heiress, in the year 1605. In which year he got charter of confirmation of these Spittels from James Denniestoun of Colgrain, superior thereof. Mungo's successor was Robert, who obtained first a tack, and after a fue-charter from Ludovick Duke of Lennox, of the lands of Meikle Tullichewn. This Robert had two sons, Robert his successor, and William, who acquired Stuckrodger. Robert of Tullichewn had one son, Mungo, who had four sons, Robert his successor; James, who acquired a part of Little Tullichewn, and had issue; Mungo, Writer in Edinburgh, who purchased Hiltown and

Auchintorly, and left issue; and William, now in Tullichewn.

Thomas youngest brother of Mungo first of Tullichewn, and third son to Robert second Blairhenachan, acquired a fue, or wadset-right of the lands of Meikle Drumfad in Glenfroon. His son was called John, designed of Drumfad, which lands this John, or rather his son of the same name sold, being ancestor to John Buchanan of Cattermiln in the parish of Kilmaronock, and others.

There are also divers of the family of Drumhead besides these mentioned, who reside in the parishes of Dunbarton, and Bonneil. William of Stuckrodger above-named, had one son, William, who mostly resided at St Ninians, who had two sons, William who left one son; and James, who went abroad.

The next cadet of Drumhead's family was WALTER, ordinarily termed Walter in Drymen, having resided the most part of his time in that village. Having no manner of document to testify the time and manner of the descent of this Walter off that of Drumhead, I must leave the same undetermined, though he is always reputed, as also owned by his progeny to be a cadet of the said family. This Walter had two sons, John, and Walter, both Notars. John had three sons, Walter the eldest, for whom he purchased the lands of Moss, being grand-father to the present Walter Buchanan of Moss, and father to

John Buchanan of Carstoun. John the Notar's second son was John, grand-father to Archibald Buchanan of Balfunning, and father to John Buchanan of Little Croy. His third son was William, who had one son who never married. Walter in Drymen's second son Walter went to Argyle-shire, and settled in Melfort in that shire, in which, and Lismore, divers of his race continue yet. Some others came thence, and settled in Drymen-parish and other places.

The last cadet of the family of Drumhead, is GEORGE, the present Drumhead's uncle. He resided the most of his time near Rapho in the county of Derry in Ireland. He purchased a pretty good interest in that Kingdom. He was a gentleman of a very good character, and very much esteemed in that place. He had two sons, the eldest succeeded to his interest, the youngest was a clergyman.

The third cadet of the family of Drumikill, was JOHN, fourth son to Thomas first of Drumikill, who for patrimony got a beneficial tack of Drumdash in Drymen-parish. He was killed by the Buchanans of Cashill, and succeeded by his son Walter, who sold Drumdash, and obtained a tack of Camochoil, and purchased the Spittel of Wester Ballat from the MacConvels heiresses thereof about the year 1552. He got also a gransoum-tack of Wester Ballat. He had two sons, John, and Duncan. John, his eldest son, had no male-issue, the beneficial tack of Camochoil by that means fell to his daughters. The eldest of these being married to one Blair, conveyed with her the Camochoil, being ancestor to Blair now of Camochoil. John's brother obtained the heritage of the Spittels, with tack of Wester Ballat. I find this John last mentioned, inserted witness in a brieve, directed to Patrick de Buchanan, sheriff of Stirling, for infefting of Robert Buchanan, nephew and heir to Robert Buchanan of Drumikill. Duncan the said John's brother was ancestor to Patrick Buchanan of Wester Ballat, who had three sons, John, the eldest, who had issue; Mr Thomas Writer in Edinburgh; and Duncan Merchant in London. Of this family is descended John Buchanan in Hiltown of Bochlyvie; Patrick Buchanan, Merchant at Kippen-kirk, with some others in these parts. There are also divers of this family in the counties of Antrim and Down in Ireland.

The fourth cadet of the family of Drumikill was JOHN of Cameron, second son to Robert second of Drumikill: He was married to Dennieftoun of Auchindinnan's daughter. He obtained the lands of Wester Cameron in tack, his son having afterwards purchased the same in heritage, which was sold by Walter, grand-father to the present William in Cameron, to Drumikill. There are few or none of this family remaining, except William now in Cameron, who hath three sons, Walter, William, and John, all married. William had a brother called George who went abroad.

There was one Angus Buchanan of Finnicktenent, reputed a cadet of Drumikill, and if so, behoved to be a third son of Robert second Laird of Drumikill. The last of that family went to Ireland, more than a year ago. There being no account whether any of that race be remaining in that Kingdom or not, there is no great occasion to insist too much upon the descent of the same.

The fifth cadet of Drumikill was WILLIAM BUCHANAN of Ross, second son to Walter fourth Laird of Drumikill; his mother being Kinross of Kippenross's daughter. He married John Buchanan in Gartincaber's daughter, by whom he had three sons, John, his successor, Captain William, and George; also three daughters, the eldest married to Cunninghame of Trinbeg, the second to Buchanan of Auchmar, the third to Buchanan of Carbeth. He purchased the lands of Ross from the Earl of Glencairn, and was succeeded by John his son, who was thrice married, first to Cunninghame of Drumquhassil's daughter, and had by her one son, and two daughters. The eldest of these daughters was married to Andrew

Laird of MacPharlane, being mother to the late John Laird of MacPharlane. The other daughter was married to Robert Taylor of Mansfield, and had issue. John of Ross was secondly married to Crawford of Kilblirnie's daughter, relict to Lindsay of Balquhuarage. He had with her one son, William, second Laird of Drumikill of that race, and one daughter married to Edward Buchanan of Spittel. He had for third Lady Anna Bickertoun, with whom he had issue.

Captain William, second son to William first of Ross was thrice married, but had no issue. He purchased the estate of Drumikill from his cousin William, eighth Laird thereof; and because he had no issue of his own, disponed that estate to his nephew William Buchanan, second son to John of Ross, the Captain's eldest brother.

This William of Drumikill married a daughter of MacAulay of Arncaple, and had by her three sons, William who died unmarried; Archibald, now of Drumikill; and George, who had no issue, also one daughter, married to Lieutenant Walter Bontein, brother to the Laird of Airdoch, who had issue. Archibald present Drumikill, married Jean Buchanan heiress of Ross, daughter of James Buchanan of Ross, his uncle, and of Margaret Stirling, daughter to Stirling of Law. With her he had four sons, and four daughters, George, third son to William first of

Ross, was killed in the year 1645, having no issue.

The sixth cadet of the family of Drumikill was WALTER of Conachra in Drymen-parish, second son to Thomas, third of that name, and fifth Laird of Drumikill. There are none of his male-issue living except Thomas Buchanan of Kirkhouse of Strablane, and his children. The said Walter had one daughter married to John Govean in Drymen, being mother to William Govean of Drumquhuassile. The said Thomas had a third son, James, who went to Ireland.

The seventh cadet of Drumikill was THOMAS, second son to William sixth Laird of Drumikill. He with his Brother George, went to Ireland, where their progeny reside.

The last cadet of that family was Dugal Buchanan, second son to Walter seventh Laird of Drumikill, and brother to William last of that race of Drumikill, and first of Craigievairn. This Dugal acquired lower Gartincaber in Buchanan-parish: He was twice married, having of the first marriage John Buchanan, Writer in Edinburgh, of the second marriage Thomas Buchanan, Peruke-Maker, in Glasgow.

The old family of Drumikill, of which William Buchanan now of Craigievairn is Representer, by any information I can obtain, for Armorial bearing carries the bearing of Buchanan; and for distinction, a

Battle-Ax in the Lion's dexter paw, pointing towards the chief proper, with Helmet in Crest, suiting his quality. The Motto, *Prosecute or Perish*.

The present Buchanan of Drumikill bears Buchanan; and for distinction, in the Lion's dexter paw, a Man's Heart proper; his Crest, a Dexter Hand holding a Sword. Motto, *God with my right*.

Buchanan of Drumhead, a cadet of the old family of Drumikill, bears Buchanan; for distinction, a Bent-Bow in the Lion's sinister-paw, and an Arrow in his dexter: For Crest, a Sinister Hand holding a Bent Bow. His Motto, *Par sit Fortuna Labori*.

AN

ACCOUNT OF

Mr GEORGE BUCHANAN.

HAVING finished my account of the family of Drumikill, I return according to promise, to give some memoirs of the famous Mr GEORGE BUCHANAN, who brought such a mighty accession of honour both to his name, and country. It agrees not with my design to give a compleat history of this great man; for that would be to give a History of Scotland during the age in which he lived, in the affairs whereof he bore so considerable a part. He was born, as he himself informs us, in the year 1506. The death of his father, and the breaking of his grand-father brought the family under very great difficulties. His mother being left a widow with eight children, did all she could for their education, though under the greatest discouragements. But it was GEORGE's peculiar good fortune to be taken notice of by a brother of his mother's, who finding him extremely capable of learning, sent him to Paris; from whence, after about two years stay, he was obliged to return, by reason of his narrow circumstances, and want of health. After his recovery he became a Volunteer in the French troops then in Scotland, but soon falling sick again, went to St Andrew's, and studied Logic under the celebrated John Major. He followed him to France the same year, and after having stayed at Paris two years struggling with his misfortunes, he was called to teach Grammar in the College of St Barbara. This he did for three years. He was brought back into Scotland by a young Nobleman, the Earl of Cassils, who had kept him with him five years in Paris. He intended to have returned again into France, but was prevented by the King's appointing him Governor to his natural son, the Earl of Murray. He had some time before this wrote a Poem, which enraged the whole fraternity of the Cordeliers against him, and raised him many enemies, with whose reproaches he was so touched, that he began from thence forward to listen more than ever to the teachers of the Reformation. About this time the King returning from France, made the Clergy very uneasy, they being apprehensive, that Queen Magdalen whom he brought along with him, had imbibed the new opinions from her aunt the Queen of Navarre. But the death of that Princess soon dispelled their fears. Sometime after a plot was discovered against the King, who upon this found reasons to believe, that the Cordeliers had not discharged their duty to him. He therefore commanded Buchanan to write some verses. Buchanan obeyed without any reluctance, but kept within bounds, and made use of ambiguous expressions. The King not pleased with those verses, commanded him to write sharper, which was accordingly done in the famous Sylva, which is called Franciscanus. Cardinal Beton hereupon plotted his ruin, and even proceeded so far as to get him thrown into prison, from whence he escaped by his ingenuity, and fled into England. But matters being in such confusion there, that one day the Lutherians were burnt, and the next day the Papists, he thought fit to retire again into France; and for fear Cardinal Beton, who was then Ambassador at that Court, should play him some tricks, he privately withdrew from Paris, and went to Bourdeaux, whether Andrew Goveanus, a learned Portuguese, invited him. He taught three years there, though not without some dread of the Cordeliers, and Cardinal Beton, which last had written to the Archbishop of Bourdeaux to secure him; but that prelate was so kind to discover the matter to some of Buchanan's intimate friends. After this he followed Goveanus into Portugal, who had orders from the King his master to bring him a certain number of persons fit to teach Philosophy, and Literature in the new University he had founded at Conimbria. All went well as long as Goveanus lived, but he dying soon after, the learned men who followed him, particularly Buchanan, were vexed all manner of ways. They ript up his Poem against the Cordeliers, and reproached him with eating flesh in Lent, though according to the custom of the country. It was also pretended, that in his discourse he had discovered some disgust at the Catholick religion. He was thus plagued with them for above a year together, till at last for fear of discovering, that they had unjustly harrassed a man of reputation, they confined him for some months to a Monastery, in order to be better instructed. It was there he undertook his admired paraphrase of the Psalms, which has been since prized at such an inestimable rate by the learned world. Having obtained his liberty, he past into England, but quickly returned to France. Some years after he entered into the service of Mareschal de Brissac, and was tutor to his son Timoleon de Cosse, to whom he has inscribed his incomparable Poem De Sphæra. The Mareschal then commanded the French Army in Piedmont. Buchanan continued five years in that employment, sometimes in Italy, and sometimes in France. He quitted it in 1560. Returning into Scotland after the disturbances occasioned by the faction of the Guises were composed, he went over openly to the communion of the Reformed Church, and was made preceptor to King James VI. in 1565.

Thus far have we an account of this great man from himself, as he wrote, and published it in his own life-time. His modesty withheld him from giving us a detail of the great honours and prosperity to which he afterwards arrived. However the Histories of that age make it evident, he was for some years in the management of our Scottish affairs. By being promoted to the post of Lord Privy Seal, he became one of the great Officers of State. And his activity in pushing the Reformation gave him such a character with our Reformers, that he was chosen by them to preside in one of their General Assemblies, as Moderator, notwithstanding of his being a Layman.

Yet these are but a small part of his honours, compared with that lasting glory he has acquired by his admirable writings. His History of Scotland, both for disposition and purity of language, has been looked upon by all good judges, to come the nearest to the ancients of any performance these latter ages have produced. I know indeed he has been blamed by some people of partiality; but the imputation has never yet been made sufficiently out upon those passages excepted against. He has also been no less censured for maintaining several principles, apprehended to be destructive of Government, in his Dialogue *De Jure Regni apud Scotos*. It is not my business either to justify or condemn him in this matter. Yet thus much may safely be said for him, That he has laid down no general Principles of Government, but what have been maintained by the greatest Legislators and Philosophers of Antiquity; and that he has been followed in them by several of the most eminent among the modern writers. If to err be a Fault, it is always allowed to be an extenuation of it, to err in good company. And this is all I shall say on the matter.

Buchanan's Poetical Writings have met with a better fate; very few having had the hardiness to detract from the worth of them, and those few that have done it, having gained so little honour by it. He has been admired over all Europe, as the many editions of his Works abundantly testify, which, as they are in every body's hands, it would be a very needless piece of presumption in me to give any character of. Nor shall I trouble either myself, or the reader, with the numerous encomiums of learned men upon him; but conclude with the single testimony of the great SCALIGER, whose praise, considering how little he was addicted to bestow it, cannot be suspected.

Imperii fuerat Romani SCOTIA Limes;
Romani *Eloquii* SCOTIA *finis erit*.

As SCOTIA's *Realms the* Roman *pow'r confin'd,*
So here their Rest Rome's Arts and Language find.

AN

Account of the Family of

CARBETH.

THERE has been a long continued pretension made by the Lairds of Drumikill, that the ancestor of this Family of CARBETH was a cadet of the Family of Drumikill. At what time this pretension was formed, how long continued, or how far acquiesced in, in more ancient times, I cannot positively determine; but am very confident, the late Carbeth, a man pretty well skilled in the Genealogy of his own, and other families of his name, did not in the least own any such matter. Tho' I must own it would be a matter of the utmost difficulty to distinguish these two families, were it not the two charters, after-mentioned, being the most ancient pertaining to this family, are so very clear of themselves; which notwithstanding does not fully satisfy some of the more nice and critical. For satisfaction of such, I shall here observe some few things, besides what I offered in the account of the family of Drumikill. That which admits of the greatest difficulty in being resolved, and is mostly objected, is a service of William, sixth Laird of Drumikill, which I perused among others of the late Buchanan's evidents, by which the said William is served heir to Walter Buchanan of Gartincaber, great grand-father to the said Walter. So that the first charter of Thomas of Carbeth's ancestor being that of Gartincaber, it is presumed, he was ancestor of both the families. For resolution of this, it is very evident, that all apenage, or tanistry lands, tho' always disponed by charter to the second sons of families, did never descend or accresce to their heirs, but did always, upon decease of him to whom these were first disponed, return again to the principal family, and were by that after the same manner reserved for, and disponed to the next second son of the same. This is so very demonstrable, by so many instances, as to need no further confirmation. So that Thomas of Carbeth, being second son to Sir Walter Laird of Buchanan, obtained from his eldest brother Patrick the lands of Gartincaber during life; after whose death Patrick gave these lands to another Thomas, his second son; or more probably, Walter, Patrick's successor, disponed these lands to the same Thomas his brother, being ancestor of the family of Drumikill, as the Tree of Buchanan plainly asserts; and by this means the service in favour of William of Drumikill is very right, whereas if he had been served to Carbeth's ancestor by designation of Gartincaber, he would be a degree further removed than Walter of Drumikill his great grand-father. Yea the cadets of the family of Drumikill, from the death of Thomas of Carbeth, possest these lands of Gartincaber till the time of this service, immediately after which, Carbeth obtained the beneficial tack of the same, or rather before this time, as is reported, having then obliged Drumikill to serve heir to his ancestor, in order to make his right thereof to Carbeth the more valid. For further illustration of this matter, it is plain, Thomas of Carbeth's ancestor obtained the lands of Carbeth in heritage some years before any charter can be produced in favour of Thomas first of Drumikill. So that if these had been one and the same, it cannot be in reason supposed, but that he had been designed by Carbeth, in some one or other of these evidents of Drumikill and Moss, in which he is always mentioned by other designations. Lastly, In that resignation by Thomas Buchanan of Carbeth of his half of Drumikill, to Robert Buchanan second Drumikill, anno 1505, he is there designed by Carbeth, without the least intimation of any relation betwixt him and the said Robert; whereas if the above-mentioned allegation were true, this Thomas the disponer behoved to be Robert's father, which could not miss to be so specified upon this occasion; whereas Robert's father in his disposition to him of the other half of Drumikill, in the year 1495, is there designed Thomas Buchanan of Drumikill, ten years before the date of this other write. So that it is very clear, Thomas first of Carbeth, and Thomas of Drumikill, were two different persons, the first being uncle to the latter; and that Thomas, who disponed his part to Robert, was cousin german to the first Thomas of Drumikill.

Judging that by what I have here and elsewhere advanced, I have put this matter in a clearer light than hitherto the same has been done; I shall proceed to the account of the family of Carbeth. The first charter I find relating to the same is, a charter by Patrick, first of that name Laird of Buchanan, to his beloved brother Thomas Buchanan, of the lands of Gartincaber, dated in the year 1461; by which it is clear that the said Thomas was second or third son to Sir Walter, third of that name Laird of Buchanan, his mother being daughter of Murdoc Duke of Albany. This Thomas was the first who acquired Carbeth, as appears by a charter granted by John Halden of Glenegeis to an Honourable Person, Thomas Buchanan of Gartincaber, of Meikle Carbeth, dated in the year 1476. There is no record to testify into what family this Thomas married; but it is pretty clear he had two sons, Thomas, and John, to whom he gave for portion the beneficial tack of Easter Ballat, which with Balwill, and Kepdourie, (the two last being confirmed by charter of Carbeth) seem to have been a part of the Arral's lands, though no evidents concerning the same, if any such were, are now extant.

To Thomas first of Carbeth succeeded his son Thomas, who gave away his half of the lands of Drumikill to Robert Buchanan Laird of the other half thereof, in the year 1505, as is already mentioned. Thomas the second's marriage is as little known as the first, if he was married at all; however he seems to have lived a considerable time, having outlived his second brother John, and at length having died without issue.

Thomas Buchanan son and heir to the deceased John Buchanan in Easter Ballat, as nearest heir to his uncle Thomas of Carbeth, obtained charter from John Halden of Glenegeis, in favour of himself and Janet Buchanan his spouse in life-rent, and of Thomas Buchanan his son in fee, of the lands of Carbeth in the year 1555. This Thomas the third of Carbeth is said to have been first married to a daughter of Douglas of Mains, by whom he had Thomas his successor; and for his second wife, was married to a daughter of the Laird of Buchan-

10. By her he had five sons, and one daughter, married to Gregor MacGregor Glengyle's ancestor. The sons were, John, Walter, William, Archibald, and Robert.

Thomas first of Carbeth was succeeded by his son of the same name, of whose marriage there is no account, nor of that of his successor being also Thomas, fifth of that name of Carbeth, who had one daughter, married to Galbraith of Balgair, and was succeeded by his son

Thomas, sixth of that name. He married a daughter of Adam Colquhoun merchant in Dunbarton, said to be a son of Luss's, her mother being Lindesay of Bonneil's daughter. He had by her two sons, John his successor, and Walter.

John, first of that name, succeeded his father Thomas; He married a daughter of William Buchanan of Ross, and had by her two sons, John his successor, and Moses of Glyn; also two daughters, the eldest married to James Forrester of Polder, the youngest to John Brice Nottar.

John, second of that name, succeeded to his father. He was first married to Cleland of Wardhead's daughter, by whom he had two daughters. The eldest of these was married to John Callender of Westertoun, the other to Thomas Buchanan of Boquhan. Carbeth was secondly married to Margaret Steven, heiress of Easter Cattar and Finnicktenant: By her he had two sons, John his successor, and Moses of Glyns; also one daughter, married to Buchanan of Auchmar.

John, third of that name of Carbeth, succeeded to his father. He married Stirling of Kippendavie's daughter, by whom he had two sons, William his heir, and Moses, and one daughter unmarried. William Buchanan younger of Carbeth is married to Kincaid of Auchinreoch's daughter, by whom he hath issue.

The first cadet of the family of Carbeth is Buchanan in Gartfarrand in Drymon-paroch, whose ancestor seems to have been son to Thomas first of Carbeth, having obtained a beneficial tack from the Lord Drummond, then proprietor of Gartfarrands, in which, and other parts of that country, divers of that race continue as yet.

The second cadet of the family of Carbeth is Buchanan of Easter Ballat, his ancestor being John second son to Thomas first of Carbeth. And altho' Thomas, eldest son to this John, fell into the interest of Carbeth, and left his brother William in possession of Ballat, yet it seems he did not quit the benefit of the tack of Ballat to his brother, till the same was sold off by Thomas, successor to the above Thomas, to Walter Buchanan son to the said William. I find this William who may be accounted ancestor of the present family of Ballat, mentioned in a discharge for 500 merks Scots by Semple of Craigbat to Buchanan of Arnpryor, for which it seems this William was cautioner, the date of which discharge was in the year 1576. That which clears the conveyance of the tack of Ballat by Carbeth, is a submission betwixt Thomas Buchanan of Carbeth and Walter Buchanan in Easter Ballat, who refer any difference betwixt them in relation to Ballat to the determination of John Buchanan in Ballacondachy, John MacLauchlan of Auchintroig, and Duncan Buchanan of Brachern, upon Carbeth's part; and William Buchanan in Baturrich, and John Buchanan Burges in Dunbarton his brother, with Andrew Galbraith in Tomdarroch, upon Walter in Ballat's part; with Thomas Buchanan of Drumikill, Oversman. The judges decerned the said Walter to pay four hundred merks Scots to Carbeth for his pretension to Ballat, and decerned Carbeth to maintain Walter's possession of these lands, and warrant him at the hands of his brethren, and all others. This submission is dated in the year 1594, and decreet was past thereon in January 1595, there being a great many other persons of repute present, besides parties, who all were obliged to sign by a Notar. For any thing I can find, this Walter had two sons, William who succeeded in Ballat, and Duncan who acquired the Dutchless. William also had two sons, William his successor, and John merchant in Stirling. William, third of that name of Ballat, had three sons, John, Walter, and Alexander. John of Ballat had four sons, William his successor, Walter now in Ballat, John and Patrick merchants in Glasgow. William late of Ballat's successor is John present Ballat.

Of Duncan the first cadet of Ballat is descended, Buchanan of Dutchless, Buchanan lately of Mid Cashlie, Buchanan in Little Kep, with divers others. John Buchanan merchant in Stirling, was father to Mr John Buchanan present Minister of the Gospel in Covintoun in the shire of Lanerk, who hath two sons, Mr John a Probationer, and Mr George Student of Theology in Glasgow. Alexander, and Walter, sons to William Buchanan in Ballat, had male-issue; as hath also Patrick Buchanan merchant in Glasgow, being uncle to the present Ballat, John his uncle hath no issue, nor Walter his other uncle any male-issue.

The third cadet of the family of Carbeth was John, first son of the second marriage to Thomas, third of that name of Carbeth. This John obtained the tack of Gartincaber. He had two sons, George and Walter; and two daughters, the eldest married to William Buchanan, first of Ross, the other to one MacAuslan. George had four sons, the eldest John, for whom his father acquired the lands of Blairluisk. John had two sons, George who went to Ireland, and William. George sold Blairluisk to his brother William now of Blairluisk, who hath two sons, George younger of Blairluisk, and John, merchant in England. George who sold Blairluisk, hath four sons; John, and William, who reside in the county of Tyrone; George who resides in Munster, and Thomas in the county of Donegall. John first of Gartincaber's second son was Walter, who had no male-issue. John had an illegitimate son, Thomas who went to Ireland, and had one son, John, whose only son, George in Glenmaqueen had four sons, John, William, Matthew, and George, who reside mostly in the counties of Derry, and Donegall. George of Gartincaber's second son George was father to Thomas Buchanan in Creithael in Buchanan-parish. He had another son, Andrew father to George, and Patrick Buchanan in Ledrish in Buchanan-parish. George's third son was Thomas, who purchased in heritage a part of Gartincaber. He had two sons, William, who acquired Ardoch in Kilmaronock-parish, and George late of Gartincaber, who left four sons, John now of Gartincaber, Thomas merchant in England, Dugal and Robert. George's fourth son was Andrew, who had three sons, two of these having gone to

Ireland, and one residing in Drymen parish. George had also a daughter married to Andrew Buchanan of Gartachairn.

Thomas of Carbeth's second son of the second marriage was Walter, who obtained a tack of Ballendeorn in Buchanan-parish. He had one son John, who, from his low stature, was termed John Beg, or Little John. His posterity reside in the parishes of Balfron and Drymen. The third son of that marriage was William, who obtained a tack of Blairnabord in the parish of Drymen; his progeny reside mostly in Blairnabord as yet, as also in other parts of the parishes of Drymen and Buchanan. There is also one Archibald, a great-grandchild of the said William, residing in good circumstances in Virginia; and there is a brother of his in the Dutch service. The fourth of these sons was Archibald, who had one son, John, a writer in Edinburgh, whose posterity for any thing I can discover reside in Mid-Calder. The fifth son was Robert, who had only one illegitimate son, ancestor to some Buchanans for some time in Sallochy, now in other parts of Buchanan parish.

The next Cadet to these mentioned of the family of Carbeth is, Walter Buchanan first of Boquhan, of the time and manner of whose descent off that of Carbeth, I am not well assured. I find him obtain a charter from Sir John Buchanan of that Ilk, of the lands of Meikle Boquhan, being designed Walter Buchanan Drumquhasle. The said charter is dated in the year 1623. He had two sons, Thomas of Boquhan, and John, who purchased Sheneglish in Kilmaronock paroch. Thomas of Boquhan had one son who left issue, being Walter, who married Lennox of Branshogle's daughter, by whom he had one son Thomas, who hath three sons, Walter, John, and George. James, and ~~William~~ Lennox dying without ~~issue~~, the interest of Branshogle fell to Thomas of Boquhan's eldest son Walter, now in possession thereof. John of Sheneglish had four sons, Walter who had one son, Walter now of Sheneglish. George who purchased Ledrishmore, leaving one son, William, now of Ledrishmore: John's third son was James, who acquired Middle Catter: His fourth son was John, in Little Tullichewn.

The next Cadet of the said family is Walter, second son to Thomas, sixth or last of that name of Carbeth. He had one son James Buchanan, portioner of Cairnock in Dundaff.

The next Cadet to this Walter is Moses Buchanan of Glyns, brother to the late John Buchanan of Carbeth. He left only one daughter married to Dennieftoun of Colgrain.

The last cadet is Moses Buchanan of Glyns, brother to the present Buchanan of

Carbeth, who is married to a daughter of Mr Archibald Govean of Drumquhasle, by whom he hath issue.

Buchanan of Carbeth bears Buchanan; and for distinction, a Dagger in the Lyon's dexter paw, pointed upward, or towards the chief, proper. For Crest, a Helmet suiting his station. Motto, *Audacia et Industria*.

An Account of the Family of LENNY.

THIS Family of Lenny is descended from the most ancient cadet which came off the family of Buchanan; and altho' by that means the most remote from the principal Family, is nevertheless preferable to some other cadets of later extract, in regard that Lenny descended at two different times off Buchanan, of which the first being son to Buchanan, married the heiress of Lenny, as did the Laird of Buchanan a second heiress; as also in regard Buchanan, now of Lenny, Represents the old family of

Lenny of that Ilk, which is reported to have been a family of good repute, as far as tradition may be relied on. But there are as few documents relating to, as there are men of that old family extant in this age, to clear this, or any other matter concerning the same. I have perused a Genealogical Manuscript of that family in the Laird of Lenny's hands, which afferts, that the Lennys, while owners of that estate, had no charters of the same, but a large Sword, with which, it seems, he, who first of that name acquired these lands, had performed some signal atchievement, being a means of his first advancement. This, and a relick, being one of St Fillan's teeth, were held in such veneration, that whoever had those two in possession, presumed he had a very good right to that estate. A tenure much like to that which is recorded of the estate of Arundel in England, that in old times whoever by whatsoever means obtained possession of Arundel-castle, was instantly acknowledged to have a sufficient title to that estate. Nor was this case of Lenny any way singular; a great many others in these more ancient times being circumstantiate after the same manner, as judging it a derogation to follicite for, or in the least rely upon written evidents for security of the possession of their estates, and far more honourable, and suitable to their inclinations, to maintain their poffeffion by their Sword, by whatever means acquired. As this fymbolical charter of St Fillan's tooth was a relick much efteemed by the ancient Lairds of Lenny; fo another relick of the fame Saint, being one of his hands embalmed, was no lefs valued by fome of our Scottifh Kings, in thofe times of ignorance and fuperftition; it being recorded of this laft by fome of our Hiftorians, that the night before the battle of Bannockburn, the Scottifh Nobles and principal officers having a conference with King Robert Bruce concerning the manner of ordering the battle next day, and being folicitous of the event, in regard of the greatnefs of the Englifh army, being more than quadruple the number of theirs, fuddenly a filver box, which was in a coffer in the tent, gave a very great clink; whereupon the King's chaplain ran to the box, and finding St Fillan's hand therein, being ordinarily kept in that box, however, cried there was a great miracle wrought, in regard he had left the hand in the King's Palace in Dunfermline, having taken only with him the empty box, left that precious relick fhould by fome mifadventure be loft, and that at that inftant the hand had miraculoufly of its own accord come, and inclofed itfelf in the box, which, in his opinion, prefaged good fuccefs to King Robert and his army in the enfuing battle. This miracle, tho' invented by the ready wit of the chaplain, being divulged through the army, added no less courage than hope to them of the prosperous event of the approaching engagement.

The first son of the Laird of Buchanan I find upon record, who married the heiress of Lenny, was Allan, second son to Gilbert Laird of Buchanan, in the reign of King Alexander III. There is no charter, or other document in Lenny's hands, that any manner of way does testify this first marriage; any discovery I obtained thereof being collected from an ancient manuscript register of the Earls of Lennox, and his vassals charters, among the records of Dunbartonshire, in which I found a charter by Malcolm Earl of Lennox, upon resignation of Allan of Lenny, in the Earl's hands, of the lands of Drumquhasle, in favour of John, son to the said Allan, for payment of four pennies of blench-duty, if demanded. This charter (as do divers other old ones) wants date, but by a subsequent charter is found to be in the reign of King Alexander III. as appears by a charter by Gilmichael MacEdolf of Wester Cameron, termed therein Cameron Timpane, to Malcolm MacEdolf his son, of the lands of Gartachorrans, dated in the year 1247. In which charter Allan is one of the witnesses, by designation of Allan Buchanan de Lenny. Drumquhasle seems to have been the patrimonial estate got by this Allan, at the time he came off the family of Buchanan, or from his father at the time of his marriage with the heiress of Lenny.

Allan's successor, as is evident by the above charter, was called John, whose successor was named Walter, as seems to appear by letters of compromise, or pacification, betwixt Maurice, and John Drummond, and Alexander Monteith, and others of that name, for the slaughter of William, John, and James Monteiths, brethren to the said Alexander, by these Drummonds. Among others whom the Monteiths include of their friends, in the said letters, is mentioned Walter Buchanan their uncle, who behoved to be either Laird of Buchanan, or Lenny; in regard there were not any other families of note of the name of Buchanan extant in that age, except those of Buchanan and Lenny. But the traditional account most generally asserted is, that the said John's son was called also John, who had a son, his successor of the same name; which last John, having no male-issue, Janet his daughter, and heiress, was married to John, the second of that name, Laird of Buchanan, as testifies a charter in the publick archives by King Robert III. in favour of John de Buchanan, and Janet de Lenny his spouse, of the barony of Pitwhonidy, dated in the year 1393. These lands of Pitwhonidy seem to have been a part of Buchanan's old estate, in regard there is no evident relating thereto extant before this one, granted in favour of Buchanan, nor is there so much as any traditional account of any lands belonging to the old family of Lenny, except those of that name in Perth-shire, and a part of those so designed in Mid-Lothian. I was for sometime surprized at Lenny's retaining the surname of Buchanan, and not rather having assumed the surname, and arms of Lenny; but observe the reason to be very plain, that the Laird of Buchanan, having married the second heiress of Lenny, would not, upon that account, change his surname; and John, his third son, who succeeded to that estate, being always termed Buchanan during his father's life-time, neglected to assume that of Lenny, as did his successors in all time thereafter, partly moved thereto, as is reported, by some disobligation put upon them by the survivors of the name of Lenny. By the death of John Laird of Buchanan's eldest son at the battle of Vernoil, and in consequence thereof, by Walter the second son's succeeding to the estate of Buchanan, the estate of Lenny was conveyed in favour of John, the third son, ordinarily designed John of Ballacondachy, being a farm-room in the barony of Buchanan, given by his father to him for patrimony, before the eftate of Lenny was conveyed in his favour. Tho' this John of Ballacondachy continued the line of the prefent Lairds and Family of Lenny, and as fuch is mentioned in the Genealogical Tree of the Family of Buchanan; yet neither by this, nor any other evident in Lenny's hands, can there be an account obtained of this John's marriage, nor whether at Allan Buchanan, his firft fon's marriage with the heirefs of Lenny, or at Buchanan's marriage with the fecond heirefs of the fame, Keir married the co-heirefs, and with her obtained the half of the eftate; that marriage of Keir by the traditional account, and with much more probability, feeming to have been at the firft of thefe two junctures. Neither is it evident by any document I could find in Lenny's hands, by what means Keir obtained the fuperiority of Lenny's half of that eftate, in regard of his being married (as is generally reported) to the younger of the fifters, or co-heireffes. All that is offered for clearing of this point, being a traditional narration, that Walter Laird of Lenny in the beginning of the reign of King James IV. had committed fome frivolous crime, which was conftrued in thefe times to be a kind of facrilege, for which being cited before the next ecclefiaftical judge, he difobeyed all citations given upon that account, till in the end being excommunicated for his contumacy, he was thereafter delated to the civil magistrate; but giving as little obedience to the one, as to the other, he was prosecuted with the utmost rigour, being not only denounced rebel, but as is reported, also forfeited, the gift of which, or more probably, of Lenny's life-rent escheat, was purchased by Keir, who reaped no advantage thereby, Lenny retaining possession of his estate by force, till in the end one Shaw in Camsmore, an intimate comrade of Lenny's, was influenced, (as the story goes) by Keir either to apprehend, or kill Lenny. Shaw, judging the first somewhat impracticable, resolved upon the last method, which he performed while at the hunting with Lenny, by stabbing him behind his back, and killing him. After which Keir obtained possession of Lenny's estate, which he did not enjoy long. For Shaw meeting Lenny's Lady and children upon a time in a very mean condition, and the Lady upbraiding him with her husband's murder, he was possessed with such horror of the fact, and detestation of Keir, his influencer, as put him upon the resolution of expiating Lenny's murder by that of Keir, which he accordingly performed by killing of Keir, as he met him occasionally near Stirling. After which Keir's and Lenny's successors adjusted the matter so, that upon Lenny's holding his estate of Keir, he should pass from any other demand he had upon the same, which being then agreed to, continues so to this day.

John first Laird of Lenny of the second line, and ancestor to the present Lenny, was succeeded by Andrew his son, as appears by * charter by James II. in the year 1458, in favour of the said Andrew Buchanan of Lenny, of the barony of Pitwhonidy, with the lands of Culenchard and Ledunchard in life-rent, and to John Buchanan his son in fee, and their heirs-male; which failing, to Patrick Buchanan of that Ilk, his other son, and his heirs-male; which failing, to Archibald, Walter, George, and Gilbert, Lenny's other sons, and their heirs-male; which failing, to Lenny's other heirs whatsoever: A very strange kind of a tailzie; Buchanan, and two of his sons, tho' he and Lenny were but cousin-germans, being preferred in that charter of tailzie to four of Lenny's sons, and his brother, if these last mentioned were legitimate. At what time these lands contained in the above charter went off from that family cannot be determined; neither is there any necessity of inserting any more of the charters of that family, some of the immediate successors of Andrew last mentioned, not being entered; so that any charters which are extant of some of the latter

---

* Charta penes Buchanan de Lenny.

Lairds, are so very late as there is not the least occasion of mentioning them. I shall therefore give account of the Laird's marriages, and of the cadets of that family, as mentioned in a manuscript collected from the charters, and other documents in the hands of Lenny, with a Genealogical Tree of his family, composed from that manuscript; it being asserted by both, that Andrew, second Laird of Lenny, was married to a daughter of Lockhart of Barr, by whom he had John his successor. He had also other four sons; Archibald, Walter, George, and Gilbert.

John, third Laird of Lenny, was married to Mushet of Burnbank's daughter, and had by her Patrick his successor; which Patrick married Semple of Fulwood's daughter, by whom he had Walter his successor, who was killed by Shaw of Camsmore. He married a daughter of Halden Laird of Glenegeis, by whom he had John his successor, who married the Earl of Monteith's daughter. This John, in company with Patrick second of that name Laird of Buchanan, with a good many others of best account of his name, was killed at the battle of Flowden, anno 1513.

To John succeeded Robert, who was first married to Graham of Inchbrachie's daughter, relict of the Laird of Ardkinglass. He had, for a second Lady, Mushet of Burnbank's daughter.

Robert, first of that name Laird of Lenny, was succeeded by Robert the second of that name, who was married to Stirling of Ardoch's daughter, by whom he had, Robert his successor, and John his second son, grand-father to the present Lenny.

Robert, third of that name Laird of Lenny, was married to a daughter of Campbell of Lawers, by whom he had one son, Robert who died unmarried, and one daughter married to Captain Archibald Campbell son to the Laird of Dunstaffnage, being mother to Doctor John Campbell of Torry.

Robert, the second of that name, had also another daughter, who was married to Mr Donald Campbell, a son of the above mentioned family, who had nine daughters; the eldest of which was married to Baron MacCorcadel, the second to MacDugal of Gallanach, the third to MacLauchlan of Kilchoan, the fourth to MacLean of Shouna, the fifth to Campbell of Inchdrenich, the sixth to Campbell of Fasnacloich, the seventh to Campbell of Fincrocan, the eighth to Reid of Achaorran, the ninth to Campbell of Feyard.

Robert, last of that name Laird of Lenny, dying without issue, he was succeeded by John Buchanan, his cousin-german, son to John Buchanan, second son to Robert, second of that name Laird of Lenny, his mother being Stirling of Ardoch's daughter. John Laird of Lenny last mentioned, married the Laird of MacPharlane's daughter, by whom he had two sons; John his eldest son, who married Lennox of Woodhead's daughter, and died without issue: His second son was Henry, who upon his brother's death succeeded to the estate of Lenny. He was first married to a second daughter of Buchanan of that Ilk. He married, secondly, a daughter of Campbell of Lawers, having by both a numerous issue.

The first cadet of the family of Lenny, according to the Genealogical manuscript of that family, was Walter, third son to Andrew Laird of Lenny. This Walter obtained a beneficial tack of Mochastel in Callender-paroch from Balfour Lord Burleigh's ancestor, then proprietor thereof. Walter's son was called Andrew, whose son Patrick had one son Alexander.

This Alexander had two sons, John his eldest, and Walter, who obtained from his father the wadset or feu-right of the lands of Glenny in Monteith; his eldest brother John, having preferred the tack of Mochastle to the heritage of Glenny, possessed the same, allowing his brother that of Glenny. The last of that race who possessed the same, was Captain James Buchanan grand-child to the above Walter, who lived a good part of his time, and died a Captain in Douglas's Regiment in France: Being never married, he sold his interest of Glenny to Walter Graham of Gartmor's family. Captain James had an uncle called Alexander, who obtained from Cunninghame of Drumquasle a beneficial tack of the lands of Gartachairn in Drymen-paroch.

This Alexander had two sons, Andrew, who feued Gartachairn from my Lord Napeir then proprietor thereof, and George. Andrew of Gartachairn had two sons, Alexander his successor, and George late Baillie in Glasgow. Alexander of Gartachairn had three sons, George now of Gartachairn, Thomas Buchanan maltman in Glasgow, and Andrew taylor in the said town. Baillie George had four sons, George his eldest son maltman, Andrew, Neil, and Archibald merchants in Glasgow.

George, second son to Alexander first in Gartachairn had three sons, John who went abroad, Alexander and William residing in Edinburgh.

John in Mochastel had two sons, Robert his eldest, and Archibald ancestor to Buchanan of Torry. Robert had one son Walter, who had two sons, John and Arthur. John the eldest sold his tack of Mochastel, and acquired afterwards the lands of Arnpryor, Straithyre, and a part of the lands of

Buchanan. He had one son, Mr Robert, who also had one son, Francis Buchanan present Arnpryor.

Walter in Mochastel's second son Arthur purchased the lands of Auchlessy. He had six sons that came to age; the eldest John who went abroad, the second James now of Auchlessy, the third Walter now Caornach, the fourth Robert who left one son James maltman in Dunblane, the fifth George who left no issue, the sixth Alexander of Dulater residing at present in his ancestor's old possession Mochastel.

John first of that name in Mochastel's second son Archibald had two sons, John of Torry, and Robert, who was killed by the English, and left one son Archibald. John of Torry had two sons, Archibald of Torry, and Robert. Archibald of Torry had three sons, John present Torry, Archibald who left no issue, and Andrew who had one son James. John of Torry's second son Robert had five sons that came to age, the eldest whereof is John of Greathil in St Ninian-paroch. His other sons were Archibald, Charles, Alexander, and Duncan. There are also of the family of Mochastel some of the Buchanans residing in Straithyre, with others in the parishes of Calender and Kilmadock.

The second cadet of Lenny's family was John Moir, or Meikle John, ancestor to

Doctor John Buchanan, who left no iſſue, and to John Buchanan in Toddellburn, with divers others about Dunblane and Straith-allan.

The third cadet of Lenny's family is Sir John of Scots-craig, ſecond ſon to Robert firſt of that name Laird of Lenny. His eſtate of Scots-craig went with a daughter of his to a ſon of the Earl of Marr, and ſince has been conveyed to divers others.

The ſame Robert had a third ſon, James merchant in Edinburgh, who purchaſed the eſtate of Shirrachal in Orkney. He had one ſon, Thomas, who ſold Shirrachal, and had three ſons, Arthur for whom he purchaſed the eſtate of Sound, John for whom he acquired the eſtate of Sandſide, and William to whom he left the eſtate of Ruſsland; all whoſe progeny is extinct, except one daughter left by Thomas late of Sandſide, being heireſs of that eſtate.

By any account I could obtain, from the two ſons of Robert, ſecond of that name Laird of Lenny, are deſcended the greateſt part of theſe Buchanans reſiding in the pariſhes of Campſay and Bathernock. One of theſe two ſons, whoſe name was John, having firſt ſettled in Bancleroch, now Kirktoun, in Campſay-pariſh, and having gone thence to Bankeir, had three ſons, whereof the eldeſt was Gilbert, whoſe poſterity continued in and near Bankeir; his ſecond ſon was William who came to Blairſketh in Bathernock. This William had a ſon of the ſame name, father to William Buchanan merchant in Glaſgow, and Gilbert Buchanan of Bankel preſent Dean of Guild in Glaſgow.

There is alſo deſcended off this family, Walter Buchanan late of Orchard, who dying without heirs-male his intereſt devolved upon his eldeſt daughter, and was conveyed by her to William Aitken merchant in Glaſgow her huſband, and now proprietor thereof. Orchard had another daughter married to Andrew Gray of Criſtoun, near Glaſgow; another to Robert Alexander merchant and late Baillie in Glaſgow; and another unmarried.

There are alſo cadets of Lenny's family of a late extract, called Alexander Roy's progeny, being only a ſmall number of the vulgar ſort reſiding for the moſt part in Calender-pariſh.

The above-mentioned being all the cadets according to the manuſcript frequently ſpoken of, or any other documents I could obtain, deſcended off the family of Lenny, who retain the ſurname of Buchanan; I ſhall, in the next place, mention thoſe of other denominations deſcended from the ſame.

The firſt, and moſt conſiderable of this laſt ſort are the MACWATTIES. The anceſtor of theſe was Walter, ſon to John, ſecond of that name Laird of Lenny. This Walter was ordinarily termed " Watty in Callintuy," being the name of the place of his residence. He had a son called John, who came to the Lennox, and resided in the parish of Luss. John, according to the ordinary custom of those, and even of the present times among the Highlanders, had his surname changed into a patronimical one, derived from his father's proper name, being thence termed John MacWatty. He having nine sons, who all had issue, was the cause of that new name's becoming in a small process of time pretty numerous. Some families of these MacWatties, after the conflict of Glenfroon, having left the parish of Luss, settled in the parishes of Killearn, and Strablain; these, quitting that of MacWatty, re-assumed their right surname of Buchanan, and those of Lenny's family in both the above parishes, with some few in the parish of Campsy descended off these MacWatties, so many of them at least as continued in the parish of Luss, and other Highland places, retain the surname of MacWatty yet, the principal person of these being Alexander MacWatty in Glenmacoirn in Luss parish. There are some of these MacWatties in the shire of Argyle, and in the county of Tyrone in Ireland.

The second cadet of this last sort descended off the family of Lenny, are, the

MacAldonichs, deriving that surname from a certain person of Lenny's family named Muldonich, being an ancient Scottish Christian name, and in some parts of the Highlands in use yet, from whose name his progeny obtained the surname of MacAldonichs, or contracted as above, and most ordinarily exprest. At what time the ancestor of these came off the family of Lenny cannot be well determined; however they always own themselves to be of the said family, and the more to remove any scruple thereanent, have mostly now, as did some of their friends the MacWatties, as already observed, assume the surname of Buchanan. So that the old surname of MacAldonich will in a short time turn into desuetude.

The last cadet of those of other denominations, descended off the family of Lenny, was the ancestor of those termed MacRobs, so denominated from one of that family called Robert, by contraction Rob, whence his progeny obtained this surname. The number and character of these are very inconsiderable, they residing mostly in the parishes of Callender, and Kilmadock, as do the MacAldonichs, mostly in the lower parts of Straithern, and Straithallan, and some other places of Perth-shire. And these are all the cadets of other denominations I could discover to be descended off the family of Lenny.

The Armorial Bearing of Buchanan of Lenny, is Buchanan, being a Lyon rampant Sable, armed, and langued Gules, within a double Treffure, flowered and counter-flowered, with *Flower-de-luces* of the second, quartered with thofe of Lenny, being Sable, a Cheveron betwixt two Bear heads erazed in chief, and a Boar head as the former in Bafe, Argent; muzzled Gules; On the chief point of the Cheveron a Cinque Foil of the firft; firft and third Buchanan; second and fourth Lenny. Creft, a Helmet fuiting his quality. Motto, *Nobilis eft Ira Leonis.*

AN

Account of the Family of

AUCHNEIVEN.

THE firft of this family was John, third son to Gilbert Laird of Buchanan, who firft affumed the furname of Buchanan, whofe eldeft fon was Sir Maurice, his fecond Allan firft of Lenny, and the third John, firft of Stainiflet, who is inferted witnefs in a charter by Malcolm Earl of Lennox, to Patrick Lindfay of the lands of Bonneil. He is alfo, with John Napeir of Kilmahew, Adam of Faflane, father to Walter of Faflane, afterward Lord of Lennox, and Maurice Galbraith, witness to a charter by the same Earl to the said Patrick, of his being Tosheagor, or principal Forrester of Lennox *. And tho' these charters want dates, yet by comparing them with those having dates granted to some of these witnesses themselves, and others in which they were witnesses, they are found to be in the latter part of the reign of King Alexander III. So that Gilbert, being the very first found by any manner of record to have assumed the name of Buchanan, and he having flourished in the latter part of the reign of King Alexander II. and a good part of the reign of King Alexander III. in which last the above mentioned John, is inserted witness by designation of Buchanan, he cannot, with any shadow of reason, be presumed, any other than son to the said Gilbert, it being clear to a demonstration there were no others designed by that surname at that time, but himself, and his children; all others descended before, as the MacAuselans, MacMillans, and MacColmans, having either retained the ancient surname, or assumed others, in use at this present time. And as it is fully evident, the ancestor of this family was a son of the Laird of Buchanan, by the continued acquiescence of the Lairds of

---

* Chartulary of Dunbarton-shire.

Buchanan, altho' there were no other evidence to that purpofe; fo hence it appears, that the pretenfion of Auchneiven's being a cadet of Lenny, can by no means be admitted, in regard Allan, who firft married the heirefs of Lenny, and the above mentioned John were cotemporaries, and both witneffes in the charter mentioned, and fome others, by defignations not in the leaft infinuating any thing at the latter's being either fon, or cadet of the former. Auchneiven's anceftor feems to have poffeffed a confiderable intereft in Dunbarton-fhire, being not only proprietor of Stainifl-, Auchinreoch, and fome other moor-lands near the town of Dunbarton, but alfo of a great deal of ground next adjacent to the town itfelf, known as yet by the name of Buchanan's Aikers; likewife a part of the ground upon which many of the houfes of that town are built, there being paid groundmail for the fame by the builders and poffeffors. Thofe lands continued with this family till about the year 1590, when John Buchanan of Stainiflet fold them with all his other intereft in and about Dunbarton, being moftly now in poffeffion of Sir James Smollet, as are alfo the moft ancient evidents that pertained to that family; all now in cuftody of the prefent Auchneiven, being only the evidents of Auchneiven, and Lecher, of a more modern date than thofe of Stainiflet.

The first of those of Lecher I find upon record, is a resignation by Neil MacIlroy heritor thereof, of the lands of Lecher and pertinents, to George Buchanan of Stainiflet, dated in the year 1482. The said right, with that of the lands of Ibert, for good service done, and to be done, was confirmed to the said George by William Lord Graham, in the year 1489.

George's successor was Patrick, whose successor was called Thomas, as appears by charter of the two parts of Lecher by William Earl of Montrose, to Thomas Buchanan, son and heir to the deceased Patrick Buchanan of Stainiflet, and Elizabeth Edmonstone, daughter to the Laird of Duntreath his spouse, in life-rent, and their heirs in fee, dated in the year 1558.

Thomas's successor was John, who sold Stainiflet, as appears by precept of Clare Constat, in his favour, as heir to Thomas his father, by John Earl of Montrose, of the lands of Lecher, dated in the year 1581. This John had two sons, Walter his successor, and Dugal, who went to Ireland, some of whose posterity having returned, reside at Linlithgow, and Queens-Ferry; and others remained in Ireland. Of this Dugal is descended William Buchanan gardener in Glasgow.

To John succeeded Walter, who was married to Edmonstone of Balleun's daughter, as appears by a seasin in her favour, in life-rent, of the lands of Lecher, by John Buchanan, father to this Walter, dated in the year 1628, by whom he had John his successor, as is clear by charter in his favour by James Earl of Montrose afterward Marquis, of an annuity of three chalder of victual, payable irredeemably out of the lands of Auchneiven, dated in the year 1630; as also a precept of Clare Constat, by James Marquis of Montrose, with seasin thereon, to the above-mentioned John, of the lands of Auchneiven, dated anno 1668. Walter of Auchneiven's second son was Walter, late deacon of the bakers in Glasgow, who had four sons, John Buchanan merchant in Glasgow, Walter maltman there, George baker there, and Thomas Buchanan master of a ship belonging to the said town. He had also two daughters, Marion married to Robert Graham merchant in Glasgow, and Janet married to George Currie merchant in that city. John of Auchneiven was married to Elizabeth Crawfurd daughter to John Crawfurd portioner of Partick. He had by her John his successor, and Walter Buchanan writer in Glasgow who acquired the lands of Teucherhill in the parish of Meikle Govan.

John of Auchneiven last-mentioned was married to Graham of Killearn's daughter, and had by her one son, John Buchanan present Auchneiven, who is married to

Graham of Killearn's daughter; and one daughter unmarried.

The Buchanans of the third of Lecher are cadets of Auchneiven; as also John Buchanan baker and late deacon-conveener in Glasgow, father to John Buchanan late deacon of the bakers there, who had three daughters, the eldest married to William Anderson merchant in Glasgow, the second to George Danzeil wright in the said town, the third to Mr Robert Buchanan of Arnpryor, whose daughter is married to the Laird of Bardowie.

Also the ancestor of those Buchanans lately in Borland, now in other parts of Buchanan-paroch, was a cadet of this family. James Buchanan uncle to these last mentioned, went to Ireland in the beginning of the reign of King Charles II. John, eldest son to the said James, being a person of good parts and education, became Lord Mayor of Dublin, and upon that account obtained the honour of Knighthood; he purchased a good estate near that city, of which his son is now in possession, who, with some other sons of his and a brother, and others of this family, resides in Linster, and other places of that Kingdom.

The latest cadet of Auchneiven's family is John, son to the deceast Walter Buchanan writer in Glasgow, being the present Auchneiven's cousin-german, and present proprietor of Teucherhill.

A BRIEF ACCOUNT OF BUCHANAN of MILTOUN; also of BUCHANAN of CASHILL, ARDUILL, and SALLOCHIE.

ALTHO' the defcent of the anceftors of thofe I am to treat of in this place be more late off the family of Buchanan, than that of fome others already mentioned, neverthelefs having obtained no manner of written document tending to the illuftration of their defcent, but only a traditional account of the fame, by which means there cannot be very much advanced concerning them; I have chofen for that reafon, not only to treat of them jointly, but alfo to place the account of them after that of others, whofe defcent can be cleared by written, and therefore more convincing documents or authorities.

As for the family of Miltoun, neither I nor any other of the name of Buchanan I had ever occafion of converfing with, had the least knowledge of, or correspondence with any such family; all found upon record concerning the same, being a description or blazon of the Armorial Bearing of Mr Patrick Buchanan, son to Buchanan of Miltoun, a cadet of Buchanan of that Ilk, mentioned in Mr Nisbet's Treatise of Heraldry lately published, in which is given no manner of account of that Family's Genealogy, but only what relates to the above mentioned Gentleman's bearing, as a cadet thereof. So that all I can offer concerning this family is founded upon a traditional account I had from a certain gentleman, who was an officer in the Laird of Buchanan's Regiment in the year 1645, at which time that Regiment being in garrison in Inverness; one Colin Buchanan of Miltoun of Peatty, a gentleman of good repute, and whose interest lay within a few miles of the town of Inverness, kept very much correspondence with Buchanan and his officers, while in garrison in that town. He was descended, by any thing can be collected from any account given them out of Maurice Buchanan's son, who was Treasurer to the Dauphiness of France in the reign of King James I. And tho' there can be no account had of any of that family's having correspondence with any other of their name in these more southern parts, in which the same is most numerous these many years by-

T

gone, neverthelefs it is very prefumeable, this family is ftill in being; at leaft it feems, by their arms, to have been fo not long ago, it being evident the late Laird of Buchanan changed his Motto from *Audaces juvo*, into *Clarior hinc Honos* in the latter part of his time, to which laft that of Mr Buchanan, Miltoun's fon, plainly alludes, his bearing Buchanan, within a double border, Gules, charged with eight crefcents, Argent, with a Rofe in Creft, flipped, Gules; Motto, *Ducitur hinc Honos*. The Buchanans of the Ifle of Sky feem to be defcended of Miltoun.

The anceftor of the Buchanans of Cafhill was always reputed an immediate cadet of the family of Buchanan; the firft of thefe having obtained the lands of Cafhill from the Laird of Buchanan, by which that family was defigned, and retained poffeffion thereof for fome ages, untill about the latter part of the reign of Queen Mary, Robert Buchanan of Cafhill, and Walter Buchanan his fon, fell at variance with Thomas Buchanan in Arduill, their kinfman and neighbour, in which conteft the faid Thomas and his fon Duncan were both killed by thofe of Cafhill, for which caufe the Laird of Buchanan difpoffeffed them of Cafhill; whereupon Walter Robert's eldeft fon went to Ireland, where divers of his pofterity remain yet. One of thefe having come thence, and settled in Argyle-shire, was ancestor to William Buchanan of Glens, who hath brethren, and some other relations in that country. William's two sons are, John Buchanan younger merchant in Glasgow, and James merchant in Tarbet. Robert of Cashill had another son, who went to Braidalbin, and was officer to one of the Lairds of Glenorchy, the present Earl of Braidalbin's ancestor, from which office his posterity were termed MacAmhaoirs, or Officer's sons, of which there were some lately in Buchanan parish, but now extinct. There are others of that name yet in Braidalbin, but they maintain no correspondence with the name of Buchanan.

The ancestor of the Buchanans in Arduill was Robert Coich, or Mad Robert, well known to be son to Patrick second of that name Laird of Buchanan, in the reign of King James IV. as by uncontroverted tradition is asserted. He was, upon account of his passionate or precipitate temper, termed Coich, or Mad, more especially from two mad adventures of his. The first of which was, his being engaged, under a great penalty, to present a certain malefactor to the Laird of Buchanan, and the person to be presented dying before the prefixed time of presentation, mad Robert's surety was charged to pay the penalty; whereupon he went to the place where the principal was interred, and having digged up his corps, carried the same, and threw it upon the court-table before the Laird and company, protesting thereupon to be free of the penalty for non-production. The Laird, and others present, being somewhat surprised at this uncommon action, frankly acquitted the penalty, lest a greater inconveniency might ensue upon refusal. The second of Mad Robert's adventures was, his killing a gentleman who belonged to the Lord Graham, for no other reason, but that the said gentleman, by his Lord's orders, was going to uplift the rents of certain lands in the upper part of Buchanan-parish, then belonged to the Lord Graham, and which Robert disdained should be possessed by any other than a Buchanan, it being contiguous to their estate.

The Lord Graham, justly incensed at this action, had recourse to Buchanan for reparation, which seeing not very practicable to be had of the actor, and Buchanan having satisfied my Lord of his not being accessory to that affair, my Lord was obliged for preventing future inconveniencies, to make an exchange of the lands in Buchanan-parish, with those of Bamoir, lying near to his other estate, and which then pertained to Buchanan.

Mad Robert had only one son, called Patrick, who, as his father had that of Coich, had the nickname of Courui, or Champion; the reason of giving that epithet to him being this, The families of Argyle and Buchanan being at variance in this Patrick's time, Argyle and Buchanan, each of them attended with a select party of horsemen, according to the custom of these times, met accidentally at Cramond-water, the one coming from, the other going for Edinburgh; these two parties standing upon each bank of the river, and neither of them adventuring to enter the same; at length Patrick Buchanan, mad Robert's son, couching his spear, and setting spurs to his horse, jumped boldly with no little noise into the river, and past thro', Buchanan with his party following him. Upon which Argyle's party stood a little aside, and left the passage clear. Upon Patrick's jumping into the water, Argyle said in Irish to the Laird of Kilmartin, who stood next him, by " St " Martin this is a Massy Champion," in Irish *Courrui*, whence Patrick was always termed afterwards the " Courrui, or Champion." He had four sons, Finlay, Alexander, Thomas, and Patrick. Of Finlay the eldest of these, are descended Alexander Buchanan, father to James Buchanan now of Cremannan, who with his sons, resides in Ireland; Mr James Buchanan who purchased the lands of Cremannan, and having no issue, disponed those lands to the present James of

Cremannan his nephew. The Buchanans, poſſeſſors for a long time of Blairour in Drymen-pariſh, of which John Buchanan in Eaſter Balfunning, Thomas Buchanan ſtabler in Edinburgh, with ſome others, are alſo deſcended off the ſaid Finlay.

Of Alexander, Patrick's ſecond ſon, are deſcended the Buchanans, for ſome time poſſeſſors of Ballantone and Gaidrew of Drumquhaſle.

Of Thomas the third ſon, are deſcended the Buchanans in Weſter Arduill in Buchanan-pariſh, ordinarily termed Donald MacThomas his race.

Of Patrick the fourth ſon of Patrick the Courrui, is deſcended Finlay Buchanan in Laggan of Tyrconnell in Ireland, who has ſome brethren, and other relations of that race, reſiding near Rapho and ſome other places of that Kingdom.

The Buchanans in Sallochy their progenitor, as thoſe others laſt mentioned, conform to any traditional account can be obtained, was an immediate cadet of the family of Buchanan, his name being Gilbert, whence his progeny were termed ordinarily MacGilberts, or Gilbertſons. The firſt poſſeſſion given to this Gilbert was Sallochy in Buchanan-pariſh, of which his poſterity retained poſſeſſion for divers generations. That Family was divided into ſeveral branches, one of theſe continuing in the old poſſeſſion, till of late years, John laſt of this branch died without male-iſſue.

Another branch of this Family went to Kilpatrick, and ſettled in Forgieſtoun, whoſe iſſue having ſpread through ſome other parts of Kilpatrick and Bathernock, any of them who yet exiſt, pretend to be of Lenny's family, ſeeing the greater part of the other Buchanans of theſe, and ſome neighbouring places are really of the family of Lenny. Beſides thoſe already mentioned there are ſome ſmall heritors, with divers farmers of the name of Buchanan in Middle and Eaſt Calder, as alſo near Langholm in the South country, of whoſe deſcent I could obtain no diſtinct account; ſo that I muſt leave the ſame undetermined.

Having compleated (conform to what inſtructions I could obtain) all I deſigned to treat of in relation to the Family of BUCHANAN, and the cadets thereof, who retain that ſurname, I proceed next to the account of the cadets of that Family, who paſs under other denominations, nevertheleſs are known, and own themſelves to be cadets of the Family of Buchanan. And tho' it be an inverſion of the method I have hitherto uſed, I ſhall begin with the moſt ancient, and moſt reputed of theſe.

AN ACCOUNT of the MACAUSELANS.

IN regard the MacAuselans are the only Sept, or Cadets of the Family of Buchanan, tho' of another denomination, that have yet retained the ancient surname by which the family of Buchanan was denominated, I shall therefore treat of these in the first place, as being the eldest cadets, and those of that name in Scotland and Ireland, complexly taken, of the best account of any other cadets of that Family whence they derived their origin. And tho' all the evidents of any considerable antiquity which belonged to the Baron MacAuselan, are long ago lost; so that all that can be obtained for illustration of the descent of that family, is a traditional account of the ancestor of the present family of MacAuselan's being a second son of one of the Anselans, generally reputed to be the first of the three so named, and who first acquired the lands of Buchanan: Yet this account, tho' the exact time of the MacAuselans descent cannot be so exactly known, is fully confirmed by the evidents of the family of Buchanan, by which it is clear to a demonstration, that their surnames for divers ages was MacAuselan, before the assumption of that of Buchanan, and that the Laird of Buchanan, as also the Barons MacAuselan, in all times thereafter owned the descent of that Sept of MacAuselans to be as above related. There was indeed a groundless pretence sometime made of the Baron MacAuselan's being the elder branch of the family, seeing he still retained the ancient Surname, being of the same import with the like pretensions made by the families of MacArture, now Campell, of Strachyr, and MacPherson of Cluny; the first pretending to be descended of the family of Lochow, while Oduin, before the assumption of Campbell; the other from that of MacCattan, before that family assumed the surname of MacIntosh, and so both the more ancient. But as these long ago, upon just grounds, ceded their pretensions; so also have the MacAuselans. Their estate, by any of their documents now extant, was never known to amount to more than the little interest of about twenty pounds Sterling of yearly rent, possest by the late Baron MacAuselan, which seems to have been the patrimony given to the first of that family, upon his descent off MacAuselan Laird of Buchanan. Nor is the supposition less groundless, that Sir Alexander, designed MacAuselan, a Knight of Lennox, who acquired the addition to the Armorial Bearing of Buchanan at the battle of Bauge, might probably have been Baron MacAuselan, and not Buchanan; seeing the latter surname was assumed some considerable time before that atchievement; but this supposition is still further frivolous upon divers accounts, it not being probable, that a person of so little interest could be knighted in such early times, while a great many of the best quality with difficulty obtained that honour; and if any of that family had so done, it is improbable, they would have allowed Buchanan to assume these arms without the least opposition at any time thereafter. It is also evident, that the Lairds of Buchanan used, and were designed by the surname of MacAuselan upon divers occasions, for a long time after the assumption of Buchanan; as for instance, in a charter by the Earl of Lennox to Finlay Campsy, of a part of the lands so named, to which Maurice Laird of Buchanan is witness by designation of MacAuselan, tho' grand-child to Gilbert, who first assumed Buchanan. So that it is no matter of admiration, that the Monks of Pluscarden, who relate the adventure of Sir Alexander, and living at such vast distance from the place of his residence, might happen to design him by his ancient surname, and best known to them, rather than by one so lately assumed.

The first of these MacAuselans I could find upon record is Malcolm MacAuselan, inserted witness in a charter by Malcolm Earl of Lennox of the lands of Luss, in favour of John Laird thereof, in the reign of King Alexander III. This Malcolm, (tho' few or none in these old charters are fully designed) seems to have been Baron Mac-Auselan, the Lairds of Buchanan having generally disused that of MacAuselan before the date of this Charter I find no more of these recorded, but a traditional account of one MacBeth Baron MacAuselan, a person of uncommon stature and strength, who lived in King Robert the third's time, and seems to have been contempary with Sir Alexander MacAuselan, or Buchannan, which makes the supposition already mentioned the more improbable; Alexander, last Baron MacAuselan, having only one daughter, who was married to a gentleman of the name of Campbell, after whose death she sold her interest to Sir Humphrey Colquhoun of Luss, her superior. The remainder of the Scottish MacAuselans reside mostly in Lennox; but the greatest number, and of best account of that name, reside in the counties of Tyrone, Derry, and Down in the North of Ireland. The ancestors of the principal men of these last were, Andrew, and John

MacAuſelans, ſons of the Baron MacAuſelan, who went out of the Paroch of Luſs to that Kingdom, in the latter part of the reign of King James VI. This Andrew had a ſon called Alexander, upon whom he beſtowed good education, by which means, becoming a prudent active Gentleman, he obtained a commiſſion in the army in time of the Civil Wars in the reign of King Charles I. At the end of thoſe wars, partly by debenture, partly by purchaſe, he acquired the eſtates of Reſh and Ardſtraw in the county of Tyrone. He had two ſons, the eldeſt whereof Oliver of Reſh was one of the moſt ſufficient gentlemen in theſe parts of that Kingdom. In the year 1698, he was High-Sheriff of that county, and influenced moſt of his own name throughout the country to ſettle in and near his own eſtate, which at firſt ſcarce amounting to L. 500 ſterling of yearly-rent, he encreaſed in ſuch a manner as to leave to his ſon a clear eſtate of L. 1500 per annum. He was twice married, and left by both a numerous iſſue. His ſucceſceſſor hath a lodging in a little town called Strabane, where he ordinarily reſides, and for which place he ſerves as Member of Parliament, as his father did for many years. Oliver's brother is called Andrew, having an eſtate called Ardocheyl, who and a great many others of good circumſtances of the name of MacAuſelan reſide in the counties already mentioned.

AN ACCOUNT of the MACMILLANS.

NEXT in antiquity to the MacAufelans is the Sept of the MacMillans; for as the MacAufelans are generally reputed to be defcended of Anfelan firft of that name, Laird of Buchanan, fo the MacMillan's progenitor is known to be fecond fon to Anfelan the third of that name. And tho' the firft be the more ancient, this in refpect of number is by far the moft confiderable of any other cadet of whatever denomination. There is no document, in fo far as I could difcover, in the hands of any of this Sept, to clear their defcent off the Family of Buchanan, but only an uncontroverted tradition, which afferts their anceftor to be brother to the firft who affumed the furname of Buchanan. Which is the more to be relied on, in regard I find the fame to agree in all refpects with a written document lately found, by which that defcent is clearly illuftrated, by a Charter by Malduin Earl of Lennox, to Gilmore fon of Muldonich, of the eſtate of Luſs, in the reign of King Alexander II. in which, Anſelan Laird of Buchanan, with Gilbert his eldeſt ſon, who firſt aſſumed the ſurname of Buchanan, and Methlan his ſecond ſon, anceſtor of the MacMillans, are inſerted witneſſes. So that notwithſtanding a fond opinion pevailed for ſome time, of their obtaining that denomination from their anceſtor's being Bald, in Iriſh *Maoilain*, and thence MacMailans or Bald-man's ſons; yet there is not the leaſt ſhew of reaſon for any ſuch ſuppoſition, after ſuch a clear evident for evincing the contrary, and a more probable reaſon of that denomination is found out. For it is clear, that MacMethlan can be no otherwiſe pronounced in Iriſh than as the MacMillans pronounce their name.

This Methlan is not found to have left his native country, but having a great many ſons, one or two of theſe went to Kyntyre, upon account of a friendſhip then much cultivated betwixt the families of the great MacDonald and Buchanan; the firſt being ſome ſmall time before allied with the principal perſon of the O'Kyans, of which family that of Buchanan was originally deſcended.

By this means Methlan's ſons, being Buchanan's grand-children, met with a very kind reception from the Lord MacDonald, who, for his ſervice, allowed to one of them a considerable estate in Knapdale, in the south west part of Kintyre, who for his heroick atchievements was termed "The Great Mac-Millan of Knap," as is asserted by an account of his family conveyed to my hands by MacMillan of Dunmore in Knapdale, being the principal man of that name, or Sept. Who further adds, that in all times bygone, as also at present, he, and his whole Sept did, and do own themselves to be descended of the family of Buchanan; and that one of his ancestors caused build a very pretty chappel in Kilmorie of Knap, for devotion and burying-place, in which there is a fine cross, with divers other figures neatly cut in stone, and a great many characters engraven thereon scarcely legible, which intimate the founder's name to have been Æneas MacMillan, who, or some of his ancestors, built a large tower in addition to Castlesuin, or MacSuin's Castle; the other part of that castle, according to tradition, being built by the progenitor of the Maxwells, upon his first coming from Ireland, and settling for sometime in Knapdale, being descended of the great Clan MacSuin in Ireland, and then naming the castle MacSuin's Castle, or Castle Suin, as now termed. It seems very probable, that upon MacSuin's leaving that country, and settling in the southern parts, his neighbour MacMillan got possession of the castle, and upon that occasion built the additional tower thereto, which he termed "MacMillan's Tower," as the firſt was denominated from MacSuin. There is a tradition, that a brother of MacMillan, who went firſt from this country with him in the time of the Civil Wars after the death of King Alexander III. went from Argyle-ſhire to Galloway, and ſettled in that country, being the progenitor of the MacMillans of Galloway. The principal man of theſe is MacMillan of Brockloch. There are alſo divers other heritors, and a good number of the vulgar ſort of the name in that country, who acknowledge their origin to be the ſame with the MacMillans of Argyle-ſhire.

The cauſe of the MacMillans loſing the greateſt part of their eſtate in Knapdale, is reported to have been their joining the Lord MacDonald their ſuperior, in aiding James Earl of Douglas in that rebellion againſt King James II. in the year 1455. Another of Methlan's ſons, being brother to MacMillan firſt of Knap, went to Perth-ſhire, and ſettled in Lawers. This MacMillan had ten ſons, whom Chalmers then Laird of Lawers, offering by force to diſpoſſeſs of theſe lands poſſeſſed by them, could not get the ſame effectuated till he obtained from King David II. letters of fire and ſword againſt them, which orders, with the aſſiſtance of the ſheriff of that ſhire, he with the utmoſt difficulty put in execution, obliging moſt of them to abandon that country, and go to their friends in Argyle-shire; whence some of these returning in process of time, obtained a part of their antient possessions in Lawers, and were ancestors to the MacMillans (though much decayed) in Ardownaig, and other parts of Braidalbine. This account is asserted by a brieve (of which I had a transcript) obtained some years ago by one Serjeant MacMillan, descended from the MacMillans of Galloway, in the grey dragoons, from one of the Kings of Arms in England. By this brieve it is further asserted, that it was Methlan himself that settled in Lawers, and that some of his sons went first and settled in Argyle-shire, upon the said letters of fire and sword being put in execution against them by Chalmers, Laird of Lawers.

A son of the great MacMillan's of Knap, who resided in a certain place in Kintyre, called Kilchammag, having killed one Marallach Moir, a certain stranger, of great account, who had settled in these parts, and seems to have been a great oppressor of his neighbours, which gave rise to the contest betwixt him and his neighbour MacMillan; for this he was with six of his friends, his associates in that action, obliged to take boat, and flee to Lochaber, and in this exigency having recourse to the Laird of Locheal, he was received into his protection, and allow-

X

ed poffeffions in his lands. Thefe changing their furnames a little from MacMillan, into that of MacGilveil, to this day retained, fome fmall time after their fettlement in Lochaber, there came one of them, and fettled in a place called Badokennan, at the head of Lochfine in Argyle-fhire, being progenitor to the MacGilveils of Glenera, and Glenfhira, with others in thofe parts.

There was another of the family of Knap, called Archibald Baan MacMillan, who having killed a certain man of repute, was fo clofely purfued upon committing the flaughter, that coming by the Earl of Argyle's refidence, he was forced into the Earl's kitchen for refuge, where the cook, being at the fame time baking, haftily caufed MacMillan to exchange cloaths with him, and fall to bake, which prevented his being apprehended, or difcovered by the purfuers; after which this MacMillan, and his progeny, affumed the furname of MacBhaxters, yet retained by them. Thofe of this name refide moftly in Cowal in Argyle-fhire; the principal man of them being Mivein MacBhaxter in Glendarowal. They term themfelves in Englifh, Baxters. Whether thofe of that name in the more lowland parts be of the fame ftem, (though it feems probable) is more than I can pofitively determine.

The principal perfon of the MacMillans

of Argyle-fhire, is Duncan MacMillan of Dunmore; his intereft and refidence is upon the fouth-fide of Lochtarbet in Knapdale in the fhire of Argyle. There are alfo MacMillans of Coura, and of Clockbrecks, with a very confiderable number of the vulgar fort difperfed through that fhire.

The MacGilveils of Lochaber are moftly planted upon both fides of Locherkek in Lochaber, and live generally under and are clofe dependants upon the Laird of Locheal, and upon all expeditions make up a company of an hundred men, with officers, all of that Sept; not reputed the worft of Locheal's regiment, being generally employed in any defperate enterprize that occurs. Thefe had a contraverfy not many years ago with another Sept, reckoned the moft defperate in all thofe parts termed MacLonvies, dependants alfo of Locheal; thefe laft having murdered one of the MacGilveils, the actors being twelve in number, betook themfelves to the mountains, being outlaws before, upon which fome of the MacGilveils addreft Locheal, telling him, if he would not allow them to revenge this murder upon the actors, they would deftroy the whole Sept without diftinction. Locheal granted their requeft, upon condition, they would only profecute the guilty, which they fo effectually did, that in a few days they either killed or brought to juftice the whole number of them, having not loft one man of their own number, though diverfe were wounded. The principal perfons of this Sept are, the MacGilveils of Murlagan, of Caillie, and Glenpean.

There are a great number alfo of the Mac-Millans in the parifhes of Leud and Armuy in the county of Antrim, and other places of Ireland. The perfons of beft account of them in that Kingdom, is Lieutenant John MacMillan of Killre in the county of Derry, having an eftate of L. 500 fterling per annum; alfo Doctor MacMillan in Lifburn, a perfon of good repute and circumftances; and MacMillan of Glenfeife, and others.

MacMillan of Dunmore carries Buchanan, for diftinction, upon a chief, parted per Barr, Gules, three Mollets, Argent.

AN ACCOUNT of the MACCOLMANS.

THE anceftor of the MacColmans was Colman, third fon to Anfelan, third of that name, and feventh Laird of Buchanan, being brother to Gilbert, who first assumed the surname of Buchanan, and to Methlan, ancestor of the MacMillans. Colman was an ordinary Christian name of old in this kingdom; As for instance, Colman bishop of Lindisfara in Northumberland, and afterwards abbot of Icolmkill, in the reign of King Ferquhard I. Also one of the Scottish nobility, who made an oration against concluding the league with France, in the reign of King Achaius.

The time and cause of this Colman's son's going to Argyle-shire is not very evident, but it seems very probable to be in the reign of King Alexander III. within a short space of his cousin MacMillan's going into that country, whose good reception there might have been the principal motive of his cousin MacColman's following him. The only written document I find relating to the MacColmans is a charter or liserent-right, granted by Duncan MacPharlane of a part of his lands to Christian Cambell, daughter to Sir Colin Cambell of Lochow his Lady, dated in the year 1395, and in the reign of King Robert III. The trustees employed by Sir Colin to see this right compleated, were, John Campbell Dean of Argyle, and John MacColman.

I had an account of the MacColmans transmitted to me by that judicious and learned gentleman, the Reverend Mr Alexander MacColman minifter of Lifmore and Appin, which juftly deferves the greater regard and credit, feeing it exactly agrees with that fent me by MacMillan of Dunmore, near the fame time, in relation to his Clan, as alfo with a written document, which came not to my hands feveral years after receipt of the faid account. That delivered me by Mr Alexander MacColman concerning the origin of that Sept, afferts, that the anceftors of the MacMillans and MacColmans were brethren of him who firft affumed the Surname of Buchanan, though the fame be not teftified by any written document, but by a continued and inviolable tradition handed down from one generation to another, with which they are fatisfied, always chearfully acknowledging their original defcent to be of the family of Buchanan, though they cannot fo very diftinctly tell the manner and circumftances of the fame.

There is alfo a very great evidence of the MacColmans blood-relation to the name of Buchanan, from this, that notwithftanding of the great diftance betwixt the refpective refidences of thefe two names, and upon that account the feldomnefs of their mutual converfe or correfpondence with one another, yet they have the fame inviolable love and entire refpect for the name of Buchanan, that they have for one another of their neareſt relations, although no preceeding acquaintance or good offices interveen.

Moreover, although the MacColmans have reſided in Mucarn, and other adjacent places in Argyle-ſhire, upwards of 400 years, yet they never gave any bond of Manrie, or other acknowledgement to, or had the leaſt dependance upon any perſon, or Clan in theſe parts, though there is no other Sept in the ſame circumſtances in all thoſe countries, but what are obliged to give ſome ſuch bond or acknowledgement. The principal places in which theſe reſide are, Mucarn, and Benedera loch in upper Lorn, in the ſhire of Argyle. The men of beſt account of them are, Mr John MacColman, ſon to the ſaid Mr Alexander, who hath a little intereſt in Liſmore; alſo another Mr John, brother to the ſame Mr Alexander, who hath ten ſons, all men of good repute.

Beſides theſe, there are ſixty effective men of that name in theſe parts.

There is another Sept of theſe MacColmans in Kintail, in the Earl of Seaforth's land, deſcended of one Mr Murdo, (or as the Iriſh term it) Murcho MacColman, who went from Argyle-ſhire into that country near two hundred years ago. Theſe are termed in Iriſh *MacAmbaiſdirs*, or Maſterſons, but term themſelves in Engliſh Murchiſons, from Murcho their anceſtor's ancient name. The principal man of theſe is

Murchison of Ouchtertyre in the parish of Locheilg in Kintail. These term themselves Dowes when in the Lowlands, and assert the Dowes upon Forth and other places to be descended of them, which Dow of Arnhall the principal person of that name in a great measure owned, there being upon that account great intimacy betwixt the late Laird of Buchanan and him; but both their estates being gone to other families, thro' want of male-issue, that correspondence betwixt the two names is ceased.

AN ACCOUNT of the ORIGIN OF THE SPITTELS.

THERE is no written document to evince the circumstances of the descent of the name of SPITTEL off the Family of Buchanan; tho' an uncontroverted tradition, and a continued pretension by the family of Buchanan to the name of Spittel, and the acquiescence of the generality of that name in the pretensions made to the same, in a great measure clear the origin of the name of Spittel to be, as is generally asserted.

The ancestor of that name was son to Sir Maurice Buchanan of that-ilk, who flourished in the reign of King Alexander III. The reason given of his assuming the surname of Spittel being, that he was admitted into that Order of Knight-hood called Knight-Templars, or Cruch Backs, which Order was instituted about the eleventh Century of the Christian Epocha, for defence of the Christian Religion, more especially of the Temple and Cross of Jerusalem, which, as the Roman Legend has it, was miraculously found by Helena mother to Constantine the first Christian Emperor, after much search made by her orders in and about the place of our Saviour's crucifixion. For preserving it the Empress caused a stately Temple to be built at Jerusalem, and dedicated to the Holy Cross, whence in after ages a great many, if not innumerable, pieces were sent by the Popes of Rome of that supposed cross, for good sums of money, to popish princes and other potentates, insomuch that one of their own writers affirms, that if the thousand part of these pieces had been of the real cross, it would have soon broken the back of Symon of Cyrene in carrying it. However the above Order of knights was chiefly instituted for defence of that cross, and having the portraiture thereof betwixt their shoulders, upon their upper garments, they were thence termed Cross-backs, or Cruch-backs, and from the Temple in which the cross was kept, Templars. There were a vast deal of lands throughout Christendom mortified to this Order, for keeping up hospitality, in entertaining such poor pilgrims, as in those days of superstition were going to the holy land, to perform their devotions; whence their Order obtained the name of the Hospitallers, and their lands Spittels, many of which yet retain that name. And though the Templars and they seem to have been originally of one Order, yet they afterwards were distinct, the Templars being afterwards known by the name of Knights of St John, afterwards Rhodes, and now of Malta. However that be, the Hospitallers became in process of time so scandalous for their wicked lives, that the Pope, upon the Pope's pretence thereof, or as some say, instigated by Philip the Fair King of France, who had formed a design of getting his sons invested in a great part of these knights lands, in the year 1330, sent his positive orders or Bulls to exterminate this whole Order, and sequestrate their lands. These orders were for most part observed, most of these knights being without mercy put to the sword, except such as were preserved by some potent friends. The Pope shortly repenting his orders in giving so many lands devoted once for sacred, to be now bestowed on secular uses, recalled his promise of giving the same to the French King and others, and thereafter mortified these lands to the Knights of St John above-mentioned. Nevertheless a great part of these lands, in despite of all the Pope could do, were kept by those Laicks who first seized the same, upon the extinction of the Hospitallers.

Among others who kept their part, was this son of Buchanan, who from these Spittel Lands possessed by him, assumed the Surname of Spittel, (his son being Adam Spittel of Ledlewans) besides which, he had Easter Baleun, Blairwhoish, and other lands in the parishes of Strathblane and Killearn, being a considerable estate with the Spittel lands. All which, having made a purchase, as it would seem, of some other place, the said Adam Spittel disponed in favour of his cousin, Walter Laird of Buchanan, by charter dated in the year 1394, and fourth year of the reign of King Robert III.

This Adam was ancestor to Spittel of Leuchart in Fife, which family since that of Buchanan was extinct, has kept no manner of correspondence with any of the name, so that neither by perusal of any of his evidences, nor by converse with the gentleman himself, could I have the opportunity of obtaining a distinct account of the time and manner of his acquiring his present estate, nor the reason of his omitting to marshall any part of Buchanan's Armorial bearing with that he now bears. The most obvious reason to me of his so doing is, that his predecessor being in orders, and by that means prohibited an armorial-bearing, his successors, if they acquired their estate by marriage, assumed those of the family they matched into; if by purchase, arms most suitable to their own inclination. Spittel of Leuchat, being a gentleman of a good estate in the shire of Fife, is the principal person of that Sept; there being, besides those in Fife, diverse of that name in the Straith of Monteath, and other places of this kingdom.

AN ACCOUNT of the ORIGIN OF THE MACMAURICES, MACANDEOIRS, MACCHRUITERS, and MACGREUSICHS.

THERE are two several Septs of these MacMaurices, descended off the Family of Buchanan at two different junctures of time. The ancestor of the first of these Septs, for any thing can be found, was an illegitimate son of Maurice, second of that name Laird of Buchanan, in the latter part of the reign of King Robert I. and beginning of King David II. The first of these I find upon record is, Arthur MacMaurice, being witness in a charter by Eugen MacKessan of Garchel in favour of Celestin MacLachlan, and Arthur MacNeil, of that part of the estate of Garchel called Auchintroig, Gartclach, &c. in the reign of King Robert III. Those of this race reside mostly in the heads of Staithern, and Straithallan, and a few of them in the parish of Callendar. The other Sept of these MacMaurices is descended of one Stooping Maurice, illegitimate son to Walter, fourth of that name Laird of Buchanan, in the reign of King

James III. This Maurice is reported to have been of a very huge stature, but withal so very coarse and unhandsome, as gave occasion for his being little regarded; so that in the time of King James IV. the Laird of Buchanan, with most of his name, having gone to the battle of Flowdon, left Maurice with some other invalids to oversee affairs at home; there being at that time some feud or variance betwixt MacKenzie Laird of Kintail and Buchanan; Kintail thought this a fit time to carry on the same, and sending for that effect one Kenneth MacKenzie, a brother, or some near relation of his own, with eighty men, to harrass Buchanan's lands, these came to a hill betwixt Drymen and Buchanan, in sight of the latter, and being fatigued, lay down among the heather, to take some little repose. Mean while Maurice getting some notice of the advance of his party, went to get surer intelligence, and passing accidentally near the hill upon which the party lay, Kenneth the Captain observing him, went alone to him, to get information of the state of the country. Maurice seeming to take little notice of him, went still on, giving no satisfactory answer to any of his demands; which at length so exasperated MacKenzie, that he gave Maurice a stroak with his sword, not being at the trouble of drawing the same; which was no sooner done, than Maurice gave him such a stroak with his battle-ax, as clave his head to the teeth, whereupon he returned instantly to Buchanan, and alarmed the country. The party in a little time awaking, and finding their Captain in that bad posture, returned with all speed back, without doing the least violence. The place where this action was done yet retains the name of Kenneth's Plain. A grand-child of this Maurice having killed a servant of my Lord Glencairn, who residing in Kilmaronock, was obliged to leave his native country of Buchanan, and go to the village of Scoon north of Tay. His posterity in these parts are termed Morreises or Morrisons. Some of these came thence, and settled upon Forth, betwixt Stirling and Culross, of whom are descended most of the Morisons in those parts. There are also some of this last Sept in the parish of Buchanan, who retain their ancient name of MacMaurice, but very few in number.

The ancestor of the Sept of the MACANDEOIRS is also reputed a cadet of the Family, being reported to be a man of prudence and sagacity, who went to Argyle-shire along with Walter Laird of Buchanan's daughter, married in the reign of King James III. to Campbell Laird of Ardkinglass; who, in regard there was no other of his surname in that country, was thence termed Deoir, or a Sojourner, whence his posterity were termed MacAndeoirs. This Sept reside mostly in a place called Arskeotnish, near the village of Kilmichael in Glasrie, as also upon the side of Lochow in MacLachlan of Inchchonnells's lands. The principal person of these is MacAndeoir of Kilchoan, near Kilmichael in Glasrie. These are dependants of the Laird of Ardkinglass, seeing their ancestor went first there with his lady.

The MacChruiters were of a long time reputed Buchanans, having for diverse ages resided in these lands in the upper parts of the parishes of Buchanan and Callendar, pertaining to the Lairds of Buchanan, but are now wholly decayed in those parts. The few of that name now extant, reside in Argyle-shire, but maintain no correspondence with the name of Buchanan. They obtained their surname from some one of their ancestor's being a harper, and were thence termed MacChruiters or Harpersons.

The MacGreusichs are so denominated from one of their ancestor's being a cordiner, termed in Irish *Greusich*, whence his posterity were thereafter termed MacGhreusichs, or Cordiner-sons. These are of the same origin with the MacAndeoirs; that Buchanan, who went to Argyle-shire with the Laird of Ardkinglass's Lady, being ancestor to both Septs. These MacGreusichs reside in Gaunnans, upon the west side of Lochlong, and betwixt that and Lochgoyle in

Ardkinglass's lands, being, as their friends the MacAndeoirs, dependants on that gentleman. There is also a small number residing upon Lochgoyle-side, termed MacNuyers of Evan Glass, or Gray Hugh's race, of the same origin with the MacGreusichs, and own themselves Buchanans. Those already mentioned are all the cadets of other denominations, directly or immediately descended off the family of Buchanan.

As for the MacWatties, MacAldonichs, and MacRobs, being all those of other denominations descended of the family of Lenny, I made mention of them in the account of that family. These cadets of other denominations descended of the family of Drumikill are the Risks, so named from their ancestor's being born upon the Risks of Drymen. The second cadets of this kind are the MacKinlays, so named from a son of Drumikill, called Finlay; those lately in Blairnyle and about Bellach are of this sort, as also those in Benachra, and about the water of Finn in Luss-parish. The MacKinlays in some other parts of these parishes are MacFarlanes. The third of these cadets was ancestor of the MacTomates, so named from one Thomas, of Drumikill's family. It is also pretended, that the Yules are descended of a son of Drumikill's born upon Yuilday. This pretension is adhered to by some of the name of Yule, by others not.

A BRIEF ACCOUNT

OF THE

Martial Atchievements of the FAMILY of BUCHANAN, and others of that Name, in the publick service of their PRINCE and COUNTRY, and upon other occasions.

THE nature of public history not permitting notice to be taken of all the gallant actions of private men, many very singular atchievements of persons bearing the name of Buchanan, have by that means been passed over in silence, so as to be capable of being vouched no otherways than by private memoirs, or traditional accounts. However, we find from these, that many of the name of Buchanan have not been wanting to signalize themselves in as eminent a manner as any of their station. For not to mention the vigorous efforts and constancy of Anselan, progenitor of that surname, in the quarrel and service of the Scottish King, and nation againſt the Danes, the inveterate enemies of both, which was the cauſe of his obtaining that firſt and ſpendid part of the armorial bearing of Buchanan; our Hiſtorians alſo celebrate the ſignal adherence of Sir Maurice, one of his ſucceſſors, to the intereſt of his country during a great part of the wars managed after the death of King Alexander, a clear evidence of which (as already hinted) is, his not having ſigned the Ragman-Roll, violently impoſed by King Edward the firſt of England upon moſt of any conſiderable account throughout this kingdom, though this gentleman at the time was honoured with Knight-hood, and upon diverſe accounts much preferable to a great many whoſe names are found at that bond of allegiance to the ſaid tyrannical King, who allowed none to refuſe it but ſuch as adventured ſo to do at their utmoſt hazard. Nor was this gentleman's ſucceſſor of the ſame name of leſs bravery and attachment to the welfare and honour of his native country, having accompanied his loyal patron, Malcolm Earl of Lennox, in all the dangerous adventures the Earl was concerned in during the reign of King Robert I. and the minority of his ſon King David II.

The next who ſignalized himſelf, for the honour of his country, was, Sir Alexander, eldeſt ſon to John, ſecond of that name Laird of Buchanan, who procured the addition after-mentioned to the armorial bearing of Buchanan. The circumstances of the adventure in which this gentleman was concerned, and the action by which he signalized himself, being briefly thus.

Charles the first of that name King of France becoming frantic, and his Queen, with the assistance of the Duke of Burgundy, making up a party against Charles the Dauphin, to whom of right the government of the kingdom did belong, and who was therefore the more favoured and supported by his countrymen; this created such jealousy in the adverse party as put them upon all imaginable methods of supporting their own interest; in order whereto they had recourse to Henry the fifth of England, an aspiring young king who had not quite lost thoughts of the old pretension of King Edward III. his great grandfather to that kingdom. He therefore readily accepted of the Queen's invitation not to invade, but to accept in a manner of the kingdom of France, of which the Dauphin, by her influence, was disinherited by his father. Upon the view of these advantages King Henry went to France with a good army, and having defeated the Dauphin's army at Agincourt, and afterwards proceeded to Paris, where he married the French King's daughter, he was constituted not only Regent of France, during the King's indisposition, but also his successor in the kingdom. Thus having ordered matters in France to his satisfaction, he returned in triumph to England, leaving his brother, Thomas Duke of Clarence, his Vice-gerent and General of the English army. The Dauphin in this exigency sent ambassadors to Scotland in the year 1419, being the last year but one of the Regency of Robert Duke of Albany, imploring aid against the English. In compliance with this request, the Regent, in the beginning of the year 1420, sent over a supply of seven thousand volunteers under command of John Earl of Buchan his own son, and Archibald Earl of Wigtoun eldest son to the Earl of Douglas. These forces arriving in France some few days before Easter, (which festival was then, and is yet very religiously, if not superstitiously, observed by the Romanists) upon which account there was a cessation of arms agreed upon for some days betwixt the Scots and English, in confidence whereof the former remained in much security: Of this the Duke of Clarence being informed by one Fregosa, an Italian, who deserted from the Scottish army, he, upon the intelligence, resolved, notwithstanding of the cessation, to take his advantage of the Scots, fearing more harm from the experienced valour of that small number, than most of the French forces besides. So keeping his design secret, upon Easter-Sabbath he ordered all his horsemen to arm, judging thefe fufficient for the enterprize, and by a hafty march arrived in a few hours at the Scots Quarters, in a little town in the province of Anjou, called Bauge, near which was a river traverft with a ftone-bridge, and guarded by a party of French, who, upon Clarence's arrival, deferted the poft. Upon this alarm, Hugh Kennedy, a Scottifh Captain, with thirty archers, advanced to the bridge, and for fome time defended the fame, untill Clarence ordered two hundred of his Cuiraffiers to difmount, and with pufh of fpear, beat Kennedy and his fmall party, deftitute of defenfive armour, from their poft. But while this was a-doing, the Earl of Buchan, with two hundred Scottifh horfemen, arrived at the bridge, which Clarence obferving, left the paffage clear to the Scots, and drew up his men in order of battle. The Scottifh General, as foon as he got his men together, advanced toward the enemy, and charged them with very great bravery, which was received by the Englifh with no lefs refolution, being fuperior both in number and experience. So that after a fharp difpute, the Scots were fcarce able to maintain their ground; till in the heat of the action, Sir Alexander Buchanan meeting the Duke of Clarence, who was very confpicuous upon account of a Coronet befet with a great many jewels affixt to his helmet, with his couched fpear with the utmoft vigour made toward him; the Duke in the same posture met his antagonist, upon whose breast plate the Duke's spear slanting, Buchanan pierced at once thro' his left eye and brain, whereupon he instantly fell from his horse, Buchanan in the mean time getting hold of the Coronet, and putting the same upon the point of his spear cried to his countrymen to take courage, for that there was a token he had killed the English General; which the English noticing, made no further resistance, but committed their safety to their horses heels, there being killed of them besides Clarence, twenty-six officers, and other persons of quality, and near 3000 soldiers, besides 2000 taken prisoners, with very little loss to the Scots, there being none of account killed upon their side.

This victory, as it gave a great check to the affairs of the English, did no less erect the drooping circumstances of the French, of which the Dauphin was so sensible, that he created the Earl of Buchan his Master of Horse, and Wigtoun High Constable of France, and rewarded all the other persons of distinction according to their merits, particularly Buchanan, whom he bountifully rewarded, and for preservation of his Heroick Atchievement, added to his former Bearing a second Tressure round the Field, flowered, and counterflowred with Flower-de-luces of the second, and in Crest a Hand coupee, holding a Duke's Coronet, with two Laurel Branches wreathed round the same; which addition was retained by the Family of Buchanan in all time thereafter.

Mr GEORGE BUCHANAN, who seems never to have been very careful in advancing the honour of his name, asserts, that the common report was, that Clarence was first wounded by Sir John Swinton, and afterwards beat from his horse by the Earl of Buchan. But the assertion of the Book of Pluscarden, and the additional arms, being so plain a monument of that action, clear the truth thereof, as above-related, beyond all manner of controversy. Buchanan is reported to have sold the Coronet to Stewart of Darnly for one thousand angels of gold, and Darnly to have pawned the same to Sir Robert Houston for five thousand angels. This gallant gentleman, with a great many more of his countrymen, was killed by the English through the treachery, desertion, or cowardice of the French in conjunction with them at the battle of Vernoile, in the year 1424.

The next of that family, who lost his life in the service of his Prince, was PATRICK, second of that name Laird of Buchanan; who, with most of his name, was with King James IV. at the battle of Flowdon, in which Buchanan himself, John Laird of Lenny, and divers others of the name were killed, in the year 1513. Though our public histories give no account of this gentleman's death, at that occasion, nor of a great many others of quality, who lost their lives in that fatal engagement, nevertheless there are accounts to be found of the same in most of the families, whose principal men were lost at that juncture.

George Laird of Buchanan, with his name and dependants, was at the battle of Pinkie in Queen Mary's minority, in which Buchanan of Arnpryor, and diverse others of the name, lost their lives. The same George was also at the battle of Langside, in which he behaved very honourably. And no less so did George, third of that name Laird of Buchanan, father to the late Laird, who being colonel of Stirling-shire regiment during the whole of the civil wars, in the reign of King Charles I. was with his regiment (most of the officers, and a good many of the soldiers thereof being of his own name) at the battle of Dunbar, as also at the fatal conflict of Inverkeithing; at the last of which Buchanan, with Sir John Brown colonel of Mid-Lothian regiment, with their two regiments, stopped the passage of the English army over Forth for some days, and would have continued so to do, till relief had come from the King's grand army, then encamped at Stirling, had not Major-general Holborn, Commander-in-chief of that party of the Scottish forces, (byassed as was thought with English gold) commanded these brave gentlemen to abandon their post, and allow the English free passage, which, when effected, the General drew on these two regiments, with that of brave Sir Hector MacLean, mostly composed of his own name, to an engagement with the best part of the English army; Holborn himself, with his regiment of horse, wheeling off without firing one shot, and leaving these three regiments of foot to the mercy, or rather merciless rage of the enemy, they, after a most valiant resistance, even much greater than could be expected from their number, were in the end overpowered, and mostly cut to pieces. The Laird of MacLean, with most of any account of his name, was killed, as also a vast number of the name of Buchanan; the Laird himself, with Sir John Brown, and some few other officers, being made prisoners, in which condition Buchanan continued unreleased till his death, in the year 1651.

It may be upon good grounds presumed, that diverse others of the Lairds of Buchanan were concerned in a great many other battles, and other grand transactions managed in this nation, though a particular account of these matters cannot be so easily obtained. However, the above-mentioned instances, of which there are accounts, are sufficient testimonies of these gentlemen's willingness, upon all occasions, to evidence their duty in behalf and service of their prince and country.

As the Lairds of Buchanan were ordinarily among the first who appeared in the public service of their country, so they were frequently obliged, according to the too general custom of the more antient times, to maintain some private quarrels with some neighbouring names, and being for the most part unjustly provoked, came very rarely off with disadvantage.

The first of these private quarrels that is reported to have been, was with the Arrals, then a numerous name in the Lennox, and whose perverse and insolent disposition was very singular, insomuch, that, upon report of any quarrel, or slaughter in these parts, in which that name resided, those not present, upon hearing thereof, ordinarily asked, Who, besides the Arrals? judging, whoever were seconds, the Arrals behoved to be first in any such adventure. Nevertheless, in that contest already glanced at betwixt the Buchanans and that name, the same was brought so low, that there scarce remained thereafter the least memory of it.

Their next contraversy is reported to be with the Galbraiths, in the reign of King James II. being the most numerous and potent name of the Lennox in that age. The reason of this contest is said to be, the Laird of Buchanan's marrying a gentlewoman of the name of Galbraith, heiress of Killearn, Bamoir, and Auchinreoch. The Galbraiths grudging very much that so good an estate should be carried off by a stranger, and in regard they could not justly withhold those lands, they resolved to take the advantage of these times, which being very turbulent, favoured such projects, to detain them from Buchanan by violence. This began the quarrel, which continued for some time with mutual slaughter, and did in the end terminate, not only in the loss of what the Galbraiths so much struggled for, but also of diverse of themselves in the action; the last of them being Galbraith of Benachra and Benraes, who resided in a little castle situated in a small island of Lochlomond, called yet "The Galbraith's Isle," whence he committed a great many hostilities upon most of the neighbouring gentlemen: And if at any time deprived of his boat, he would swim with his cloaths and arms tied betwixt his shoulders, and in that manner take a boat from the next adjacent shore, and carry the same into his Isle. Of this practice Buchanan being informed, caused plant an ambush in the next Isle to Galbraith's, which intercepted him while in his swimming posture, and dispatched him, to the no small satisfaction of his neighbours.

There were divers other hostilities carried on betwixt that of Buchanan, and some other neighbouring families, not necessary here to be mentioned; as there were also betwixt the family of Lenny, and two several neigbouring Clans, at two different junctures; betwixt the family of Drumikill, with the like number of Clans; and also betwixt Carbeth and a certain Clan in their neighbourhood. In all which contests, tho' after a great deal of bloodshed, those families came off with the same honour and advantage, that the principal family were wont to have in their encounters.

The name of Buchanan was so numerous in heritors, and the castle of Buchanan so centrally placed in respect of the interests and residences of these heritors, that the Laird of Buchanan could, in a summer's day, call fifty heritors of his own name to his house, upon any occasion, and all of them might with conveniency return to their respective residences against night, the furthest of them not being above ten miles from Buchanan.

The name of Buchanan, since the principal family became extinct, consists of, or is classed into four classes, or families; The first of these, being a certain number of heritors, and their dependants, who are immediately descended off the family of Buchanan, or the latest cadets thereof, who, though they keep entire friendship with, yet have no dependance upon any other family of the name. The principal person of these is, Buchanan of Auchmar, there being of this class ten heritors. The next is the family of Drumikill, the principal person or head of which is Buchanan of Cragievairn, there being of this family seventeen heritors. The third is Buchanan of Lenny, of which family, himself included, there are ten heritors. The fourth is the family of Carbeth, of which, Carbeth himself included, there are fourteen Heritors. The Heritors of the MacAuselans, MacMillans, MacColmans, and Spittels, all immediately descended off that of Buchanan, being added to the First Class, makes the same the most considerable of the Four.

A BRIEF ACCOUNT OF Some LEARNED MEN of the Name of BUCHANAN.

THERE have been several learned men of the name of Buchanan, besides Mr GEORGE of whom already; particularly, Mr THOMAS BUCHANAN of Ibert, nephew to Mr GEORGE, upon whose demission the said Mr Thomas succeeded in the office of Lord Privy Seal: Before which he was a Preacher, and a learned and eminent Divine: Being a great promoter of the Reformation, he was consulted in all points any ways difficult that occurred in those times; upon which account he is very often mentioned in the Histories of Knox and Calderwood.

There was another Mr THOMAS BUCHANAN, son to Thomas second of that name young Laird of Drumikil. He was minister of Syres in Fife in the reign of King James VI. and was of the greatest learning and esteem of any of his time.

Mr ROBERT BUCHANAN Provost of the Collegiate Church of Kirkheugh in St. Andrews, in the beginning of the reign of King James VI. was very famous for Philosophy and Theology, being, for any thing I can find, of the old family of Arnpryor.

Mr DAVID BUCHANAN, second son of William Buchanan of Arnpryor, was a gentleman of great learning: He flourished in the latter part of the reign of King James VI. and beginning of the reign of King Charles I. He wrote a large Natural History, which was not compleated at the author's death, and therefore never printed, to the great loss of the learned and curious. He wrote also a large Etymologicon of all the shires, cities, rivers and mountains in Scotland, which was printed, tho' not in many hands; from which I find Sir Robert Sibbald quotes some passages in his History of the Shires of Stirling and Fife.

FINIS.